A Narrative Approach to Business Growth

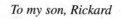

To my son, Rickard

A Narrative Approach to Business Growth

Mona Ericson

Jönköping International Business School, Sweden

Edward Elgar
Cheltenham, UK • Northampton, MA, USA

Published by
Edward Elgar Publishing Limited
The Lypiatts
15 Lansdown Road
Cheltenham
Glos GL50 2JA
UK

Edward Elgar Publishing, Inc.
William Pratt House
9 Dewey Court
Northampton
Massachusetts 01060
USA

A catalogue record for this book is available from the British Library

Library of Congress Control Number: 2009941264

Mixed Sources
Product group from well-managed
forests and other controlled sources
www.fsc.org Cert no. SA-COC-1565
© 1996 Forest Stewardship Council
FSC

ISBN 978 1 84980 043 3

Typeset by Cambrian Typesetters, Camberley, Surrey
Printed and bound by MPG Books Group, UK

Contents

Foreword: Thickness/realism – openness/usefulness – participation/ relevance: reflections on the difference a narrative approach makes

Daniel Hjorth, The Department of Management, Politics and Philosophy, Copenhagen Business School

The distinctive quality of a narrative approach, when part of a qualitative research tradition, so I have suggested (Hjorth, 2008), is that it significantly increases language's capacity to keep and carry the sense of occasion of the studied event (its 'eventness') to the reader. The purpose would be to allow for the intensity of – in this case – the entrepreneurial event to live in language, with the result that readers' chance of experiencing (and not simply reading about) what took place in another time and place increases dramatically. 'The task of understanding then depends not on the extraction of an abstract set of principles, and still less on the application of a theoretical model, but rather on an encounter with the singular, the specific, and the individual' (Greenblatt and Gallagher, 2000: 7).

This foreword aspires not so much to anticipate the themes or arguments of the book as to endorse the approach with a somewhat widely gesturing signature. By this I mean to proceed as if Greenblatt and Gallagher's note above gave me a gentle push in my back, suggesting that our capacity to make what we study knowable to a more general audience lies in the narrative's power to connect the singular, the specific and the individual to the broader landscape of storied experiences and the productive resonance that emerge from this contact. I want to elaborate, as an inspired reader of this book, on three themes that I see as important challenges immanent to the art of practicing an edifying narrative approach: thickness/realism, openness/usefulness, and participation/relevance. The prefacing qualities of this maneuver lie in the fact that the arguments for the selection of these themes are indeed to be found through your reading of this timely and important contribution to business growth studies.

THICKNESS/REALISM

The distinction between the thin and the thick description seems to me still important for the difference that a narrative approach makes to the reader with ambitions to understand the text beyond the representational. Greenblatt, reporting on Geertz, phrases this in terms of the former (thin) being 'merely describing the mute act' while the latter (thick) is 'giving the act its place in a network of framing intentions and cultural meanings.' We recognize the circularity – the thick description is thick because it is written into a network of other small stories (petit récit, as Lyotard, 1984, puts this) in the context of which a more rich meaning is achieved. The Lyotard mention is significant here as I believe there is work of resistance, on the part of the writer, which is importantly linked to the networking capacity of the story. To the extent that the writer succeeds with placing the description into a network of intentions and cultural meanings (that is, in a network of other small stories), this is a matter of defending it against greedy theoretical models or abstract sets of principles, and such grand narratives that seek to further their explanatory power by colonizing a 'new piece of land.' To the extent that we learn something new from Mona Ericson's study – and indeed, in several respects, we do – this is a result of her capacity to resist this tendency, which always offers itself up as an easy solution to all academic writers as they sense the loneliness of the one holding in her hand a set of small, loosely connected, flowing stories in a world of giant, solid, and stable theories. On the level of the analytical strategy, we learn from this book the prize that results from winning such multiple small battles: new and deeper meaning.

'Thickness is not in the object; it is in the narrative surroundings, the add-ons, the nested frames' (Greenblatt, 2000: 25). Our 'raw' stories, recorded in the field, will thus always be given sense and meaning in the particular style that is the result of the entwining of the writer's peculiar way of driving the pen, and the research field's cultured ways of understanding its reality. So, for instance, a description such as: 'The banker had five children,' is likely to be implicative of an opportunity (to finance a toy store), in the network of entrepreneurship research's way of understanding its reality. An anthropologist, however, may find this description to be full of complexities related to 'ways of living' that primarily do not suggest the presence of an economic opportunity. Neither of the two senses is the true one. Statistical certainty would not help one try to make sense of or discriminate (on the basis of accuracy) between the two descriptions. Both, instead, are part of the richness and complexity of the acted documents that are social life.

One's capacity as a writer to keep the sense of event in the studied piece of life alive depends to a large extent on whether one is acquainted 'with the imaginative universe within which their [those that are studied] acts are signs'

(Geertz, 1973: 11). Here, again, we are reassured by Ericson's style that she is acquainted with the imaginative universe within which the locals' acts that she has studied are signs. This does not provide her with the urge or possibility to close her stories, to finalize them, to determine what they are essentially about. Instead, the richness of experiences, narrated and contextualized, invites the reader as writer – as someone made competent (by the style of the text) to go on writing these stories into their own imaginative universes, telling others those stories that were not delivered by (in this case) Ericson's pen. This generosity towards the reader is a distinct quality of the text Barthes called 'writerly' (Barthes, 1990); the text that foregrounds its meaning-making progresses via several voices, and does not shy from heterogeneity of sense. Ericson emphasizes, with the help of O'Connor, that idea that stories have a 'life far beyond the single occasion of its telling,' as she, towards the end of the book, reflects upon a narrative dynamic conceptualization of business growth.

We thus learn that thickness is a matter of realism. Not scientific-realism (boiling down to the view that science generates knowledge about phenomena that are theory independent), but realism that we find in William James' pragmatism as well as in contemporary post-structuralism, proceeding from the conclusions that participation precedes recognition, and relation precedes position (Massumi, 2002). It is this already relationally engaged position that a narrative approach embraces and explores in its thicker descriptions. The result is that research is speaking to us in a realistic voice.

OPENNESS/USEFULNESS

This is also where research, speaking in this voice, becomes relevant and useful. Usefulness, I will suggest here, is secured by the style we have identified above as producing the writerly text, which foregrounds its meaning-making, is multivoiced and proceeds along the realism of heterogeneous sense. Here is where openness – and the generosity toward and faith in the reader's own lived experience of making sense that this openness addresses – is related to usefulness. The narrative approach is not about 'staying in language,' for there is no way not to stay in language (which is not to deny nature or emotions – we never arrive at nature, however, except with culture as a necessary companion; Latour, 1993; 1999). Usefulness is based on the narrative approach's insistence on the knowledge-creation capacity of everyday life. 'All bare facts,' Massumi (2002: 214) reminds us, 'are born factoid.' The question is not whether it is real or constructed, says Latour (1999), but whether it is constructed well enough, according to the practices of science, to pass as fact. The question is not about the status of language. The question is to what extent the academic study asks us to join that particular practice of making knowledge over which it has established control historically, or whether it seeks to remain – as long as possible – in the realm of storied knowing. The narrative approach we are acquainted with in the book you have started to read is of the kind where the precision of narrative wit is held as dear to the knowledge-thirsting, curious mind, as ever the abstract-aspiring fact-making of scientific rationality.

Now, again, it is not a matter of constructing a dichotomy and proceeding as if correctness would be bestowed upon those keeping to one side of the construct. Indeed, it is the work of scholarly endeavors – call this more precisely a quest – to strive toward the well-constructed fact. The fact is defendable and meaningful, beautiful and workable. A narrative approach, however, is distinctly about what Greenblatt (2000: 31) describes as 'making the literary and the non-literary seem to be each other's thick description,' by which I here mean: make the narrative and the scientific seem like each other's thick description.

You may object by saying this means a narrative approach loses its uniqueness. Admittedly, it characterizes qualitative research more generally, this 'dialogue' between the scientific (abstract principle, theoretical model) and the empirical data (Morgan, 1983). We find it as an ideal in hermeneutically oriented approaches, and Gadamer speaks about the fusion of horizons (horizon being the historically derived situatedness from which understanding and interpretation takes place) so that we come to understand the other and reach an agreement. However, it is precisely the problem of the other that was underestimated in hermeneutics and which emerged in its fuller politico-ethical complexity with Levinas (1987) and postcolonial theory (e.g. Bhabha, 1990).

Anthropology, which inspired research on culture as it bloomed within management and organization studies in the early 1980s (Smircich, 1983) intensified our awareness of this problem as it illustrated the challenges. The interest in the 'native's' phrasing of his reality (the emic view, as anthropological literature calls this) was as much a colonial gaze in spite of its well-meaning intentions. 'Each other's thick description' is therefore a more demanding task than it may first seem. A genuine dialogue, as Bakhtin (1981) has shown in the case of Dostoevsky's novels, requires a polyphony that results from a writer who embraces what we have called above the heterogeneity of sense. Dostoevsky's literature is in this sense good literature as it makes (in Greenblatt's words) the literary and the nonliterary seem to be each other's thick description.

In perspective of this discussion, I would say that the keyword in Ericson's narrative approach is participatory, which is the aim and value that makes it useful as well as relevant.

PARTICIPATION/RELEVANCE

When emphasizing the importance of participation, I mean to draw attention to the continuity of experience – from Latin *experientia*, meaning 'the act of trying.' Continuity is achieved by how actuality, as intensity, as registering potential (the virtual) binds our world together. The glue, Massumi (2002: 220) suggests, is affect (which is not emotion, but rather intensity, or capacity to act). Participation is always a matter of response. The time spent in the field is an investment in actuality, in the becoming of practices you study. Affect binds this situation to the narration of it, and the subsequent addressing of people and processes that is part of how you feed back your research. The logic is almost the opposite of classical idea(l)s of objectivity, where (artificial) detachment was seen as the basis for correct knowledge coming out at the end of the research process. From the perspective of a narrative approach, precision as well as relevance is instead made possible by the continuity that affect brings. It is not a matter of losing oneself to the local, contextual, singular, specific, or individual. Again, it is not about the emotional. A narrative approach has better chances of being relevant, precise and meaningful to the extent that it registers and explores how bodies' capacities to act increases and decreases. This is how a narrative approach can be participative; by working with affect (and so, make room for potential).

When I once sketched out a way (method) to follow as a poststructuralist analyst (Hjorth, 2003), I suggested that genesis – repetition – participation provided workable guidance. Participation – to take part – was also there a gesture towards the shared experience. That is, the scholar that finds engaging with empirical studies necessary because of her interest with everyday practices needs also to aspire to participation in shaping those practices, or, more often, shaping how those practices are imagined. Participation, of some kind, is one way of testing the relevance of your thick descriptions. It is a way of checking how 'writerly' your knowledge of the local field of practices is, how useful it can become in the unfolding into networks of intensions and cultural meanings that practitioners 'do' to it. It is, as Ericson correctly points out, a matter of dialogue.

Relevance, however, is in no way exhausted by usefulness. The small story's power to affect the other is immensely important for the other's capacity to become affected. What is brushed off one day as useless, can the next day be the key to one's receptivity towards the unexpected, the unpredicted, to the registering of potential – the world's becoming. A story that knows how to generate affect can be as participative as the one that is immediately embraced as useful. A 'scar' of intensity – the duration of the image's effect, as Massumi (2002) defines this – left on the surface of an organizational culture will often have tactical impacts on the social. Like de Certeau's (1984) 'transformative insinuation' (as Ahearne described de Certeau's concept of tactics, 1995: 163), it affects the movement so that a surprising effect is achieved. This is one important argument for a narrative approach – that something remains for the writing. That writing is a process of becoming relevant of the researcher, and this relevance is a matter of working with affect (intensities, capacities to act; Deleuze, 1995) as binding experiences – 'ours and theirs' – together.

REFERENCES

Ahearne, J. (1995), *Michel de Certeau – Interpretation and its Other*, Stanford: Stanford University Press.
Bakhtin, M. (1981), *The Dialogic Imagination: Four Essays*, ed. Michael Holquist, trans. Caryl Emerson and Michael Holquist, Austin: University of Texas Press.
Barthes, R. (1990), *S/Z*, Oxford: Basil Blackwell.
Bhabha, H.K. (1990), *Nation and Narration*, New York: Routledge.
de Certeau, M. (1984), *The Practice of Everyday Life*, Berkeley: University of California Press.
Deleuze, G. (1995), *Negotiations – Gilles Deleuze*, New York: Columbia University Press.
Gallagher, C. and S. Greenblatt (2000), *Practicing New Historicism*, Chicago: The University of Chicago Press.
Geertz, C. (1973), *The Interpretation of Cultures*, New York: Basic Books.
Greenblatt, S. (2000), 'The touch of the real', in C. Gallagher and S. Greenblatt (eds), *Practicing New Historicism*, Chicago: University of Chicago Press, pp. 20–48.
Hjorth, D. (2003), *Rewriting Entrepreneurship – For a New Perspective on Organizational Creativity*, Copenhagen, Malmö and Oslo: CBS Press, Liber and Abstrakt.
Hjorth, D. (2008), 'Nordic entrepreneurship research', *Entrepreneurship, Theory and Practice*, March, 313–38.
Latour, B. (1993), *We Have Never Been Modern*, Cambridge, MA: Harvard University Press.
Latour, B. (1999), *Pandora's Hope: Essays on the Reality of Science Studies*, Cambridge, MA: Harvard University Press.
Levinas. E. (1987), *Time and the Other*, trans. Richard A. Cohen, Pittsburgh, PA: Duquesne University Press.
Lyotard, J.-F. (1984), *The Postmodern Condition – A Report on Knowledge*, trans. Geoff Bennington and Brian Massumi, Manchester: Manchester University Press.
Massumi, B. (2002), *Parables for the Virtual*, Durham, NC and London: Duke University Press.
Morgan, G. (ed.) (1983), *Beyond Method – Strategies for Social Research*, London: Sage.
Smircich, L. (1983), 'Concepts of culture and organizational analysis', *Administrative Science Quarterly*, **28** (3), 339–58.

Acknowledgments

This book presents a study that is part of a research program, 'The Process of Growth – Organizing, Strategizing and Entrepreneurial Activities', at Jönköping International Business School. The program contributes to the knowledge of those firms that have shown sustainable, long-term growth.

Many thanks go to Leif Melin, Professor of Strategy and Organization, Leader of the Growth Research Program, for giving me the opportunity to study business growth in Hilding Anders and to him and the other members of the research program, Leona Achtenhagen, Olof Brunninge, Jenny Helin, Anna Larsson and Lucia Naldi for their valuable comments on the drafts of my manuscript!

I also wish to thank Professor Daniel Hjorth, Copenhagen Business School, for initial encouragement in the development of a study employing a narrative approach.

With great appreciation, I acknowledge the contribution of Bengt Adolfsson, Olle Andersson, Rikard Eriksson, Lars Haux, Bertil Henningsson, Anders Hultman, Claes-Göran Jönsson, Arne Karlsson, Tomas Modén, Anders Pålsson and Mats Östergård. Many thanks for making it possible for me to gain valuable and interesting insights into a rich variety of growth activities associated with the Hilding Anders business.

Special thanks go to Karin Hedman, Norra Skåne and Kenneth Palmgren, Hästveda Servicekontor, for providing me access to archived material that brought alive past activities lived by people associated with Hilding Anders.

Moreover, I am grateful to Björn Kjellander, who copyedited my text. Many thanks, Björn!

Finally, I wish to thank Jan Wallanders and Tom Hedelius Foundation for their financial support that allowed me to carry out the study!

Mona Ericson
Jönköping, January 2010

1. Toward a narrative dynamic conceptualization

This book conceptualizes business growth through a narrative approach that uses a story-like representation of growth. A narrative has a rich potential for enhancing our understanding (Rossiter, 1999) of growth and the emotionally charged changes (Orbuch, 1997) that come with growth. A narrative dynamic conceptualization builds on a communicative structure that corresponds to people's ways of experiencing life (Demers, Giroux and Chreim, 2003). Practitioners' tellings invite us to an interpretation and understanding that make it possible to capture a multidimensional character of growth, opening up previously marginalized sides in research on growth. Interpretation and understanding mediate a participative and dialogically structured world. In such a world, experience denotes an integrative ongoing process in the life of the practitioner, relating the practitioner to other human beings and to the cultural past.

The book also includes the organizing and shaping of a pattern of growth, using 'plot' as a means of interconnecting practitioners' growth-related activities and concomitant changes. Generally plot 'functions to transform a chronicle or listing of events into a schematic whole by highlighting and recognizing the contribution that certain events make to the development and outcome of the story' (Polkinghorne, 1988: 18–19). Nevertheless, if we keep our ears open to a variety of utterances among practitioners, more than one plot is presented. Apparently there is no schematic whole and no one single plot that maps and analytically portrays growth through a casual, linear and coherent arrangement of stories (Boje, 2000). The plots flow with the practitioners' stories, elevating a rational complexity of business growth that reconciles calculative rationality and emotion.

The plots interconnect into a business growth narrative that stretches back to before 1940 and forward into this millennium. Projecting many practitioners' narrative voices can give us some insight into growth with reference to the business firm Hilding Anders International AB (Hilding Anders), founded in 1939. By the year of 2009 – through people's comments and documents – Hilding Anders is presented as a group of companies (the Group) with 4,600 employees and 30 subsidiaries around the globe. About 20 brands are sold in Europe and Asia (Hilding Anders, 2009d). The Group has followed a profit-driven, focused growth strategy to become the world-leading bed and mattress manufacturer. Striking a balance between growth and profitability, performance exhibited a turnover of SEK7.059 billion in 2008 (Hilding Anders, 2009c).

The business growth narrative, characterized as multivoiced and multiplotted, portrays growth as a strategic matter. It exhibits sensitivity to the different kinds of changes that managers and others promote when carrying out activities in the name of Hilding Anders as they take the business forward. Strategy, not merely reduced to the notion that growth is a matter of winning battles with competitors, accounts for relationships between people, their actions and interactions (Nordqvist, 2005; Watson, 2002). Accordingly, the firm is not the point of departure for the business growth narrative presented in this book.

Through a narrative approach, I hope that my study, despite the severe limitations of its fragmentary exposition of growth-oriented activities, has the potential to make a valuable and interesting complement to the existing body of growth research. In previous research on growth, the firm is often a starting point for an analysis. When a study is preoccupied with collecting firm-level data and measuring correlations between research variables (Bamford, Dean and Douglas, 2004; Begley and Boyd, 1987; Boeker, 1997; Cho and Pucik, 2005; Goddard, Tavakoli and Wilson, 2009; McMahon, 2001; Shepherd and Wiklund, 2009; Singh and Mitchell, 2005) there can only be limited space for a story-like representation of practitioners' involvement in activities related to growth. Firm-level data and variables are not very receptive to the idea of bringing in narrative voices and plots. Fundamentally grounded in a verificationist epistemology, logical-scientific explanations are provided about the study object: the firm. A verificationist view of knowledge supplies the basis for causality, leaving out a narrative reason for action and interaction (Bruner, 1990). Firm-level data and growth variables tend to disregard the richness of human expression, including emotions and the context in which interactions and activities are situated, as well as the contextualization of the interactions and activities that people communicate through their stories.

Deeper insights into how growth occurs and patterns emerge through practitioners' involvement in and stories about growth require pulling back the firm-level curtains. Significant gaps in our understanding of growth as human interaction and activity necessitate a move beyond firm activity, accentuating a need for a study that allows the firm as a social reality to emerge through practitioners' accounts, a study that also furthers the notion of narrating practitioners' reasonable activities by adding the emotion dimension. As shown in my previous study of business growth (Ericson, 2007), activity reflects social practice, denoting an intersubjective relationship in social interaction among individuals (Fichtner, 1999) who consider themselves to represent (or in one way or another being associated with) a business. While appreciating an integral relationship between activity and social practice, the present study too transcends a dualistic description of context and activity. The firm is not 'out there', ready to be studied. The 'firm' (or the 'company') is a world of practice that the practitioners relate to through their lived experience.

> Activities are not organized as outcomes or products of human actions and interactions, and there is no context characterized as an activity system consisting of a subject and an object, internal and external tools. Upholding a distinction between a subject and an object, and between the internal and the external is not of relevance under the assumption that the world of practice is not detached from the practitioner. (Ericson, 2007: 33–4)

In a constantly moving network of activities we can point to specific moments of change that from the practitioners' perspectives promote growth. The term 'growth' is often used interchangeably with 'expansion', to signify change through increases in sales, turnover, market share, employment, profitability and productivity. As Penrose (1959: 1) adds, the term growth implies 'an increase in size or an improvement in quality as a result of a process of development, akin to natural biological processes in which an interacting series of internal changes leads to increases in age accompanied by changes in the characteristic of the growing object.' However, how expansion, increase and development happen through the activities that practitioners' enmesh themselves in has not received much attention. Although we are apt to treat growth and firm in a reified language, we need to dwell on what we actually understand by 'growth'. Business growth, conceived of as a social phenomenon, stems from and is constituted by human interaction and activity. Human interaction and activity bring into existence business growth as a meaningful social reality.

By taking a narrative approach, a dynamic conceptualization of growth is proposed, grounded in a relational multivoiced (Fletcher, 2007) and multiplotted exposition of growth. The emphasis here is on coming to an understanding through listening to practitioners' stories. The intention is then not to dissect but to connect further (Steyaert, 2007) through plots, the bits and pieces that people involved in business growth activities communicate in their stories. The study complements my previous study on business growth (Ericson, 2007) where I, inspired by the style of a Bach fugue, presented a flow of activities closely interconnected through themes. The so-called principal theme is carried by voices associated with the global corporation Nefab introducing the fugue and is followed by other alternating voices that allocate different versions of the principal theme, which then is continuously announced and varied through transpositions into different keys, to use a musical term. The present study builds on more fragmentary material that does not allow itself to be organized and structured in fugal themes.

As a complement to current strategic and business growth thinking, a narrative approach is well-positioned to capture the presence of multiple interlinked realities (Barry and Elmes, 1997). Practitioners can make sense of their realities in a variety of ways, providing many different accounts about growth. Nevertheless, the development of knowledge has long been influenced by the voices of those who advocate a logical-scientific explanation rooted in a verificationist epistemology.

NARRATIVE AND STORY

In studies that try to grasp reality 'out there' one clearly recognizes the impact of the empiricist and rationalist traditions. 'Dissidents' have challenged these traditions but the development of knowledge is far more influenced by the voices of the empiricist and the rationalist than by the voices of the dissidents, Bruner (1990) asserts. In the pursuit of true knowledge, empiricists focus on the interplay between the human mind and the external world, whereas rationalists try to discover how the human mind gets a reliable fix on the world for the principle of right reason. With little effort going into a human being's construction of reality, rationalists' main interest is in how reality is represented in the act of knowing. Mind is regarded as an instrument of right reasoning and capable of empirical verification. Nevertheless, logical-scientific explanations subjected to verification (Mumby, 1993) ignore narrative voices, allowing little room for intentionality (Bruner, 1990).

Although the 'cognitive revolution' that took place in the late 1950s centered on how a human being constructs and makes sense of the world, 'computing' became the model of the mind. According to Bruner (1990), the original intention of the cognitive revolution was to prompt psychology to join forces with its sister interpretative disciplines in humanities and in the social sciences: anthropology, linguistics, philosophy, literary theory and history. Yet, the emphasis shifted away from meaning and meaning-making to information and information processing. The terms 'input' and 'output' replaced the behavioral terms 'stimulus' and 'response' without dealing with mental processes.

The subordination of the cognitive revolution to the ideal of computability neglected the constitutive argument of culture. Treating the world as a flow of information and the human mind as a computational program provides no place for the narrating human being's action and intentional states such as believing, desiring, intending, sense-making and meaning-making. As Bruner (1990: 19) maintains, human action, as opposed to human behavior, is 'situated in a cultural setting, and in the mutually interacting intentional states of the participants.' In accordance with Weber (1947), if behavior is not oriented to meaning it is not an action. The narrating human being participates in and realizes herself through culture. 'Behavior' takes sense-data as the main unit of cognition (Czarniawska, 2004). It is accordingly important to distinguish between behavior and action. Drawing on MacIntyre (1981), Czarniawska emphasizes that descriptions based on sense-data would imply that we are confronted with an uninterpreted and even an uninterpretable world: 'Such a world would indeed be a world of "behaviors", both meaningless and mechanical, because if sense-data were to become the basis for the formulation of laws, all reference to intentions, purposes, and reasons – all that which changes behavior into a human action – would have to be removed' (2004: 3).

As indicated, the concept of action as intentional acts can be related to narrative. The term 'narrative' is closely linked to story. Stories 'express movement, interpret ideas, and describe from the storyteller's perspective how things used to be and how they are, as well as how they should be,' Feldman et al. (2004: 150) declare. Stories demonstrate how multilayered human expressions are and provide context and meaning.

Story is viewed as a part of a narrative,[1] responding to the question of what happened and what activities mean to the storyteller (Feldman et al., 2004; Riessman, 1993) but is also used interchangeably with narrative (Brown, Stacey and Nandhakumar, 2008; Downing, 2005; Nisker, 2004; Polkinghorne, 1988). As Spence (1982) points out, Freud, the first psychoanalyst, made us aware of narrative as a well-structured story that fills the gap between unrelated events and makes sense out of nonsense in the search for meaning. In the narrative tradition of psychoanalysis we are prone to discover the underlying plot while listening to sequence, coherence and transformation. From the viewpoint of Polkinghorne (1988), plot is the organizing theme that weaves together a complex of events to make a single story. Less well structured, a narrative shatters into many small stories characterized as multivoiced (Boje, 2000).

Both narrative and story are meaning-making mechanisms. Stories bring to individuals a framework for making sense of and learning about daily activities and changes in activities (Weick, 1995). Going even further, narrative constitutes 'a basic element of our being and of our living in the world' (Lämsä and Sintonen, 2006: 107). A human being has an innate primitive predisposition to narrative organizing that makes narrative 'one of the most ubiquitous and powerful discourse forms in human communication' (Bruner, 1990: 77). 'For we dream in narrative, daydream in narrative, remember, anticipate, hope, despair, believe, doubt, plan, revise, criticize, construct, gossip, learn, hate and love by narrative' (Hardy, 1968: 5). Human beings are storytellers – *homo narrans*. The idea of human beings as *homo narrans* posits the generic form of all symbol composition. In accordance with Fisher (1989: 63), this idea 'holds that symbols are created and communicated ultimately as stories meant to give order to human experience and to induce others to dwell in them in order to establish ways of living in common, in intellectual and spiritual communities in which there is confirmation for the story that constitutes one's life.'

Homo narrans as a symbol-using and symbol-making creature takes the front seat in a variety of studies. The idea of social and individual life as a narrative is found in many texts throughout history, as Czarniawska (1997) tells us. During the past two decades, literary theorists, in particular, have become increasingly interested in this concept, involving in discussions of narrative and story their underlying structure and centrality in human experience and existence. Since a narrative theory developed within the field of literature has relevance for a range of other studies (Polkinghorne, 1988) such as studies of business growth, it is important to provide some historical glimpses of the main literary traditions. It is through the development of literary narrative theory that we can see how the locus of study has broadened from a concern exclusively on the structure on narrative text to a communication process. Its more recent attention on human existence (Gadamer, [1960] 1989) informs the way I look at business growth.

Historical Glimpses

Since the 1960s, literary theorists have been engaged in discussions inspired by the traditions of Russian formalism, American new criticism, French structuralism and communication theory in connection with hermeneutics, as Polkinghorne (1988) points out. Russian formalism, as represented by Vladimir Propp, used structural analyses to find the archetypal type, that is, the single deep structure underlying the whole body of Russian fairy tales. The meaning of narrative was thought to depend on how basic functional units such as the subject, verb and adjective of a sentence were arranged and repeated in the different tales.

The American new criticism approached the literary text, poetry and drama and later on the novel as an autonomous whole without reference to a historical context. Nevertheless, Polkinghorne (1988) reveals that, with Northrop Frye's inductive study of stories in the Western world, a major shift in the view of narrative occurred in the United States. In the search for an evolutionary scheme in the history of literary expressions, from myth to realism, Frye placed narrative as the overarching form of the prose discourse.

French structuralism borrowed research methods from linguistics to provide more rigorous and systematic studies, which led to the new literature science called narratology, as Polkinghorne (1988) points out. Structuralists such as Noam Chomsky, Claude Lévi-Strauss and Roland Barthes were interested in uncovering 'a tightly structured, lawful operation behind the surface appearances of flux, change, and development' (Polkinghorne, 1988: 81). The underlying assumption was that the structure of a narrative resembles the structure of other linguistic expressions and that the code in which a message is communicated can be identified and separated from the content of the message. Structuralists believe in a closed grammatical system based on rationally ordered functional units. They are advocators of the view that language using this structure helps divide the world into stable units. However – as Polkinghorne notes – structuralists, overlooking the surface of ambiguities of stories, face problems when they try to describe how and why stories are different.

The interest in narrative has also moved through the point-of-view use of communication theory, linking the sender, the message and the receiver together in a single speech event. As opposed to the structuralists' focus on the author of a story as the grammar constructor, point-of-view theorists hold that the author is a creative force in the construction of a story. With reference to Jacobson's theory, Polkinghorne (1988) directs attention to the whole act of communication and to the function of a message. The theory, shifting the focus from the underlying plot structure, concerns a contact, a code and a context. Polkinghorne clarifies:

> There can be no communication unless there is contact with the sender's message. … Messages are communicated through a code, which involves more than the connection of meanings with sound or letter combinations, but includes as well the organization pattern of the discourse as a whole. …The context of the message … it is the broader meaning that is meant to show through in the communication. (Polkinghorne, 1988: 33–4)

The author's point of view involves a relationship with the story characters. The message sent will produce a meaning that depends on the intended function. In accordance with Jacobson's theory, the referential function points to an external referent. In a conative function, the meaning is to convince or move the receiver to act. A phatic function concerns the contact between the sender and the receiver. The metalingual function recognizes the communication process per se. In the poetic function, the poetic message is the prime concern. A referential function accordingly is only one of several possible functions of storytelling.

In addition to the author (the sender) and the message, a communication structure must include the reader (the receiver). Reception theory, advancing the point-of-view use of the communication theory, ascribes to the reader of a narrative text a central position (Polkinghorne, 1988). It refers to the interactive process that takes place between the reader and the text. Polkinghorne mentions the reception theorist Jauss, who, inspired by Gadamer's ([1960] 1989) more advanced hermeneutics in the form of philosophical hermeneutics, situates literary work in its historical-cultural context. With reference also to

Barthes, Polkinghorne emphasizes the reader's relationship to the text. Understanding the text is a temporal activity that undergoes change during the reading process. Through reinstalling the writer and the reader in contemporary narrative literature theories, interpretation and understanding of narrative and story as a hermeneutic process is elevated.

Spreading beyond literary theory to humanities and social sciences (Czarniawska, 1997, 2004) narrative theory has become useful in organization studies. Business growth scholars have not paid much attention to narrative traditions and *homo narrans*, but an increased interest in narrative and story can be noted in studies that focus on learning and knowledge sharing, values, norms, culture and meaning-making in organizations. These studies are not unlike business growth studies, and are worth looking into when we are further clarifying in which direction to work.

Related to Organization

Czarniawska (1997, 2002, 2004) is prominent among scholars using a narrative approach in her studies of the Swedish public administration and city management in three European capitals. She posits that 'narrative knowledge constitutes the core of organizational knowledge, that it is an important way of making sense of what is going on in the everyday life of organizations' (1997: 167). Several organization scholars agree on the idea that a narrative approach offers an excellent means for learning and sharing knowledge among the members of an organization (Denning, 2002; Hummel, 1991; Reissner, 2005; Sole and Wilson, 2002; Taylor, Fischer and Dufresne, 2002). As Lämsä and Sintonen (2006: 107) say, 'narratives foster learning since they are rememberable, easy to understand and deal with human-like experience that we regard as a credible source of knowledge.' A knowledge-sharing story facilitates the exchange of contextually and culturally embedded knowledge. It provides surrogate experience insofar as it gives the listener an opportunity to develop an understanding of a situation experienced by the storyteller. Due to its social and communicative properties, a story can be used for problem solving, chunking experiences into workable segments while imputing causal relations between events (Herman, 2003).

A review of organizational story and storytelling studies, undertaken by Boyce (1996), elicits three perspectives: the social construction of reality, the organizational symbolism and the critical perspective. From the perspective of the social construction of reality, stories are largely seen as tools for socialization (Louis, 1980; Wilkins, 1984). As argued, through storytelling much is learned about collective centering and collective sense-making. Storytelling is an 'effective form of communication for the construction of a collective sense and for connection with deep meaning,' Boyce (1995: 107) maintains.

Following Berger and Luckmann (1966), social constructionists hold that individuals through their interactions engage in constructing and collecting experience about reality. Also acknowledged are two dimensions of being, namely connectedness of universe and freedom of will. By incorporating these dimensions into the social constructionist perspective, fundamental differences can be uncovered in how people view reality, McWhinney (1984) remarks.

From the social constructionist perspective, narrative is seen as a primary source of organizational meaning-making and learning (Lämsä and Sintonen, 2006). Organizations facing the challenge of dealing with workforce diversity in terms of gender, age, religion and ethnicity need to enable interplay and dialogue between various perspectives of diverse people. The participatory narrative approach developed by Lämsä and Sintonen helps promote intentional organizational learning processes that take place in various social negotiations among people.

> People should understand how interpretations of the spoken and written narratives are affected by the position of whoever makes the interpretation. Because people belong to different groups, each indicating particular ways of thinking, behaving, speaking and valuing that are often accepted as self-evident 'truths' and 'rights' morals, it is essential that they can identify and reflect critically on potential domination and inequality potentially existing in the dominant narratives within the organization. (Lämsä and Sintonen, 2006: 113)

In constructing the approach, they draw on narrative theory and learning theory. As a fundamental structure of human meaning-making, narrative creates a space for the representation of diversity in organizations. The participatory narrative approach organizes experiences and knowing while stimulating empathic orientation, which helps people in organizations become aware of differences among them. It enables the transfer of theoretical and abstract ideas from one time and place to another. As exemplified:

> the same problems of friendship and human relationships can be recounted in a film about a community of homeless men living under city bridges, as in a novel about competition in the business world between top executives. Similarly, the same ethic or gender issues can be addressed in narratives which can equally well take place in the past or the future. (Lämsä and Sintonen, 2006: 109)

A key to synthesizing heterogeneous elements is emplotment. Through the plot, it constitutes the logic of the integration of events into a single story. Emplotment provides a structure that frees us in time and space. Building on Ricoeur's (1983) idea of a three-fold present, Lämsä and Sintonen (2006) assume that the temporal qualities of the past and the future exist in the present. As Ricoeur (1983: 7) posits, 'time has no being since the future is not yet, the past is no longer and the present does not remain.' Narration brings in the past as memory and the future as expectation, placing the past and the future within the present.

Of special interest to Downing (2005) is the social order of a firm and the dramatic quality of narrative processes that take place among the entrepreneurs and their stakeholders. Drawing on Giddens' (1979) reasoning about the dual structure of rules and resources, a holistic framework is proposed, emphasizing entrepreneurship as a social activity based on culture as an open-ended process of communication. The social construction of entrepreneurship offers an understanding of the social order of the firm 'as it is variously manifest in the concepts of social embeddedness, social capital, social networks, business models, entrepreneurial personal theory, vision, and innovation,' as Downing (2005: 196–7) propounds. Personal theory refers to the entrepreneurs' active learning from experience and relationship (Frank and Lueger, 1998).

With reference to Berger and Luckmann (1966), Downing further claims that communicative networks hold a dramatic enactment of roles. The realization of a drama depends on how the actors play their roles and how actions and identities are coordinated. The framework thus centers on narrative dramatic processes that account for patterns in the expression of emotions, identities, understanding and coordinated action. Such processes produce and transform the social order of an organization, its constitutive rules and resources.

Communicative networks are also evident in Wigren's (2003) work. Applying a social constructionist perspective to a study of the 'Spirit of Gnosjö', she focuses on culture as created in and through social construction in different arenas in the Swedish community of Gnosjö: the business firm, the multifaceted arena of business-related activities, the church and the local theater association. She highlights a sociocognitive dimension of culture. By listening to and analyzing stories from different groups of people who act in the different arenas defined as spheres of interest or activity, Wigren explores a network of meanings that is emotively manifested in values and norms. A 'fellow feeling' denotes that people in some contexts hold on to the same values and norms. Yet, value pairs such as inclusion and exclusion, cooperation and competition, equality and inequality entail a number of inconsistencies within the 'Spirit of Gnosjö'.

Moving beyond the grand narrative 'Spirit of Gnosjö' described in the media, popular science literature and in the regional marketing material for a successful business region with a homogeneous culture, Wigren (2003) analyzes four stories from the four arenas. The analysis results in three value sources: religion, the family and the heritage of the region. The focus on espoused values and values deduced from people's acting and interpretation of their surroundings – so-called inferred values – reveals that people talk in one way and behave in another. Wigren (2003: 215) observes: 'The everyday knowledge a person shares, influences whether or not a person is included in a certain context. People who are not familiar with the norms and values in the community might find it difficult to have fellow feeling with the community.'

Akin to the social constructionist perspective, the rhetorical approach, furnished by Feldman et al. (2004), directs attention to the construction of meaning with an attempt to grasp the indepth meanings of a story. It incorporates the concepts of opposition and enthymeme. Opposition refers to the fact that meanings are extracted from the implicit contrast between two elements of a story. Meaning thus lies in the opposites embedded in a story.

> For example, a sign saying "Exit" only has meaning in the context of other signs or other potential signs that say "Entrance". Thus, what you are meant to do when you see the sign "Exit" makes sense because of your understanding that you are inside something and, therefore, there is presumably an entrance as well as an exit. In the same way, a storyteller can create a sense of what is right about something without even talking about it only by talking about what is wrong with its opposite (Feldman et al., 2004: 151).

Enthymeme refers to a syllogism, a part of which is missing in a story because of unspoken taken-for-granted facts and conclusions left out. Enthymeme can therefore simply be described as a plausible argument, Feldman et al. (2004) hold. Syllogism construction helps sort through a mixture of meanings, making an argument explicit. The identification of indepth meanings requires also the generation of storylines. According to Feldman et al., a storyline is a clear and concise sentence that clarifies what the narrators are trying to say about the phenomenon that is being studied. A storyline might emerge, however, as less clear and concise. As Downing (2005: 193) submits: 'Storylines are emotionally resonant stories that are remembered and repeated. They reflect actors' positioning of individual and collective identities and understanding of actions and events.'

In keeping with the rhetorical approach, drawing on a narrative material based on 15 interviews, Feldman et al. (2004) identified nearly 400 oppositions and 800 syllogisms as micro interpretations. By using inductive and iterative thematic data coding, they integrated the micro interpretations into an overall understanding of organizational change – the subject matter at hand.

The perspective of organizational symbolism holds that stories are symbol-bearing aspects of organizational life, accentuating the function of the symbol for sustaining social order in an organization. Organizational symbolism relates storytelling to organizational culture (Boyce, 1995; Dandridge, Mitroff and Joyce, 1980; Morgan, 1997; Pondy et al., 1983; Smircich, 1983). Following Dandridge, Mitroff and Joyce (1980: 77), symbolism 'expresses the underlying character, ideology, or value system of an organization.' Through stories, this character is revealed. Powerful as stories are in passing on a culture, they serve as social maps to help people learn how things are done. Wilkins explains:

Perhaps the simplest reason for the power of stories is that they are often all we have to go on. That is, we can wait to learn about the organization through our own trial-and-error experience but that takes time and we can make costly mistakes. Stories are the experience of others which can potentially fill in the gaps in our experience. So if they come from a credible source or if they give us a particularly good example of what we already suspected, we tend to believe what we hear. (Wilkins, 1984: 48)

From the critical perspective, attention is directed to the ways in which organizational stories are used to bind the individual to the organization, promoting and reinforcing a dominant management ideology or a managerial metamyth that basically substitutes meaning for motivation (Bowles, 1989; Ingersoll and Adams, 1986). The beliefs central to this myth are that 'work processes can and should be rationalized, that the means for achieving objectives are of overriding concern and should receive maximum attention in organizational life, and that efficiency and predictability are of primary importance in the hierarchy of organizational priorities' (Ingersoll and Adams, 1986: 377).

The critical perspective emphasizes a rational-technical orientation of work, the concern of which is the individual's motivation. In the fragmentation of work and reification of a human being that takes place because of rational-technical orientation, there is apparently little awareness of what makes work meaningful. Sievers adds:

The invention of motivation took place in a situation in which through the division and fragmentation of work into jobs and isolated activities, the possibility of actualizing for oneself and others any meaning through work became lost by an increasing percentage of the employed. As meaning is lost and with it the ability or quality of meaning as a co-ordinating and integrating source for one's own actions as well as for the interactions with others, motivation has to be invented. (Sievers, 1986: 344)

As indicated, storytelling has multiple functions, performed as knowledge-sharing, collective centering, sense-making, meaning construction, symbol-bearing and the passing on of managerial metamyths. Narrative and story seem to be valuable sources of insight into organization, organizational processes, culture and ideology. Nevertheless, narrative and story do not necessarily presuppose an objectively framed exposition of an organization. A story has a narrative voice and does 'not have the "sudden death" quality of objectively framed expositions where things are portrayed as "they are",' as Bruner (1990: 54–5) contends. The organizational symbolism and the critical perspective assume the existence of an organization. Both are concerned with an ideology of an organization without addressing the question of how, in the receptivity to the 'otherness' of the past, it takes shape in individuals' activities. While some social constructionists attend to what happens within an organization, others suggest extending the boundaries of the organization. As Wigren (2003) admits, social construction reaches across and beyond the defined boundaries of an organization. A focus on social construction within an organization appears to prioritize, ontologically, stability as a constitutive feature of organization. Insofar as the weaving and reweaving of activities is an ongoing process, an organization (or a firm) is always becoming (Tsoukas and Chia, 2002). The organization is a discursive space that is constituted in the telling and retelling of stories (Brown, Humphreys and Gurney, 2005). Emerging through people's communication and day-to-day relationships, fluid and mobile, organization is then not a being (Taylor and Van Every, 2000).

The social constructionist rhetoric approach illuminates how story helps the move from surface observation toward the underlying and not directly observable plane from which meaning can be extracted in 'opposition' (Feldman et al., 2004). It is interesting to note that meaning closely relates to opposition. Nonetheless, the move that comes with the extraction of meaning need not take an analytical route, probing into the construction of syllogisms for sorting through meanings. When following such a route one might end up losing oneself in an overwhelmingly large number of micro interpretations, fumbling to grasp an understanding without conceding the simultaneity of interpretation and understanding. Simultaneous interpretation and understanding necessitate a move beyond the relativistic stance inherent in social construction. As Gadamer ([1960] 1989) posits, interpretation – the explicit form of understanding – is always influenced by cultural tradition. A relativistic stance fails to appreciate that 'tradition, through its sedimentations, has a power which is constantly determining what we are in the process of becoming,' as Bernstein (1983: 142) clarifies.

Story and storytelling play a central role in the different narrative approaches applied to organizational studies but it is not clear how story and narrative relate to each other. The social constructionist, the organizational symbolism and the critical perspective seem also negligent of the fact that story could resist narrative and be thought of as *ante*narrative. While drawing on a participatory narrative approach one acknowledges how multilayered human expression and reality are. The participatory narrative approach, as presented by Lämsä and Sintonen (2006), invites a diversity of people and stories, and helps to bridge the stories from different times and spaces. It opens up the option of antenarrating, taking narrative as something that comes after story and adds plot. Boje (2000) makes a distinction between story and narrative. Existing before narrative, story is then before narrative. Antenarrative deals with the prevalence of fragmented and polyphonic storytelling, suspending time sequence, coherence and closure.

Appropriated to Business Growth

Particularly relevant to my study of business growth is a participatory narrative approach. It originates in an understanding of practitioners' emergent orientation toward the things they see, experience and construct as reality. The organization, firm or company is not already 'there'; it emerges through practitioners' telling, accounting for interplay and communication between the narrators. It conveys the relational idea of how people come to be and interactively know the world (Fletcher, 2007). 'Participatory' assumes joint performance of and intersection between those telling of their direct involvement in growth and the researcher as listener and interpreter (Barry and Elmes, 1997; Boje, 1991, 1995; Lämsä and Sintonen, 2006).

While acknowledging how multilayered human expression and reality are, the participatory approach embraces different social worlds and meanings adhered to in these worlds (Bruner, 1990; Mumby, 1993; Shotter, 2003). It sincerely appreciates a hermeneutic process, which takes cultural tradition as its starting point. As purported by Gadamer ([1960] 1989), cultural tradition refers to the sphere we stand in and belong to. By introducing the concept of *Erfahrung* – as distinguished from *Erlebnis*, which refers to a psychological understanding of experience and thus to the enduring residue of moment lived – Gadamer provides the basis for intersubjectivity and interrelational interpretation and understanding. In this way, one avoids the problem of how to bridge individual, collective and organization levels, Küpers (2000) comments. But Gadamer, going even further, attributes to interpretation and understanding an ontological status. No longer thought of as a subdiscipline of humanistic studies or as the method of *Geisteswissenschaften*, hermeneutics in the advanced form (philosophical hermeneutics) presented by Gadamer ([1960] 1989) pertains to questions of our belongingness to the world (Bernstein, 1983).

By using the term *Erfahrung*, Gadamer ([1960] 1989) refers to an ongoing integrative process related to effective historical consciousness. This suggests a turn away from a focus on thoughts and beliefs as central in human life, toward a participative and dialogically structured world where 'meanings arise inevitably and inexorably in people's living, responsive reactions to the "callings" of events occurring around them,' Shotter (2003: 440) clarifies. The aim of interpretation and understanding is obviously not to grasp the subjective intentions of historical agents (Bernstein, 1983).

In line with the participative and dialogical, Gadamer ([1960] 1989: 446) relates a human being's life movement to language, promoting the idea that language has its 'true being only in dialogue, in *coming to an understanding*.' The hermeneutical task of understanding, inevitably bound to interpretation, connects fundamentally with language. Language is not a mere means in a communication process, underlines Shotter (2003). As a universal medium, it actualizes effective-historical consciousness, meaning that we are always standing in a hermeneutical situation affected by history. To be able to understand business growth as human interaction and activity, it is essential to add an existential dimension to the participatory narrative approach. We cannot neglect a past that in a philosophical hermeneutical sense always is shaping our lives.

Social constructionist researchers taking a relativistic and subjective stance refer to meaning as if it imposes on reality, leaving out the existential dimension of humans in their relation to the world, Crotty (2003) remarks. It is argued that through 'experience and accumulated knowledge each person develops a personal set of labels to give meaning to present and future social situations' (Chell, 2000: 69). In making the process of intentional consciousness far less cerebral, as Crotty puts it, intentionality denotes 'a radical interdependence of subject and world' (2003: 45). Embracing the notion that human beings intentionally relate to their world is to reject relativism and subjectivism.

In sum, the participatory narrative approach brings together narrative theoretical ideas applied by scholars using a social constructionist perspective but also encompasses an existential dimension that directs the attention to experience as an integrative life process. Language unfolds this lived experience, mediating past and present. As Shotter emphasizes (2003: 444), world and language are 'all *internally* related participant parts of a larger, indivisible, dynamic whole, a ceaseless stream of ongoing activity, of understandable-being in motion.' Further, the approach considers 'antenarrating' as central to building on a multivoiced interpretation and understanding of business growth. Narrative in its post-story guise is bound with becoming. Instead of remaining stationary with regard to a particular organizational context, the narrative varies with people's activities, free of restrictions in time and space. The business growth narrative thus comes after the stories that people provide and is presented without a proper plot sequence and coherence, which is traditionally preferred in narrative theory.

The participatory narrative approach sets the overall directions in which I work. It assumes joint performance of and intersection between those people recounting their direct involvement in growth and the researcher as listener and interpreter. In the co-construction that subsequently takes place, I also make theoretical concerns throughout the text, entwining these with the bits and pieces that people who are engaged in growth activities supply by their stories. In this way, the unfolding narrative of business growth blurs a sharp distinction between theory and practice. In the interface between theory and practice and through the dialogues promoted by theory and practice, the business growth narrative is worked out. Theory is applied when considered relevant for bringing about an interpretation and understanding of the activities and changes that practitioners share and participate in and tell about.

SUMMING UP

This introductory chapter points out that the aim of this book is to provide a valuable and interesting complement to the existing body of business growth research. In reference to narrative approaches employed by organization scholars, it clarifies which direction we should work in. In close relation to the social constructionist perspective, the chapter introduces a participatory narrative approach, emphasizing interplay and communication between different human voices, including the voice of the researcher and author of this book. Inspired by Lämsä and Sintonen (2006) and Wigren (2003), the participatory narrative approach builds on oral and written stories to which is attributed the ability to open up to different social worlds and the meanings attributed to these worlds. As underlined, its interpretative orientation makes this study differ substantially from a logical-scientific way of explaining business growth that relies on firm-level data and statistical techniques to produce verifiable results. While focusing on Gadamerian interpretation and understanding, the narrative approach also clearly deviates from a relativistic and subjective constructionist view.

Ascribed a participatory character, the narrative approach has the potential to foster a dynamic conceptualization of business growth. Not particularly well-structured in a traditional narrative sense, the business growth narrative is characterized as multivoiced and multiplotted. Based on Boje's (2000) distinction between narrative and story, story appears as antenarrative. This makes the business growth narrative afforded in this book a post-story.

THE REMAINING CHAPTERS

The next chapter looks into earlier research on growth, illustrating that much interest is dedicated to the firm and to what occurs within the firm with regard to entrepreneurship. In addition, it emphasizes the need to move beyond the firm level, complementing existing studies with a narrative dynamic conceptualization of growth. It promotes the idea that business growth research must shed light on human activity, including emotion, while taking into account a context in which activity also locates the context of activity that practitioners draw up and impart by means of their stories.

The third chapter points out that the participatory narrative approach encloses an existential dimension that is concerned with an intersubjective character of reality. The framework allows us to be sensitive to the practitioners' voices as they articulate their lived experience and notions of growth. Attributed to a participatory character, the framework also permits the researcher and author of the book to entwine theoretical threads continuously with the practitioners' stories. Since much of the practice of growth takes place through language, a dividing line is not made between language and practice.

Thereafter, four empirical-oriented chapters weave together bits and pieces that practitioners associated with the Hilding Anders business communicate about growth through their stories. The chapters portray a wide range of activities in connection with theory. They expose growth in reference to strategically important changes, labeled turning points and route followers.

The final chapter delineates plots by interconnecting the turning points and the route followers already exposed in the empirical-oriented chapters, and proposes a narratively framed rationality that reconciles intellect with sense, calculative rationality with emotion. The chapter further discusses plot in reference to pattern and the way in which pattern has been outlined in earlier research on strategic change and growth. As emphasized, a dynamic conceptualization of business growth, drawing on many voices and many plots, is founded in a narrative rationality that makes explicit the underlying intersubjective and interpretative character of business growth as human interaction and activity.

2. Toward implies from

A move toward a narrative dynamic conceptualization requires a clarification of what instigates this move. A 'toward' necessarily implies a 'from'. Previous (nonnarrative) growth research suggests here a preliminary location to depart from. It is also important to note that insights gained from earlier nonnarrative theoretical frameworks, empirical foci and concepts could prove useful for catching nuances in the practitioners' stories. The words they use might bring together issues dealt with in both narrative and nonnarrative literature. The participatory narrative approach does not confine itself to a specific growth theory.

This chapter shows that in most business growth literature the firm is at the center and that a major assumption regards a firm's natural evolution in the sense of linear moves from one stage to another. Moreover, it emphasizes that to generate competitive advantage, the firm must use resources efficiently and build capabilities to release positive synergies between resources. By referring to entrepreneurship, this chapter also incorporates a dimension of growth that trains the spotlight on the individual in the firm. By highlighting the dynamic character of entrepreneurship, it further directs attention to relational ideas that are concerned with how people come to constitute and interactively know a world. The chapter concludes by stressing that it is important that we throw more light on human interaction and activity.

THE GROWING FIRM, AND INSIDE IT

An extensive body of research directs attention to the firm, underlining the importance of definitions and measurements for understanding and explaining growth (Delmar, Davidsson and Gartner, 2003; Shepherd and Wiklund, 2009). Reviews of literature on business growth display a richness of studies that examine internal and external determinants of firm growth and performance (Gibb and Davies, 1990; McKelvie, Wiklund and Davidsson, 2006; Merz, Weber and Laetz, 1994; Smallbone, Leigh and North, 1995). There seems to be a broad agreement among growth scholars on the relationships between firm growth, competitive advantage and performance although their use of measures announces limited consensus on formulae and time spans. Based on an extensive review of empirically oriented articles published in highly regarded management journals[2] during 1992–2003, Shepherd and Wiklund's

(2009) work illustrates that the most frequently appearing firm growth performance measures are sales, number of employees, profit, assets and equity. The performance construct is generally recognized as multidimensional. The lack of convergent validity means that an independent variable could be positively related to one performance measure and negatively related to another (Bamford, Dean and Douglas, 2004).

Studies show that the firm attributes successful performance to growth and to the achievement of sustainable competitive advantage (Pfeffer, 2005; Rouse and Daellenbach, 1999), using profit as an indicator of success (Delmar, Davidsson and Gartner, 2003). Together with product and market development, the growing firm pursues a strategy for investment and management of production (Smallbone, Leigh and North, 1995). Without the support of different resources and the development of competencies and capabilities, it is unlikely that the competitive advantage will be enduring. In a growing business, it is therefore important, according to King, Solomon and Fernald (2001), to test whether the manager's potential capabilities, representing the highest current level of mental complexity, correlates with the manager's job performance. As growth also results in increased financial challenges, firms need to rely on more frequent financial reporting in order to monitor performance, concludes McMahon (2001). The choice to grow (Peng and Heath, 1996) implies staying ahead of competition, improving market orientation (Golann, 2006) and engaging in value innovation by discovering new sources of value for the customers (Kim and Mauborgne, 1997). As Gibb and Davies (1990: 22) posit: 'All growth must of course come through the market place.'

Firm growth, profitability and market value depend on innovation spurred through the application of knowledge to produce new knowledge to ensure product and service quality (Cho and Pucik, 2005). A growing firm needs to expand its customer base, products and services continually (Sexton and Seale, 1997) in order to secure and maintain a competitive position (Claver, Andreu and Quer, 2006). A fit between the firm's resources, strategies and market attractiveness plays a key role in the firm's success, Chandler and Hanks (1994) argue. A misalignment between a firm's strategy and environment is indicative of poor performance (Boeker, 1997). Alignment requires management actions to adjust to changes in the firm's external conditions (Smallbone, Leigh and North, 1995).

Through the focus on fit, it is clear that the firm and its environment represent poles as separated by a dualism.[3] A fit concerns the positioning in the market in relation to the resource base of the organization. Yet, changes in strategy and structure might be accompanied by changes in the organization's values and management processes, which make a fit difficult to obtain since both strategy and structure reflect the administrative heritage of the organization (Bartlett and Ghoshal, 1991).

Reviews of literature on business growth also exhibit the assumption of a firm's linear moves as portrayed by life-cycle models. The assumption holds that it is inherent in the firm's actual existence that it must grow continuously in order to sustain a competitive position in the environment (Claver, Andreu and Quer, 2006). Based on the premises of natural evolution, business growth concerns a number of stages and a set of factors that prompt the firm's transition from one stage to another (Adizes, 1988; Churchill and Lewis, 1983; Gibb and Davies, 1990; Greiner, 1972; Helms and Renfrow, 1994). Sequentially ordered stages are frequently characterized as changes in market, finance, control, management style and organization (Gibb and Davies, 1990; Merz, Weber and Laetz, 1994). A simple three-stage progression captures the evolutionary essence of the firm's life cycle. The first stage covers the founding of the business; the second stage includes expansion and stability of operations into routines; the third and final stage represents maturity with modest expectations on growth (Gersick et al., 1997).[4]

The deterministic trend of the linear series of stages has attracted severe criticism. Scholars have criticized stage models for failing to acknowledge that there are erratic and unpredictable ways of growing (Geroski, 1999) and for neglecting alliances and other partnering arrangements that lead to complex configurations of strategic choices (McCann, 1991). When a firm proceeds from one stage to another it may encounter a complex transition due to integral interdependencies among strategy, structure and situation variables (Miller and Friesen, 1984). In addition, demographic variables such as firm size, firm age, industry and ownership allow for substantial differences in growth patterns, as Delmar, Davidsson and Gartner (2003) admit. As an example, firms exhibit patterns labeled 'steady sales growers' when they have positive development in absolute sales but negative development in employment; they are labeled 'acquisition growers' when showing strong development in absolute sales and total employment; and are labeled as 'erratic one-shot growers' when they have negative development in absolute sales and employment. As Penrose (1959) adds, firms have no determined size in the long run. To understand the dynamics of firm growth, one needs to shift the focus away from stages and sequences of a life cycle to a firm's collection of human and physical resources and to how the resources interact with the administrative organization to expand the firm's productive opportunity, suggests Penrose.

As pointed out next with reference to the resource-based view, the Penrosian distinction between internal and external growth, a firmcentric and a multifirm capability approach, firm growth comes through the firm's use of resources, entrepreneurial orientation and development of capabilities. Yet the firm is at the center, manifesting its existence as an independent unit that interacts with the environment as it appears 'out there'. A 'mindset' is even attributed to the firm.

A Focus on Resource and Capability

A focus on the firm's resources, relationships between resources, competition and profitability, amounting to the resource-based view, reflects a resurgence of interest in the work of Penrose (1959). Although Penrose's role in the evolution of the resource-based view has been contested (Rugman and Verbeke, 2004), her work has been widely acknowledged as central to providing the foundation of the resource-based view (Lockett and Thompson, 2004). In accordance with this view, the firm must use available resources efficiently. The 'costly-to-copy attributes' described by the managers translate the resources into economic rents and drivers for the performance and competitive advantage of the firm (Barney, 1991). Applied to small business growth, the resource-based view explains that growth depends on the managerial resources that are available over time to plan and manage growth (Dobbs and Hamilton, 2007).

Penrose's (1959) theory of the growth of the firm holds that the firm's capacity to maximize profit depends on how it makes use of productive opportunities based on internal resources and on the discovery of external environmental changes. This capacity can be captured empirically in a firm's degree of entrepreneurial orientation, with small firms more entrepreneurially oriented than large ones, as McKelvie, Wiklund and Davidsson (2006) illustrate. Large firms as opposed to small firms have access to financial and managerial resources that make them more inclined to grow through acquiring productive resources from external sources. Small firms' growth is financed almost exclusively through retained earnings (Oliveira and Fortunato, 2006). Limited cash flow imposes financial constraints, and less managerial slack available make firms reluctant to get involved in acquisitions. Instead, they commit themselves to organic growth by taking advantage of productive opportunities through recombining resources and utilizing slack resources, explains Penrose (1959). Entrepreneurial orientation and use of knowledge-based resources are critical in that respect, enabling the firm to overcome environmental and financial constraints. Entrepreneurial orientation, which explains the mindset of firms that pursue new opportunities (Lumpkin and Dess, 1996), yields a positive relationship between knowledge-based resources and firm performance, conclude Shepherd and Wiklund (2005).

Penrose (1959) draws a line between internal, organic growth and external, acquired growth but also acknowledges that the more integrated an acquired firm becomes the more similar organic growth is. McKelvie, Wiklund and Davidsson (2006) refer to the Penrosian internal–external distinction, and to the resource-based view as a fruitful way of understanding why firms of various sizes pursue different growth strategies:

Organic and acquisition growth are different processes, requiring different explanations in terms of the firms' resource endowments and usages. Entrepreneurial resources, reflected in the firm's entrepreneurial orientation, are important to organic growth, whereas the size of the firm's resource pool, as seen by financial capital and managers, is important to acquisition growth. (McKelvie, Wiklund and Davidsson, 2006: 189)

Moving beyond the resource-based view, Eisenhardt and Martin (2000) direct attention to how firms build competitive advantage in situations of unpredictable and rapid change. The resource-based view has generally been criticized for not explaining how and why resources contribute to competitive advantage in dynamic markets where long-term advantage is most unlikely. By questioning the path-dependent strategic logic of the resource-based view, Eisenhardt and Martin (2000: 1118) point to the fact that it 'not only lacks a logic of change that is crucial in dynamic markets, but also underplays the difficulty of predicting the length of current advantage and the sources of future advantage.' Concentrating on dynamic capabilities, linked to knowledge-creation processes and organizational routines, they describe how the firm gains, reconfigures, releases and synthesizes resources. As Grant (1991: 122) clarifies: 'capabilities involve complex patterns of coordination between people and between people and other resources. Perfecting such coordination requires learning through repetition. ... A capability is, in essence, a routine, or a number of interacting routines.'

To grow the business and strengthen its market position, a firm must engage in the development of dynamic capabilities, taking into consideration the capabilities that are embedded in organizational processes and routines. From the viewpoint of Eisenhardt and Martin (2000), dynamic capabilities can be used as tools to move into a new competitive position employing a path-breaking logic of change. A constantly and globally redefined corporate environment suggests variation in product innovativeness. Strong entrepreneurial firm-level behavior promoting innovativeness could be demonstrated through the management's exploitation of market opportunities in a pre-emptive and aggressive fashion, Avlonitis and Salavou (2007) propose. When operating in dynamic markets it makes sense to produce innovative resource configurations, generating a series of temporary advantages rather than striving for long-term competitive advantage. In such contexts, the managers are affected by the pace of experience. Just as infrequent experience can lead to people forgetting what was previously learned, experience that comes too fast can make it difficult to absorb what occurs in an unpredictable and rapidly changing market, to transform and consolidate experience into learning, Eisenhardt and Martin (2000) emphasize.

In providing a useful complement to the firm-centric (corporative) capability focus, Moore, Autry and Macy (2007) use a multifirm perspective in the design of a capability-based approach. A multifirm capability approach originates in the notion of interpreneurial capability, with attention directed to value added through interorganizational relationships. To grow a business, a firm can employ an internal growth strategy in the form of corporate venturing, product development, organizational change or process innovation. At the same time, it can rely on an external growth strategy such as vertical alliance, establishing strong relationships between customers and suppliers for combining interfirm resources across the value chain. By introducing the concept of interpreneurship, Moore, Autry and Macy draw on both intrapreneurship, referring to entrepreneurship within an organization, and alliance entrepreneurship, which concerns the identification of and response to partnering opportunities.

Social capital is particularly important for gaining competitive advantage through leveraging entrepreneurial capability via strategic alliances.[5] 'An interpreneurial capability is an intangible, socially complex capability that organizations leverage in order to innovate and is created by combining entrepreneurial and relational capabilities. In this case, the combining of entrepreneurial (e.g. proactiveness) and relational (e.g. social capital) resources results in an innovative, interpreneurial capability' (Moore, Autry and Macy, 2007: 75).

Related to Internationalization

Firm-level explanations of growth build also on insights from studies of cross-border mergers and acquisitions (Cartwright and Cooper, 1996; Larsson and Risberg, 1998; Nahavandi and Malekzadeh, 1988; Very, Lubatkin and Calori, 1998) and from internationalization theories acknowledging that competitive advantage stems from resources and capabilities, especially knowledge-based intangible assets.[6] Peng (2001: 819), using a citation-based approach when documenting the extent to which the resource-based view has penetrated research in international business, draws the conclusion that it has provided 'a powerful theoretical perspective.' A large number of diverse research topics, ranging from the global strategies of multinational corporations to entrepreneurial activities of start-ups employ the resource-based view.

Insights drawn for internationalization theories help broaden the focus on the exploitation of a firm's advantage and have far-reaching implications because of the shift in frame away from transaction to capability, as Madhok (1997) points out. Traditionally, the internationalization perspective on mode entry into a foreign market has been closely related to the transaction cost theory (Williamson, 1975), which is concerned with minimizing transaction costs and conditions underlying market failure. Transaction cost theory is driven by the assumptions of opportunism and bounded rationality whereas a

capability approach, based only on bounded rationality, operates independently of the assumption of opportunism. A capability frame emphasizes the
dynamic process by which a firm's knowledge base is developed and integrated into the functioning of the organization, explains Madhok.

Going even further, Naldi (2008) argues that different types of knowledge
highlighted by internationalization scholars could be brought together by
Penrose's (1959) theory of the growth of the firm. In close connection to the
capability-based approach, rooted in the resource-based view, she directs
attention to the exploitation of a current advantage and the development of
new ones:

> In the organizational capability framework, the ideas that firms are broader sets of
> fungible resources and that expansion involves a balance between exploitation of
> existing resources and development of new ones relate directly to Penrose's theory.
> Thus, both Penrose's theory of the growth of the firm and the organizational capa-
> bility framework offer useful insights for complementing the internationalization
> perspectives and make inroads into the internal expansion, partially into the direc-
> tion of such expansion, and into the dynamics beneath firms' knowledge-based
> ownership advantages. (Naldi, 2008: 44)

Every firm can be described as a bundle of resources and capabilities, assert
Erramilli, Agarwal and Dev (2002). In line with the capability approach, they
argue that the transfer of a resource or a capability needs to be internalized to
ensure imperfect imitability. Knowledge embedded in complex social interactions and team relationships cannot easily be coded and transferred through
intimate social activity.

The overview of internationalization research provided by Naldi (2008)
illustrates that earlier research pays much attention to the formation of multinational enterprises (MNEs) and to how they deal with different kinds of
market imperfections. In the pursuit of monopolistic advantage, a MNE is one
way to organize international change. Another stream of research focuses on
the actual process through which a firm expands internationally and increasingly involves itself in a specific foreign market as it gains experience from its
current activities, as Naldi says. Such a process is captured through a stage
model that describes international progression from no regular export to the
establishment of independent representatives abroad (Johanson and
Wiedersheim-Paul, 1975). Studies of the expansion process also depict a
circular process that takes into account how market knowledge and commitment affect the decision to engage in international activities (Johanson and
Vahlne, 1977). Through the development of a network approach, the focus
centers on the establishment of a firm's relationships and positions in a foreign
market (Johanson and Mattsson, 1988).

The more recent international entrepreneurship stream of research investigates young firms, so-called international new ventures. Oviatt and McDougall define this venture '*as a business organization that, from inception, seeks to derive significant competitive advantage from the use of resources and the sale of outputs in multiple countries*' (1994: 49, original emphasis). Drawing on Oviatt and McDougall, Naldi (2008) points to a growing number of early internationalization firms that base their competitive advantages on the ability to spot and act on emerging opportunities, on knowledge of markets and suppliers and on the ability to establish networks with business associates. Accordingly, three groups of international market makers are identified. The first group is comprised of new ventures in the form of export/import start-ups or multinational traders that serve a few nations with which the entrepreneur is familiar. The second group attends to the specialized needs of a particular geographical region, and the third group, the most radical one, coordinates multiple value chain activities in different foreign places. The third group contains global start-ups that require skills at both geographical and activity coordination to be able to respond to globalizing markets but also act proactively on opportunities in these markets. Once established, 'they appear to have the most sustainable competitive advantages due to a combination of historically unique, causally ambiguous, and socially complex inimitability with close network alliances in multiple countries,' contend Oviatt and McDougall (1994: 60).

So far, this chapter has devoted little attention to human interaction and activity. The firm has played a major role as a collective agent that exploits and develops resources and capabilities to generate competitive advantage and grow. The discussion that follows elevates the entrepreneurship dimension of growth, indicating that entrepreneurship is a complex construct. It mentions a number of entrepreneurship and corporate entrepreneurship studies that address the individual level and the firm level, referring to factors that influence entrepreneurship and the processes through which entrepreneurial activities are encouraged. As also noted, previous research on entrepreneurship and corporate entrepreneurship gives little attention to the intersubjective relation in social interaction among individuals.

On the Entrepreneurship Dimension

As the field of firm growth has progressed, researchers have realized that there are growth advantages accruing to small firms and entrepreneurs (Dean, Brown and Bamford, 1998). Firm growth has become increasingly accepted as an indication and a continuation of entrepreneurship within a firm (Davidsson, 1991; Merz, Weber and Laetz, 1994). Analyses broaden to include the individual level. Scholars introduce an entrepreneur as the person who founded an enterprise (Begley and Boyd, 1987). They highlight the entrepreneur's instrumental function by interlinking entrepreneurship and enterprise with self-employment and small business ownership (Curran and Blackburn, 2001; Dale, 1991; Sexton and Smilor, 1986) with limited concern for intersubjectivity and relationality. This can be exemplified in Peay's and Dyer's (1989: 49) definition of the entrepreneur as 'an individual who has been instrumental in founding at least one organization for profitable purposes, and who maintains a major ownership position and directs managerial control for the enterprise by virtue of the position held, such as president or chief executive officer.'

Studies also elevate the process of entrepreneurship. Gartner (2001) describes entrepreneurship as 'organizing', arguing that it is through the study of firm creation that entrepreneurship can be understood. Davidsson, Low and Wright (2001) refer to the processual aspect of entrepreneurship when using the term 'emergence'. But a substantial body of small business research attests to the qualities of just one person who scans for opportunities and exploits opportunities that others miss (Bateman and Crant, 1993; Kirzner, 1973) and is highly skilled in promoting and implanting radical change (Nystrom, 1995). The entrepreneur is introduced as an agent of change, who, driven by self-interest, operates in the private sector in a market economy and attempts to maximize profit. The entrepreneur sometimes earns an image as a heroic swash-buckling business adventurer (Casson, 1982) whose frantic dealings have somewhat piratical connotations (Hobbs, 1991). From the broader, societal perspective, the entrepreneur acts as the prime mover in economic development, not only adjusting to markets but also making them and destroying them (Schumpeter, 1934). Profit is regarded as a reward to the risk-taking and risk-averse entrepreneur (Timmons, 1994) for bearing the costs of uncertainty and risk. The entrepreneur is 'someone who has the ability to perceive and exploit previously unrecognized profit opportunities' (Bygrave and Minniti, 2000: 25). In many cases it is, however, difficult to identify an individual who acts as an entrepreneur. Added to this is the complicating factor of identifying what a single individual does. As Schumpeter (1951) underlines, entrepreneurship concerns building aptitudes, which no single individual combines, into an organization.

Entrepreneurship is portrayed as a type of behavior that concentrates on opportunities rather than on resources (Thurik and Wennekers, 2004). Opportunity can be defined as 'a future situation which is desirable and feasible' (Stevenson and Jarillo, 1990: 163). The mere discovery of an opportunity is obviously not sufficient. The potential entrepreneur must decide to explore and exploit an opportunity, believing that 'the expected value of the entrepreneurial profit will be large enough to compensate for the opportunity cost of other alternatives (including the loss of leisure), the lack of liquidity of the investment of time and money, and a premium for bearing uncertainty' (Shane and Venkataraman (2000: 223). Opportunity exploration includes testing a product and a market, and exploitation refers to production start-up and full-scale operation (Choi, Lévesque and Shepherd, 2007). In this opportunity context, 'entrepreneurial judgment' plays a significant role as an input to growth (Penrose, 1959). Entrepreneurial judgment refers to managers' ability to see and take advantage of productive opportunities through recombining resources and utilizing slack resources, discerning ways to meet changing market conditions and customers' altered preferences. A most crucial question then pertains to how to make an opportunity productive. Depending on the manager's entrepreneurial judgment, connections are made between resources and the services produced by the resources. Individual differences between the managers, regarding values, expectations, interest and knowledge, shape the entrepreneurial image of the opportunity available in the environment, Penrose asserts. Through the design of jobs and positions, the provision of resources and positive inducements, the organization and its management can make individuals specifically able to detect and willing to exploit opportunities (Stevenson and Jarillo, 1990).

To pursue growth opportunities the managers must show a positive attitude toward growth, believing in growth (Wiklund, Davidsson and Delmar, 2003), and be aware that their displays of positive and negative emotions affect the employees' willingness to act entrepreneurially (Brundin, Patzelt and Shepherd, 2007). The individuals' motivation and intention to grow the business also depend on other psychological factors such as their need for achievement, locus of control and risk-taking propensity (Begley and Boyd, 1987). Moreover, entrepreneurship studies point out that changes that occur over time in individuals' perceptions of external competitive conditions and their cognitive style modify their initial growth intentions, influencing the degree of growth or the individuals' risk averseness. Cognitive style influences the interaction with the environment, determining how a person processes and evaluates information and makes decisions. A risk-averse individual takes a more cautious, incremental approach to decision making, relying on prevailing norms whereas a less risk-averse individual is more inclined to break norms, Dutta and Thornhill (2007) claim.

From a social constructionist perspective, ontologically oscillating between subjectivity and objectivity, Chell (2000: 74) argues that 'the creation *and* pursuit of opportunity are fundamental to the entrepreneurial persona' and that cognitive psychology can help improve our understanding of entrepreneurs' thinking and their different sense of time and space. Opportunities are not 'out there' but part of a process of entrepreneurship that accounts for a mental space between the entrepreneurs and their perception of reality. With reference to behavior and perception, it is unclear, however, how the entrepreneurs participate in and realize themselves in an interpretable world where human action goes beyond behavior (Czarniawska, 2004),[7] and experience as an integrative life process exceeds a subject's perception. By including an existential dimension our understanding accounts ontologically for intersubjectivity rather than an oscillation between subjectivity and objectivity.

Applied to the corporate setting, entrepreneurship includes corporate venturing, strategic renewal and innovation (Guth and Ginsburg, 1990). A firm is entrepreneurial if it develops new products or new markets or utilizes new technology (Jennings and Lumpkin, 1989). It might engage in diversification through reconfigurations of resources (Burgelman, 1983), extending its domain of competence (Covin and Slevin, 1991). Corporate entrepreneurship refers to organizational renewal with regard to four classes of variables: external, internal, strategic and performance.

Based on a review that mainly directs attention to developments during the 1980s and 1990s, Sciascia and Naldi (2004) introduce corporate entrepreneurship as the study of firm-level entrepreneurship and as a subsection of the wider entrepreneurship field. Employing an analytical process perspective, they put forward the idea that corporate entrepreneurship needs to be more closely related to research on entrepreneurship. This means incorporating both the firm level and the individual level, accounting for the process through which the individual pursues opportunities found within the boundaries of the firm as well as in the external environment. Sciascia and Naldi hereby build on Shane and Venkataraman's (2000: 218) work which implies taking into account 'how, by whom and with what effects opportunities to create future goals and services are discovered, evaluated and exploited.'

Briefly, entrepreneurship is a complex construct that represents a rich array of activities and dynamic interplay between opportunities and actions within the firm and outside. In the words of Bratnicki:

> The heart of entrepreneurship is creating, shaping, recognizing, and interpreting unformed opportunities followed by will, ability, desire, competences, responsibilities, and initiative to seize and pursue these opportunities. Entrepreneurship includes both opportunities and actions. Actions are a general label for bundles, sets, or sequences of behaviors aimed at resource mobilization and deployments, initiatives, responses, moves, deals, investments, and developments. They include ideological, political, economical, legal, and administrative social behaviors over time oriented to change the way people live or work. (Bratnicki, 2005: 19)

To enhance the dynamic character of entrepreneurship in organizations (organizational entrepreneurship), contributing to the traditional field of corporate entrepreneurship, Bratnicki (2005) focuses on dialectic reconciliations, enabled by managers who intend to grow their business. Organizational entrepreneurship is a process that transforms individual ideas into collective action through the reconciliation of contradictions: 'opportunities and actions, vision and venture, resources and organizational architecture, achievement of long-term equity value and short-term profitability, creativity and discipline, internal and external aspects of managing change' (2005: 22). According to Bratnicki, organizational entrepreneurship co-evolves and co-aligns with the environment through the reconfiguration of internal resources and organizational architecture including elements of culture, power, leadership, strategy, people and structure elements.

A firm's entrepreneurial behavior and the individual entrepreneur's discovery and exploitation of opportunity generally associate with the allocation of resources in productive directions (Delmar, 2000). The entrepreneur produces conditions for new markets to develop while acting as catalyst for economic activity. Entrepreneurship contributes to the growth of the economy as a whole (Bygrave and Minniti, 2000) and seems to have merely positive macroeconomic implications. Depending on prevailing laws, legal procedures and social habits, entrepreneurial activities could, however, operate in ways that in the end yield unproductive effects (Baumol, 1959; Bygrave and Minniti, 2000). Looking into the business development of the 20th century in Sweden, Glete (1988) concludes that the market is far from being a neutral meeting place. Entrepreneurial activities performed by financial actors influence the stock market and the adjacent credit market. Some entrepreneurs intervene in the market through bold and ruthless actions, unexpectedly changing the price of a product while others respond to a quoted price by changing their buying and selling plans. What makes an opportunity productive and a corporate setting entrepreneurial is a complex issue that must be addressed from different angles and time horizons.

MORE LIGHT ON HUMAN ACTIVITY

Notwithstanding the usefulness and value of firm-oriented growth studies for advancing our knowledge, it is pertinent to note that studies concerned with the phenomenon of growth (Dutta and Thornhill, 2007) and with human intersubjectivity and relationality are notably absent. As indicated in this chapter, although firm-growth studies submit that competitive advantage builds on individuals' activities, there is little notion of how growth and competitive advantage emgerge through interindividual processes. The firm is the main actor that predefines an organizational context within which individuals perform activities. Managers' entrepreneurial judgment, their descriptions of costly-to-copy resource attributes and their transformation of experience into meaningful learning to accelerate the formation of dynamic capabilities take place within a firm that is ascribed the means of generating profitability, competiveness and growth. The firm provides a room for complex routines that emanate from sequences of people's coordinated actions. The firm pursues a strategy, stays ahead of competition, engages in value innovation and passes from one stage to another, growing. The firm possesses, reconfigures, synthesizes and utilizes resources. The firm tries to achieve a fit with the environment 'out there', monitoring performance. The firm interacts with other firms in order to leverage capability through a combination of entrepreneurial and relational resources. Endowed with the capacity to speak for themselves, 'firm' and 'resource' become reified as fixed, predetermined and independent entities.

In the pursuit of knowledge development, studies employ an analytical methodology that has limited recognition of a story-like representation of practitioners' involvement in growth-related activities. Statistically significant relationships are sought between firm growth variables (for example, Bamford, Dean and Douglas, 2004; Begel and Boyd, 1987; Boeker, 1997; Cho and Pucik, 2005; Goddard, Tavakoli and Wilson, 2009; McMahon, 2001; Shepherd and Wiklund, 2009; Singh and Mitchell, 2005). Although there are studies that use a social constructionist perspective, concerned with how entrepreneurs contest, construct and deal with a business reality through language (Chell, 2000), studies of growth that explicitly point to the entrepreneurship dimension display a preference for firm-level dependent variables. Even a study highlighting the social dynamics of entrepreneurship relies on hypothesis testing and mathematical tools (Bygrave and Minniti, 2000). A previous literature review, covering 389 entrepreneurship-oriented articles, published between 2003 and 2005 in well-regarded journals in the United States and Europe, announces that a majority of studies employ statistical techniques and use large-scale secondary databases when investigating financial outcomes of firm-level performance (Brush, Manolova and Edelman, 2008). The recent request for theoretical advancement and knowledge accumulation, emphasizing robustness across different operationalizations of growth constructs (Shepherd and Wiklund, 2009), further points in the direction of a strengthened focus on measurements.

In growth literature including the dimension of entrepreneurship, the individual level receives plenty of attention. The analysis broadens to include individual entrepreneurs, their intentions and actions (Davidsson, 1991; Shepherd and Wiklund, 2005; Wiklund, Davidsson and Delmar, 2003). Yet many entrepreneurship studies, implicitly or explicitly, assume the existence of a firm. The firm defines the context within which the entrepreneurs realize their intentions and take action. With reference to the entrepreneurship dimension, processes through which individuals pursue opportunities and individual ideas transform into collective action receive attention. These processes, lacking narrative intersubjective sensitivity, frequently result in imposing boundaries that separate the firm from the environment, designating the internal as opposed to the external. A dynamic interplay between opportunities and actions occurs within the firm and outside. This interplay even singles out people as an element separated from other elements such as strategy and culture. Interaction between organization and environment, variables and elements, the internal and the external, represent the individual entrepreneur's reality as poles separated by a dualism. As I have underlined elsewhere:

> Dualism permits opposites to be depicted and tensions to emerge between opposing poles, while denoting a territory between the poles simply by being ignorant of it. Then, the dualism serves as a tool for dividing, keeping apart and putting some distance between phenomena, thereby also exaggerating the characteristics of each phenomenon under study. (Ericson, 2004: 13)

Transcending a dualistic relationship requires appreciating an integral relationship between elements, and the external and internal, while – in view of activity as social practice – highlighting the intersubjective relation in social interaction among individuals. As Hjorth and Johannisson (2000) contend, entrepreneurship is rather something that is left out and marginalized by a focus on the organzation and the processes occurring within the organization. The dualistic opposition relaxes through 'world-openness', which means that human beings take part in enacting reality and applying concepts to what they experience. In accordance with Gergen (1999: 11): 'The world does not produce our concepts, rather our concepts help us engage that world in various ways.' Reality cannot be taken for granted as existing 'out there' as something that surrounds the individual. The individual's relationship to her environment is characterized by world-openness (Berger and Luckmann, 1966).

There is a need for more conversation on dualisms, theoretical perspectives and underlying assumptions. Wiklund, Patzelt and Shepherd (2009) propose a two-layered ontology that encompasses mental models on the one level, and individual capabilities and attitudes of small business owners on the other level. They draw a 'big picture model' that constitutes a basis for deriving hypotheses for empirical testing. Their study illustrates that managers' attitudes, the entrepreneurial orientation of the firm and the dynamics of the task environment – as regards characteristics such as customer and supplier concentration, and export – have a significant influence on firm-level growth. However, it is also important to direct more attention to entrepreneurship as dialogues that constitute human interaction and activity (Hjorth and Johannisson, 2000). Berglund (2007), introducing a broader view of entrepreneurship, also refers to a web of thinking and acting in dialogues between people such that no dualism is admitted between the world and the people. In that which occurs between people, 'reality' transforms, Berglund posits.

From the viewpoint of Gartner (2001), it is essential to increase our awareness of the assumptions that drive research and recognize significant differences in our beliefs about entrepreneurship. To Gartner, it seems that:

> Efforts at theory development in entrepreneurship have some similarity to the 'Blind Men and the Elephant' story. Six blind men touch different parts of the elephant and come away with very different descriptions of an elephant's characteristics. The story offers a syllogism for thinking about the problems of integrating differing views of a large and complex phenomenon. (Gartner, 2001: 28)

Referring to the current debate on progress within the field of entrepreneurship, Welter and Lasch (2008) identify a need for a perspective that directs attention to the context in which entrepreneurship research takes place. They argue that: 'Context matters not only for entrepreneurship as such, because it is influenced by culture, political, and economic environments, thus explaining cross-national differences in themes and topics, but context also matters for the institutionalization of entrepreneurship research and research communities' (2008: 242).

Although growth scholars are encouraged to engage in theoretical and ontological conversations, there seems to be little incentive to develop an alternative in the form of a narrative-oriented theoretical and methodological perspective that constitutes an ontology that prioritizes an interpretation and understanding that mediates past and present in a participative and dialogically structured world. This suggests that extending the conversation beyond the two-layered ontology proposed by Wiklund, Patzelt and Shepherd (2009) would be necessary in order to become more sensitive to the different ways that reality can be constructed (Fischer and Reuber, 2003). It includes problematizing the relationships between firm, growth and entrepreneurship. Studies not taking the firm for granted invite individual narrators and allow for a new problematization of entrepreneurship (Ahl, 2007; Fletcher, 2007; Hjorth, 2007; O'Connor, 2007; Steyaert, 2007). By approaching entrepreneurship as a tactical process of differentiation, the interest shifts toward everyday stories as a form in which invention emerges. Living life in a tactical way, people make creative use of existing orders to open up new opportunities (Hjorth, 2007).

To strengthen the dynamic character of growth further, including the dimension of entrepreneurship, one must move out of the modernist managerial perspective (Hjorth, 2007) which – with its emphasis on organizations as entities, economic resources and instrumental functions – dominates studies of growth and entrepreneurship. The modernist dedicates interest to how reality is represented in the act of knowing, from a cognitive viewpoint looking at the human mind as an instrument for right reasoning and capable of empirical verification. 'Stories of Modernist life depict the administered, rationally planned, grand society that harnesses premodern passion, subjectivity, and choice' (Boje, 1995: 1003).[8] Rather, we should consider that the individual and the world are interrelated through the individual's lived experience of the world and that we cannot experi-

ence the world as an object that we apprehend (Chia, 2004). In a participative and dialogically structured world (Shotter, 2003), experience denotes
an integrative ongoing process in the life of the practitioner, relating the
practitioner to other human beings and to the cultural past. Always shaped
by effective-history, experience is then not the discovery of facts but a
living historical process that constitutes our existential being in the world
(Gadamer, [1960] 1989). In other words, we should be aware that when we
'enter human life, it is as if we walk on stage into a play whose enactment
is already in progress' (Bruner, 1990: 34).

SUMMING UP

This chapter reveals that an extensive body of growth research places the
firm at the center, analyzing external and internal determinants of firm
growth while attributing successful performance to growth and the achievement of sustainable competitive advantage. Moreover, it shows that growth
concerns a number of stages and a set of factors that prompt a firm to move
from one stage to another. Further, the chapter directs attention to theories of
resources and capabilities in a single-firm context as well as in a multifirm
context and to how these theories relate to internationalization theories. By
incorporating the entrepreneurship dimension of growth, the individual level
is addressed. In earlier research, the individual entrepreneur gains much
attention. However, as the chapter points out, there are studies referring to
entrepreneurship as firm creation and a type of behavior that concentrates on
opportunities rather than on resources. In reference to corporate and organizational entrepreneurship, both the firm level and the individual level are
considered.

The chapter acknowledges the usefulness and value of firm-oriented
growth studies for advancing our knowledge but argues also that individuals' interaction and activity should receive more attention from researchers.
As noted, growth scholars are encouraged to engage in theoretical and ontological discussions. Nevertheless, there seems to be little encouragement to
develop an alternative, narrative approach that transcends a dualistic relationship between the external and the internal in the view of activity as
social practice while elevating the intersubjective relation in a social interaction among practitioners.

A narrative approach to the study of business growth could prove valuable as a complement to the existing body of research, advancing our understanding of the business growth phenomenon while taking into account a
context in which interaction and activity are situated. It could also be a
context for interaction and activity that practitioners draw up and impart by

means of their stories. To shed more light on business growth, the next chapter explains in more detail what a participatory narrative approach is about and how it helps weave together the bits and pieces that practitioners narratively communicate.

3. Weaving narrative bits and pieces

The participatory narrative approach mediates an ontology that enables consistency throughout the text in this book with a world of lived experience and a human being's belongingness to cultural tradition – the historical past. This belongingness makes tradition a partner with which a human being can enter into a dialogue, bringing the past and the present together (Gadamer, [1960] 1989). Ontological consistency then implies that the empirical–theoretical interlaced discussions and the methodological discussion in this book enclose an existential dimension[9] that throws light on individuals' relationality. Given the historicity of experience, *homo narrans* as relational selves become part of the world and coexist with it. In the words of Gadow (1999: 62): 'Individuals are intrinsically relational; existential subjectivity is intersubjectivity.'

A relational narrative extends beyond the particularity of a person alone but also beyond one particular growth theory. The narrative embodies intersubjectivity, which is an alternative to both the subjectivity of immersion and the objectivity of detachment, as Gadow (1999) propounds. The narrative invites different voices to make themselves heard and different theoretical threads to be woven into their tellings. Not confined to a prespecified growth perspective ready to be applied when generating and weaving togther the bits and pieces practitioners narratively communicate, the participatory narrative approach allows for the use of growth concepts rooted in narrative as well as in nonnarrative theories. With the emphasis on intersubjectivity, an interpretation and understanding of business growth emerges through a plurivocality that permits a move beyond a monovocal growth theory.

More clearly, the ontological dimension manifests in two propositions. The first is that individual and world are interrelated through the individual's lived experience of the world, which implies that organization and environment, organization and individual, practitioner and practice, actor and activity are not dealt with as separate entities of a dualism. The second is that learning with reference to the broadening of horizons (Gadamer, [1960] 1989) is a fundamental and integral part of growth activities. I do not, however, accentuate the learning aspect in the present study as I have already provided an illustration of (developmental) business growth as dynamically residing in 'human activity and relationships with learning intimately connected with the broadening of horizons' (Ericson, 2007: 150).

From a narrative viewpoint, grounded in the intersubjective world of human lived experience and practical accomplishment (Prus, 1996), it is important in the actual research to frame carefully the bits and pieces practitioners supply, and to realize a dialogical authorship. A framing and a dialogical authorship help communicate an interpretation and understanding that account for practitioners' interactions and activities, and their construction of and involvement in changes. Here interpretation and understanding signal application. A central theme in philosophical hermeneutics is that interpretation and understanding shape our practical lives. There is an inextricable connection of the theoretical and the practical, according to Gadamer ([1960] 1989).

The participatory narrative approach represents a qualitative methodology that clearly distinguishes itself from other qualitative methodologies that center on experience: ethnography and grounded theory. An ethnographic methodology suggests taking part in and experiencing a range of activities over an extended period. By socializing with individuals in a specific cultural setting, the researcher discovers and deduces what is significant in that setting, gaining an understanding about and inferring meaning from individuals' activities and lives. The cultural descriptions provided are based on detailed fieldwork that draws on different kinds of data such as observations, interviews and photographs. The systematizing and synthesizing of the data gathered (Moustakas, 1994) are guided by a verification procedure that views data as reified entities. This denies the kind of truth that speaks in cultural tradition (Gadamer, [1960] 1989). With a focus on the verification of collected data not much attention is dedicated to a philosophically based grounding of theory and method.

The overall aim of a grounded theory methodology is to discover theory from empirical data. The emphasis is on theory as an ever-developing entity, subsuming verification of the emergent theory. As Glaser and Strauss (1967: 28) argue: 'when generating is not clearly recognized as the main goal of a given research, it can be quickly killed by the twin critiques of accurate evidence and verified hypotheses.' To arrive at a theory one needs to take apart the story within the data collected, unraveling the elements of experience and their relationships. A comparative analysis is conducted in which data collection and coding into categories are activities that occur simultaneously and continue as long as new categories emerge or data emerges that fits an existing category. Categories and their specific properties are elements and aspects of the developed and integrated theory, which can also yield discussions presented in the form of hypotheses, as Glaser and Strauss contend.

An attempt to understand what business growth is about must echo openness to a mode of experience in human life that goes beyond what can be verified. It is in the receptivity to the otherness of the past and the way it takes shape in an individual's talk and action that a truth can be claimed, as Gadamer ([1960] 1989) purports.

A FRAMING NARRATIVE AND 'COMPLETENESS'

It is common practice, according to Shklovsky ([1909] 1990), to apply the structure of 'a framing story' to the accumulation of motifs. Motifs, the simplest narrative units, are woven together to make up a theme for which the term plot is used. Drawing on literary criticism, the romance, tragedy, melodrama and irony plot can be defined (Downing, 2005). While the hero, introduced by the romantic plot, succeeds in establishing harmonious relationships between the characters involved, the hero in the tragedy plot suffers a fatal setback. The melodrama plot places at the center stage a hero whose struggle culminates in a battle where evil is defeated. The irony plot reveals the incompetence of the hero. While several heroes and heroines could be identified in a business growth narrative, it would nevertheless be difficult to describe the battles they fight to separate good from evil, highlighting their triumphs and fates or ironically illustrate incompetence.

The plot often follows a sequential logic, teleologically shaping story material toward a particular end; but other ways of representing a story found in the literature incorporate nonlinear and nonteleological sequences (Richardson, 2002). Apart from sequentiality, different forms of parallelism occur. In an adventure novel, Shklovsky ([1909] 1990) explains, one plot proceeds while there is another at the same time or at a quicker tempo, prompting the reader to cross over to another narrative time. An additional way of illustrating plot is through the parallelism of antithetical relationships that pit different groups of people against each other or build on kinship bonds that give people a feeling of being close to one another. While making a distinction between narrative and story with story conceptualized as antenarrative, plot serves as a device for weaving stories together. Plot dresses story in a post-story narrative guise (Boje, 2000).

As illustrated in this book, the business growth narrative as post-story interconnects plots that mainly adhere to a temporal chronology. The plots essentially constitute people's involvement in activities bunched together along the timeline, with the past toward the left and the future toward the right. Nevertheless, in some situations the narrators' experience of time and provision of a multitude of fragmented stories suspend a chronological basis. This means that the business growth narrative also conveys a sense of continuity that redefines the present in the light of the past and the future, inserts the past onto the present (Demers, Giroux and Chreim, 2003) and bridges time gaps when it is not able to supply chronologically rich descriptions of activities. With the temporal dimension of narrative relating to meaning-making, it cannot be taken for granted that time consists of a linear succession of events. As Rossiter (1999: 63) maintains, 'narrative suggests a flow of time that accommodates the confluence of past, present, and future in the process of meaning-making. The "having been" of the past and the "not yet" of the future both suggest the meaning of being in the present.' A threefold present places the past as memory and the future as expectation within the present (Ricoeur, 1983). Stories do not require beginnings, middles and endings in the formal and restrictive definition of stories (Bruner, 1990; Steinmetz, 1992). History cannot be reduced to testable proportional forms (Bruner, 1990). History cannot lose sight of history in a philosophical hermeneutical sense, which means that the recalling of the past is a dialogical function (Gadamer, [1960] 1989).

Business growth narrating implies no precise starting and ending points. Nonetheless, it rounds off in a way that might evoke in the reader a certain feeling of 'completeness'. The way it is told allows the plots to make sense in relation to each other, admitting room for action and counteraction (Shklovsky, [1909] 1990). Instead of law-type statements that invite falsification or verification on a statistical scale (Czarniawska, 2004), the narrative leaves open the connection of activities and changes entailed in activities into different business growth plots. A feeling of completeness might nevertheless vary a great deal because of the ongoing revision taking place between storytellers. Boje (1991: 124) explains: 'Both teller and listener are sending cues to manage how much of the story is told, how much is left to the imagination, and what interpretation is applied.' People immerse themselves in incremental refinement and reinterpretation that sometimes lead to abbreviated and succinct simplification. In the case of terse telling, the storyteller alludes to a shared understanding of a social context and uses the shortest form of a story when saying to another person: 'You know the story' (1991: 115). Extended glosses could also be included in order to sell a particular point of view, adds Boje.

In relation to the business growth narrative, action and counteraction refer to the dialogues between the narrating individuals involved in different kinds of growth activities and the researcher and author of the book. The provision of stories promotes action whereas counteraction grants the switching of the researcher's role from a listener to an interpreter commenting on and interweaving theoretical threads with the stories the practitioners provide. The business growth narrative proceeds through the dialogues, communicating through the medium of language. It is thus at the interface of practice and theory, and practitioner and researcher, that the business growth narrative is worked out.

Etymologically, the word 'dialogue' derives from 'dia' and 'logos', which mean 'through' and 'word' respectively (Herman, 1995). The we-sphere, holding the encounter of an 'I' with a 'you' in the dialogue, is a fundamental condition of intersubjectivity (Gadamer, [1960] 1989) and implies both action and counteraction (Shklovsky, [1909] 1990).

The Narrative Material

The business growth narrative emerges in the light of the different voices speaking of a rich array of growth-related activities at face-to-face meetings, via telephone and email, and through documents. Hilding Anders International AB (Hilding Anders) exists as a bed and mattress producer in people's talk and in documents, extending through the following business areas: Nordic, Central & West, South, East, and Asia (Hilding Anders, 2009b). Approximately 4,600 employees engage in operations on 27 European and 13 Asian markets (Hilding Anders, 2009d). The practitioners' stories presented in the empirically oriented chapters (Chapters 4–7) are witness to sustainable growth thoughout the years. Ever since the 1950s, the Hilding Anders business has grown in terms of steady increases in sales accompanied by increases in profitability. As presented on the website the strategy of Hilding Anders is to: 'Create profitability through organic growth and acquisitions; Create synergies and economies of scale by coordinating purchasing, production, logistics, IT and R&D; Base marketing and product development on local conditions and customer desires' (www.hildinganders.se).

The narrative material was generated in 2006–9 during my visits to Malmö, Helsingborg, Alvesta, Hästveda, Osby and Tibro, in the southern part of Sweden. My first contact was with the CEO Anders Pålsson at the headquarters in Malmö. Anders Pålsson provided me with company-related stories that mainly focus on Hilding Anders' strategy, business concept and the expansive phase the company faced at the time. I also received from him documentary material on a wide range of business operations. Contacts with people presently involved in top management activities then took me to Helsingborg, where I met with Bengt Adolfsson, the former CEO. In Alvesta, I talked with Lars Haux, the former production and purchasing director. Encouraged by interesting and informative dialogues with these people to gain deeper insight into growth and to learn more about activities that would bring the past alive, I went to Hästveda to meet with Olle Andersson, the son of the founder of Hilding Anders. Having participated in various activities over 40 years, he supplied rich stories about the expansion of the business, including changes of different kinds. While paying a visit to the factory in Hästveda I talked with Tomas Modén and Claes-Göran Jönsson, both directly involved in the production of beds and mattresses. Olle Anderson recommended that I contact the former production manager Bertil Henningsson – for which I went to Osby. To gain some insights into the brand aspect of growth, I got in touch with Rickard Eriksson, production manager at Tibrobädden, located in Tibro. Via telephone and email I was provided with interesting stories by Anders Hultman, one of the former chairmen of Hilding Anders, Arne Karlsson, the CEO of Ratos and former business area manager of Atle, and by Mats Östergård, the managing director of the Finnish Unituli. In addition, I met with and talked to other people whose names are not mentioned in this book.

To prepare for the meetings, I spent time in a local library, reading about the historical development in the region where the Hilding Anders business started up. I also spent time in the local newspaper office, looking into and summarizing articles published about Hilding Anders and people associated with Hilding Anders. Practitioners provided me with additional material via email and telephone. Due to the time pressure and unforeseen turbulent conditions that practitioners presently associated with the Hilding Anders business encountered in their daily business life, it was almost impossible for me to access these practitioners and generate material about ongoing activities. Daily business life can, however, present itself in differing degrees of closeness and remoteness, as Berger and Luckmann (1966) point out, meaning that the reality of everyday life is not exhausted by immediate presences. To get a grasp of what is happening, one does not always need to be present or be in the middle of things as they take place.

Through my visits to different places, telephone calls and emails, numerous dialogues took place. Communications that can best be described as tacit dialogues were performed in relation to documentary texts in order to generate material, asking what could be made of the texts in the construction of a business growth narrative. The questions were then: 'What do they lend themselves to becoming' (Crotty, 2003: 50), and what practitioners tell of in these texts. I gathered many pages from documents such as newsletters, press releases, company information and overviews dispersed in various locations on the internet. In these documents, practitioners announced their opinions on different strategic matters. As Demers, Giroux and Chreim (2003) argue, these kinds of documents can be read as narratives.

Before the first contact and meeting with a person, I prepared by listing a few questions (based on the material accessed through the local library, the local newpaper office and the internet) to be used for the guidance of our talk. I expected the actual meeting to unfold through questions and answers as in a traditional interview. When the talk turned in an unanticipated direction the interview evolved into a dialogue; a more spontaneous and nonpredictable form of interaction with the practitioner took place. As opposed to an interview, which is commonly regarded as a tool for transmitting insight, experience and facts (Alvesson, 2003), a dialogue is a spontaneous form of interaction (Herman, 1995).

Several practitioners make themselves heard in this study; there were around 30 in all. Although the voices of CEOs, directors and managers dominate the study, the participatory narrative approach – emphasizing antenarrating – promotes a move beyond managerialism perpetuated by a hegemonic narrative. A hegemonic narrative tends to be monovocal and monologic, based on a 'simplistic assumption that managers are an amorphous mass that have one view – the "right" view' (Vickers, 2008: 550). Despite appearances of hegemonic narratives, multiple versions of 'reality' exist. As Brown, Humphreys and Gurney (2002: 323) argue, the power structures instantiated in such narratives 'are always in a permanent state of becoming.' The business growth narrative worked out in this book, starting from the assumption of relationality and intersubjectivity, is polyvocal in character and does not aim for coherence and closure.

The practitioners construct a reality that facilitates sense and meaning in interaction with the listener. The relational issue of maintaining the participants' engagement (Rae, 2005) entails a two-way communication in which it is important to be aware of a story's seductiveness and particular perception (Sole and Wilson, 2002). A storyteller can speak eloquently and provide rich detail, yet present a one-sided picture. To avoid falling into the traps of seductiveness and single-sided perception, I met with and talked to people involved in a variety of activities stretching over a period of nearly 70 years. In connection with theory, I reflected on the words and perspectives of the storytellers. The participatory narrative approach leaves itself open to a variety of theoretical threads to be woven into a practitioner's story. I also realized that the richness of experience and accomplishments of a practitioner are hard to capture in interaction with theory within the scope of this study. The business growth narrative builds only on fragments cut out of people's lives and their engagement in growth activities.

The face-to-face dialogues lasted from half an hour to four hours, and relied mainly on what Feldman et al. (2004) describe as the convention of story in narrative, namely the then-what-happened convention. Dialogues via email continued for several months. The bits and pieces supplied by the dialogue partners emerged chronologically for the most part, over the course of the dialogue. Here time relates to the being of time (Ricoeur, 1983), suggesting that time appears as a quantitative element, implied by conventional devices such as the calender and the clock (Sztompka, 1993). Yet, the past was also brought into the present, and gaps between the past and the present were bridged when making the past come alive in the present talk, attributing a narrative temporal quality to time. As Ricoeur (1993: 52) postulates, 'time becomes human to the extent that it is articulated through a narrative mode, and narrative attains its full meaning when it becomes a condition of temporal existence.' Since past and present experience and the visual are hard to put in words, and experience might be too fleeting to be captured in a proper language (Spence, 1982), it is only possible to capture some fragments of growth practice.

I tape-recorded the face-to-face dialogues, apart from talks over lunch, coffee breaks and outdoor visits, and transcribed them verbatim. I translated these dialogues, the dialogues performed via telephone and email, and parts of the documents that were presented in Swedish into English. The face-to-face dialogues, those via telephone and email and the tacit dialogues performed in relation to the documentary material focus on the involvement of the founder's son in business activities, the making of and realization of expansion plans in interaction with others, the generation shift, the merger activities, the building of a brand portfolio and the changes of ownership. Thus, the empirical–theoretical interlaced discussions in Chapters 4–7 are structured according to these foci. Guided by the participatory narrative approach that allows different theoretical threads to be woven into the empirical-oriented material, I draw on a variety of narrative and nonnarrative theories and concepts. Previous studies that explicitly use a narrative approach in combination with nonnarrative firm-focused studies give an insight into the different growth aspects that are brought up by the practitioners orally and in the written form. As an example, nonnarrative firm-growth theory applies to utterances in which the practitioner describes how the firm adapts to changes in the environment. To register a practitioner's utterance with interpretation and understanding, I thus continually supply theoretical connections without aiming at closure in a narrative traditional way. This describes a process of 'in-betweens', through which the business growth narrative is worked out. The process involves more than one visit to Hästveda, and renewed contacts via email with people directly involved in the study as well as giving them the opportunity to comment on the parts of the manuscript that referred to our dialogues. The context that helps provide an interpretation and understanding is constructed out of what takes place in the temporary we-constellation, which is made up of the practitioners and the researcher, with the researcher led by the practitioners through their accounts and comments on the material at hand. Based on the practitioners' comments some changes were made in the manuscript. After these practitioners confirmed that I had made the changes they required, they consented to my publishing the material.

The participatory narrative approach does not supply a coherent account of a set of business growth activities. The weaving of narrative bits and pieces allows for the delineation of more than one plot. Ontologically grounded in cultural tradition (Gadamer, [1960] 1989), there is no analytical situation in which the practitioner as an unbiased reporter has privileged access to the past, and the researcher as an unbiased listener hears a story that resembles a coherent and finished narrative. An analytical situation presupposes 'a kind of naive realism that is hard to imagine, harder to practice, and runs counter to everything we have learned about the way we come to understand the world' (Spence, 1982: 25). Naive realism pertains to a narrative tradition that is compelling in the sense that it smoothes out discontinuities and inconsistencies.

Dialogical Authorship

Meetings and talks with people made me – a listener and interpreter – visualize a world of practice (Denning, 2002). In addition to the spontaneous form of interaction, a dialogue is characterized by a move 'from interaction to participation through a pool of "common meaning" developed and accessed by those engaged in direct encounter,' as Ballantyne (2004: 117) explains. The face-to-face dialogues allowed the co-creation of a shared imagining of business growth constituted in a rich array of activities, accepting that there is no 'grand narrative' or case based on the conventional wisdom that a narrative or case represents a set of real events (O'Connor, 2007). This implies a comprehensive understanding that differs from an understanding of language as a mirror of an objective reality. As Ahl posits:

> In fact, that which the word is thought to represent can be said to be accessible for human experience and comprehension only as far as there is a suitable expression for it. Even when such an expression is at hand, the meaning invested in it is likely to vary between different people, contexts and times as it was human-made in the first place. In this manner language circumscribes (and makes possible) what one can think and feel and imagine doing. (Ahl, 2007: 677)

To be able to realize a dialogical authorship one must try to be self-reflexive about one' s own hegemonic moves in the writing – a most difficult challenge, as Boje, Luhman and Baack (1999) emphasize. The term 'hegemony' refers to the power of a story (as grand narrative) to 'ascribe a meaning onto our existence that can be imprisoning' (Boje, Luhman and Baack, 1999: 341). Case studies have traditionally been presented in a brief narrative form based on an authoritative voice as if they are facts (Carson, 2001; Nisker, 2004; Pattison et al., 1999). A monovocal, hegemonic presentation obscures alternative voices in that it 'reconstructs and replaces "stories" of the flux of experience with a "narrative" plot and a "moral" to be comprehended as a sequential whole' (Boje, 2000: 8). The business growth narrative problematizes a monovocal case and a grand narrative that represent real events. It consists of a web of bits and pieces provided in dialogues with practitioners and documents. Dialogue refers to a discourse characterized as interaction (Herman, 1995) *and* participation (Ballantyne, 2004). Participation denotes the furthering of interaction, manifesting in the co-creation of a shared interpretation and understanding of growth. In the move from interaction to participation, the dialogue is formed through intersubjective interpretation and understanding of business growth. It takes place through a continuous exchange between the practitioner and the researcher. In this exchange, the practitioner listens to the researcher's questions and comments, and the researcher listens to the practitioner's stories and comments on the researcher's comments and theoretically grounded interpretations.

Each narrative voice makes itself heard in coexistence with other voices and with my researcher voice as I continually try to put in place a dialogical authorship (Barry and Elmes, 1997) with the text manifesting intersubjective and relational concerns. There is a multiplicity of utterances, and meanings are attached to the utterances that make up the business growth narrative. There are numerous stories providing insight into people's everyday lives (Wigren, 2003). A story-like representation of business growth activities is a participatory (ante)narrative process that pulls away from a grand narrative that could easily become the narrative of a studied case, as Wigren emphasizes.

The co-construction of a shared imaging of business growth thus detracts from a representative view of knowledge (a verificationist epistemology) that predominantly assumes a dualistic ordering in categories that can be operationalized to represent phenomena with a concrete existence in the world (Knights, 1997). The world is not separated from the knowing individual. It is through action, counteraction, reaction and interaction that a 'common space' emerges, visualizing a world of practice:

> Stories invite the listener to visualize a different world and in the imagining, to add value to the activity. The shared imagining of the teller and listener creates a common space. As the storyteller watches the reactions of the listeners, he instinctively builds on and emphasizes the elements that are resonating with the listeners, thereby encouraging the phenomenon of co-creation. The audience senses that the storyteller is interacting with them, and they respond to it with more reactions. (Denning, 2002: 4)

A dialogical authorship requires the researcher to take a processing role, listening to different voices, illustrating in the written format how they narrate their notions about growth and their involvement in activities and changes related to growth. Thereby 'acceptability' and 'tellibility' take precedence over a logical necessity that relies on time-linear, cause–effect relationships (Bruner, 1990).

Acceptability refers to a narrative truth judged by its verisimilitude rather than its verifiability. Acceptability thus implies sensitivity to narrative voices, articulating their lived experience and notions of growth. Hence, the business growth narrative depends less on the identification of growth factors, evolutionary stages and performance measures, and more on the persuasiveness of the narrative and whether it subscribes to tellibility and invokes retelling. 'What the story revolves around, how it is put together, and the way it is told all determine whether it becomes one worth listening to, remembering, and acting upon' (Barry and Elmes, 1997: 433).

Delineating Plots

The participatory narrative approach mediates 'patterns' in the form of 'plots'. Plots are fundamentally sense-making devices (Downing, 2005). Lacking a pre-existent basis for emplotment, the plots are not distilled into analytical elements identified as storylines that generate an expected pattern and outcome. With a focus on plots, I remain receptive to the flexibility reflected in the stories, maintaining their antenarrative character (Boje, 2000). The business growth narrative as post-story thus flows with the many voices and the many plots, refraining from becoming trapped in a coherent pattern such as growth stages. While we are engaged in fragmentation and multidimensionality, more than one plot is constructed.

The plots direct attention to what the practitioner emphasizes when telling of activity involvement and changes. I regard changes as turning points and, interconnected, they dynamically drive a plot. Change thus refers to a turning point that defines itself in activities instigating a move in a new direction. I look for moments (depicted as points) where change develops and emerges as growth is continually promoted. These moments, point-like as they are, can be described as temporary, frozen and condensed human interaction and activity. Often conflict laden and emotionally charged, they emerge from encounters between people who articulate conflicting views on strategic matters. By also attending to activities that construct contexts in which the corporate strategy of Hilding Anders is supposedly strengthened – following a route already set by the top management – I highlight a type of change I label 'route follower'. Route follower, as opposed to turning point, denotes a more protracted movement. It unfolds a process involving interactions and activities that continuously enhance and strengthen the focus on growth, fully in line with a predefined growth strategy. Interconnected, the route followers also constitute a plot. Bits and pieces narratively communicated by the practitioners thus provide the material from which changes with reference to both turning points and route followers are extracted. The business growth narrative is accordingly scattered and fragmented into a multiplicity of voices and plots that combine turning points and route followers. Cut out from practitioners' lived experience are fragments that constitute the business growth narrative and its plots.

There could be a never-ending array of turning points and route followers making up plots. As interpretation and understanding proceed, plots emerge from activities that constitute contexts in which calculative rationality and emotions come to the fore. My concern is then not with an analysis of syllogisms inherent in a story. Rather than analytically dividing the narrative material, formulating concise storylines and categorizing units for data coding, I reflexively and metaphorically walk hand-in-hand with the practitioner through the processes of interpretation and understanding. Interpretation and understanding occur simultaneously (Gadamer, [1960] 1989). Understanding is apparently not distinguished from an interpretation

outlined as micro interpretations, subsumed under an overall understanding
first achieved when the walk terminates.

Narrative, embodying intersubjectivity, exposes business growth by using
language. Since much of growth practice takes place through language, there
is no need to distinguish between language and practice. *Homo narrans* lives
and constructs reality through language that carries both calculative rationality and emotion. As Mumby (1993: 4) postulates: 'We are never neutral,
dispassionate observers of behavior but are always heavily implicated in the
construction of the narratives (petit or grand) that provide insight to the social
reality that we inhabit.'

Central to the participatory narrative approach is the idea that 'self' is
constructed, not governed by logical rules (Gergen, 1999). Self is a transac-
tional relationship between people; it is dialogue dependent, argues Bruner
(1990). When moving into the future from the past, the action of the self could
very well be to preserve itself in the face of changes. When moving from the
future to the present, the self might instead become open to alteration while
being receptive to possibilities of the future (Crites, 1986). As Rossiter (1999:
64) maintains: 'The present moment is the meeting place of the past and
future. It is the balance point between identity and self-transcendence, the
decision point between continuity and transformation.'

SUMMING UP

The participatory narrative approach mediates an ontology that permeates the
empricial-theoretical interlaced discussions and the methodological discussion
in this book. This means that ontological consistency is promoted throughout
the text to a world of lived experience and a human being's belongingness to
the historical past. The existential dimension that is enclosed conveys an intersubjective character of reality and offers a nondualistic and interrelated interpretation and understanding of business growth. Growth is lived by the
practitioners and is shown in their activities, relationships and in their
constructed and laid-out contexts. Practitioners as *homo narrans* become part
of the world and coexist with it. The participatory narrative approach assumes
joint performance of and intersection between those telling of their direct
involvement in practice and the researcher as listener, interpreter and author of
the book.

This chapter further reveals that the bits and pieces practitioners narratively
impart define different kinds of change that can be captured by turning points
and route followers. Turning points and route followers interconnect into
plots. Business growth serves as a framing narrative that encloses within itself
plots that mainly adhere to a sequential logic since the dialogues performed

with people associated with the Hilding Anders business largely rely on the then-what-happened convention. But the business growth narrative also redefines the present in the light of the past and the future, and brings the past and the present together while transcending temporal and spatial limits of practice.

To face the challenge of what to do with fragmentation of lived experience reflected in the stories supplied orally and in a written form by the practitioners, antenarrating is emphasized, which means that the business growth narrative comes after stories and adds plots. The plots dress the practitioners' stories in a post-story narrative guise. Since much of growth practice takes place through language, a dividing line is not marked between language and practice. The narrative approach allows sensitivity to voices that articulate their lived experience and notions of growth. Because of its participatory character, the approach also permits the researcher and author of the book continuously to entwine theoretical threads with the practitioners' telling, as the next four empirical-oriented chapters illustrate.

4. To begin the business growth narrative

In response to the ongoing nature of business growth, the 'beginning' and 'ending' of the business growth narrative become issues of unpredictability and construction, since it does not have a beginning or an ending. As Hjorth (2007: 723) puts it, 'the beginning is always a result of preceding beginnings flowing into a subsequent one, related not chronologically like rills relate to streams.' Without recourse to a metanarrative the business growth narrative also lacks a definitive ending. 'The old metanarratives sinned in their ambition to end a conversation by trying to predict its outcomes. If a canon is already known, there is nothing left to talk about,' Czarniawska (2004: 13) notes.

The beginning of the business growth narrative is constructed and made sense of in the dialogue with the son of the founder of the business. In its call upon the past, it engages in an interpretation and understanding made through the lived experience of the founder's son.

FATHER AND SON

Today in his 80s, Olle Andersson looks back on a time when he, as a very young man, was involved in different activities. Being in charge of the business for 30 years, all through 1957–87, he also shared the ownership of the business with his wife Britta.

To begin with, the narrative provides glimpses of Hilding Andersson and the 1939 starting-up of a business for manufacturing beds, sofas, chairs, tables and rocking chairs. The place was Bjärnum, a municipality situated in the province of Skåne in the south of Sweden. Prospects were none too good at the time with limited demand for furnishing. The survival of the business was even at stake, Olle Andersson recounts:

> My father started up the furniture business in 1939, shortly before the Second World War broke out. I know that very well, I was 11 years old at the time. In the present state of things, demand for furniture fell considerably. This, my father had to face, trying to find a way to financially survive. Fortunately, he received an order for interior fittings for a poultry farm. There is no denying that the order rescued my father from a very difficult situation.
>
> Gradually, people got accustomed to the war and began to spend money on furniture. The Swedish Co-operative Union Kooperativa Förbundet (KF) placed a large

order to meet the needs of the refugees, who came from war-ravaged regions in Europe and settled into new homes that the farmers in Skåne made available for them. Each new home requested a suite of furniture for which my father charged just under SEK100. The KF order meant that he narrowly escaped from a situation in which the business could have run at a loss as matters stood at the time. Sales volume was limited, however, but money was rolling in so we pulled through and were able to get on.

My father was a very nice man. He was a hardworking man but didn't make a great profit on the business. It was just enough to provide for the big family, sustaining a reasonable standard of living. (Olle Andersson, personal communication, 1 September 2006)

Andersson introduces the family of six children; four boys and two girls who spent time working in the factory. Olle, the youngest one, already at an early age helped out in the factory from time to time.

There were six kids, four boys and two girls, and since there were many other families competing for jobs in the region where we lived, my father thought it was a good idea, as we were growing up, continuously to involve us in the business. We worked in the factory, helping out from time to time. I made myself useful in the factory when school was over for the day, and during holidays.

The more children assisted in production, the lower the production costs. We certainly noticed that this was a fact because we did not get very good pay for the job we did. (Olle Andersson, personal communication, 1 September 2006)

Andersson continues by telling of the investments plan made in his 20s. He refers to the growing realization that changes in production had to be undertaken but also to the feeling of disappointment when acknowledging that his father disliked the plans for change. But, as he was able to take on more responsibility, Olle Andersson followed up on the investment plans, rerouting and streamlining production and as a result, profitability increased.

I was the youngest one and actually the only one who stayed on after my brothers and my sisters left the business. I made investment plans in the hope that I would be able to realize these plans, increasing sales and improving profit. However, the investment plans were subjected to a disagreement between my father and me. I saw no other way out than to contact an engineer, as a consultant used to be called back then. He came up with calculations that showed that the rocking chair was the only product that paid its way, but the quantity of rocking chairs produced annually amounted to just 50. By calculations, it was further shown that the bedstead was the most profitable product. Of course, I stripped down production to bedsteads, using material and a production technique that substantially lowered the production costs. Because of the actions taken, I was able to offer the customers a price that was nearly 40 percent lower than the price charged by my colleagues in the furniture industry. Eventually sales went up and I made money. By concentrating on bedstead products, profits were yielded which encouraged me to make further investments in the business. (Olle Andersson, personal communication, 1 September 2006)

In 1957, at the age of 29, Olle Andersson took over the business from his father. The willingness on his part to run the business is justified in a context where managerial activities were allied with 100 percent ownership, which implied full control over business operations. From Andersson's viewpoint, such a context promised better growth opportunities. By assuming a position as owner-manager, he would have every chance to succeed in expanding the business further, he thought. The founder's son had ideas of what he would be able to do independently and was eager to put the ideas into practice. The current situation did not feel right since he envisioned the expansion of the business as depending on him being in total control. Eventually Hilding Andersson, at the age of 70, agreed to leave the business. Arguably, the dimension of control added to the self-belief of the son when he was left with the owner-manager position. As Hall (2003) argues, business is a means of individuation. To express the self, proving his own capability seems here to be an important driving force for Andersson. Drawing on Hall, the reluctance of Andersson to continue working with his father suggests an active differentiation and distancing of the self.

The conception of self apparently includes a tension between current and future (identity) self. In entrepreneurial stories, there is often dissatisfaction with the existing reality, according to Rae (2005). Tension between current and future identities describes an emotionally charged situation in which a person becomes an entrepreneur. The current reality does not 'feel right' since it is connected with the rejection of an unsatisfactory present and an urge to create a new reality and identity.

> I took over after my father. Yet my father and one of my sisters were still involved in running the business. The business was called Hildings at the time. Fairly soon one of my brothers joined me. Since the business was not financially viable we applied for a bank loan. A limited company was formed and we changed the name from Hildings to Hilding Anderssons Möbelfabrik AB. Now we were shareholders. When my brother and sister left the business, my father Hilding and I were the only owners of the company. As I was willing to assume full responsibility for the business, I preferred to be the company's sole owner. As it turned out, Hilding had a hard time letting go of the business but a colleague of mine succeeded in persuading Hilding, convincing him that everything would be just fine if his youngest son took over. A wholly owned company managed by me as the sole owner could account for better possibilities to expand the business further, I thought.
>
> In order to get total control, I bought out Hilding. I paid him well for the shares and I saw to it that he got out of debt completely. Hilding was born in 1887. He left his position as the owner-manager in 1957. In 1961, I moved the business to Hästveda, not very far from Bjärnum where Hilding first started the business. (Olle Andersson, personal communication, 1 September 2006)

In 1961, the name of the company changed to Hilding Anders Möbel AB. In 1969, Hilding Andersson died. Based on the stories, provided by Olle

Andersson, turning points, suggesting a move in a new direction, can be constructed.

Turning Points

Turning points can be constructed out of the activities Olle Andersson recounts. Activities expose different kinds of change and relate here to the founder and owner-manager Hilding Andersson as he faced the challenge of not being able to continue running the business he had recently started. Further, activities relate to the rerouting of production, and the son assuming the owner-manager position. The turning points are strategically important and prospectively making sense through holding the potential of continuous growth. Here growth means 'expanding the business', in Olle Andersson's words.

A precarious situation emerged, clouding the future as the survival of the Hildings business was at stake. This was an emotionally charged and stressful situation that allowed for a turning point, demonstrated by Olle Andersson in his description of the rescue of his father. This turning point proposes a way out of a situation that most likely would have had disastrous consequences for the family. The order for poultry farm interior fittings unexpectedly constructed an opportunity to continue business operations. Arguably, sense was made prospectively in a context of activities that formed between Hilding Andersson and the purchaser of the equipment. While drawing on a future-oriented frame, sense is prospectively made (Boland, 1984; Wright, 2006). Conceptualized as 'the rescue of my father', the son indicates a sense-made context entwined with emotions. The expressions 'survival at stake' and 'rescue' clearly denote that emotions of fear were induced: fear of what would happen in the near future as well as relief combined with hopes for the future. Associated with the making of sense is a turning point that refers to the moment in which Hilding Andersson realized that he certainly would be able to survive financially.

The disagreement between father and son that arose about which direction to go in the future is a critical juncture that defines the turning point of rerouting production. The disagreement indicates the involvement of emotions. To justify a changed direction, the son made plans, engaging a consultant who calculated which product would be the most profitable. Based on the calculations, a context emerged in which sense was made prospectively. Related to this sense-making context, the turning point suggests a move away from a focus on the production of a diverse range of furniture to a focus that centered on a product that considerably lowered production costs.

Furthermore, a turning point refers to the hurdles Olle Andersson overcame when assuming full responsibility of the business. Through him drawing up an imaginative space of action, opportunities were constructed to expand the business without the father interfering. Imaginative space refers to a non-geographical distance to which one can travel in one's mind while being located in the here and now (Lämsä and Sintonen, 2006). Implied in this is the turning point of gaining total control. The turning point seems to hold a move away from a conflict-laden and emotionally charged interaction between father and son toward a more consensual interaction that paved the way for the son to take over, running the business as his own.

According to Davis and Tagiuri (1989), the work relationship between a father and a son in a family-owned company varies as a function of their respective stages of life and can be very problematic and conflict laden during certain stages. The turning point actually reflects such a stage in life where the father, turning 70, might have felt that leaving the business would be losing a major source of meaning and legacy in life. When approaching the age of 65 and 70, men are usually reminded of the loss of meaningful activities when they leave their company, Beveridge (1980) explains. Retirement often only occurs with death, say Davis and Tagiuri:

> Founders or heirs of companies, who probably feel more attached to their organizations than other men do and who have the power to mold a competency legacy, may become more determined than ever in this period of life to leave their stamp on their organizations. In this period, the owner-manager is likely to want to assert his power strongly over others, and he will probably struggle with those who exacerbate his self-questioning and reduce his feeling of control over his legacy. (Davis and Tagiuri, 1989: 523)

Olle Andersson was in his late 20s. This stage of life is generally characterized by the son feeling held back in his desire to make a change, and the father feeling unappreciated, according to Davis and Tagiuri (1989). Strongly believing in himself, Olle Andersson managed to argue his way with the assistance of a person who knew his father well and helped persuade his father to sell the business to his youngest son. A period between the ages of 28 and 33 – the so-called 'age thirty transition' – is a time when men normally feel some urgency to face their lives and settle down (Levinson, 1978). As Dumas (1989) underlines, the key developmental issue for a son is authority achieved through the differentiation of self from the father. It can be argued that Olle Andersson achieved authority when assuming the owner-manager position, which allowed for full control over business operations.

A qualitatively different turning point refers to the death in 1969 of the founder of the business. How this particular turning point relates to the expansion of the business, the founder's son does not relate.

REALIZING EXPANSION PLANS

When still in Bjärnum, a situation emerged that placed a major obstacle in Olle Andersson's path. The decision to move to Hästveda, situated not very far from Bjärnum, was a way to master this situation and respond to the disapproval of the local government in Bjärnum to the expansion plans outlined. Andersson tells of the move:

> It was necessary to move production to Hästveda where I had the opportunity to establish new facilities. I had plans to build a new factory in Bjärnum but my prospects of marketing the products were none too good since a new building would not be very well placed on the outskirts of Bjärnum, which seemed to be the only option at the time. So I contacted the local government to be granted permission to extend the business at a more attractive site in Bjärnum. However, I was not very content with the offer I got from the local politicians and therefore I decided to move production to Hästveda. I bought my workers a Mercedes van to run as a commuter shuttle so they still could live in Bjärnum where they had their homes and their families. I was lucky to have the most competent workers and I really wanted to keep them even if production moved to another place.
>
> The move to Hästveda offered better transportation possibilities and gave higher visibility to the business and the products, which was of great advantage for marketing the products, and for sales – which virtually exploded. There were sudden and rapid increases in turnover and we kept straight on, feeling very confident about the future. Our only concern was in calculating with the number of millions that sales would accrue from then on. In comparison to other furniture firms, sales showed up as high revenue per employee. While keeping production costs sufficiently low, revenue per employee amounted to SEK1 million. (Olle Andersson, personal communication, 1 September 2006)

In Hästveda, Britta and Olle Andersson, the married couple and the owners of the business, together with their employees engaged in various growth-oriented activities. While being utterly sensitive to the customers' needs and wants, Britta Andersson served the customers efficiently, her husband emphasizes. Steadfastly, she held on to the idea that it was crucial to meet the customers' expectations quickly. Other 'ladies' were also engaged in sales activities, as Olle Andersson remarks (personal communication, 1 September 2006), and since the customers certainly benefited from the contacts with the female sales representatives, he learned to encourage strongly the ladies in their dealings with the customers. A narrative frame of meaning (Reissner, 2005) emerges, placing the customer at the center.

> My wife Britta was of great help to me. She was involved in sales and was very sensitive to the customers' needs and wants. Being extremely customer-oriented, she helped sustain long-term relationships with the customers. She served the customers efficiently by providing them with the products they requested at an acceptable price level while also being highly concerned about the quality of delivery. The key was satisfying the differing requirements of the customers.

In order to sustain high delivery quality, Britta argued for keeping a stock of goods. This was a contentious issue because the board of directors held the view that the supply of goods needed to be cut down considerably. My wife thought that the board had little say in this matter. It was essential to meet the customers' expectations quickly. Being out of stock meant that we could not ensure that orders and deliveries would be expedited on time.

Besides, Britta kept an accurate account of money, carefully noting how much we earned. It was important to her that the customers paid well for the products we offered. She knew how to charge, which I greatly appreciated.

Other ladies were engaged also in sales activities. They were strongly aware of the value of meeting the expectations of the customers and keeping promises. They even strived to deliver the goods ordered earlier than requested by the customers, exceeding the expectations of the customers.

In the 1960s and 1970s, largely due to the male dominance in the furniture industry, one did not show much confidence in the women's business dealings. The male customers hardly wished to talk to a woman. Instead, they turned to me but I learned that the customers actually benefited from talking to a female sales representative. Therefore I saw it was necessary to support the ladies fully in their contacts with the customers. (Olle Andersson, personal communication, 1 September 2006)

According to the local newspaper, Mrs Britta Andersson had an excellent command of everything concerning the business. She was involved in exports to the Nordic countries, the UK, France, Germany, Canada and the United States. Through the American representatives, contacts were established with customers who wanted Hästveda beds for their summerhouses in the Bahamas (*Norra Skåne*, 1969).

In realizing the expansion plans, the son of the founder constructed the machinery needed to try out new ideas and methods. An open exchange of information between spouses, friends and customers made possible the technological exploitation of a technical invention that resulted in the development of the interior-spring mattress. When recounting the development of the bed base, Olle Andersson supplies details about the advantages and disadvantages of putting the bed base at the edge of the bed. Moreover he refers to the challenges faced when trying to obtain the right to manufacture and sell a product.

All the time, I experimented and developed new products. My wife, Britta, who had close contacts with the customers, noticed that some customers wanted a bed with an interior-spring mattress. The only supplier of this product was KF and since I was lucky enough to be closely related to some people employed by KF, I had access to valuable information about the product. By exploiting a technical innovation that was made in Germany, I succeeded in obtaining the right to manufacture that particular bed but did not personally obtain a patent. At the time, a friend of mine and I were the only producers of the bed in question. My friend was a supplier of KF and I was a supplier of private furniture stores. The production of beds with interior-spring mattresses was essential for spurring continuous development and growth. Then, the bed base came into it.

The bed base could be put at the edge of the bed or further inwards where you could, however, easily hurt your toes. My wife discussed the bed base matter with our customers, that is, the furniture dealers, and found out that their views diverged a lot. From our perspective, the bed base should be put at the edge of the bed, with the bed frame put on thereafter. Because of this construction, a more solid bed could be offered but in order to adjust to the requirements of our customers we saw no other way out than to make movable bed bases.

I applied for and obtained a patent to protect my invention. When attending the trade fair for furniture manufacturers in Stockholm, I was nevertheless in for a big surprise. Both Dux and Ikea exhibited bed designs that used a movable bed base, a copy of my invention. 'How would I deal with this?' I asked myself. I consulted a lawyer. We made an agreement with Dux and as a result Dux paid for the encroachment on my right to sell this particular bed product. We contacted the wholesalers by letter in which we politely asked them to provide us with information on those who bought beds with the copied design of the movable bed base. They agreed on what the letter stipulated so there was no need to make a claim in court against the manufacturers of the product. They paid for the harm done and I received about SEK1 million in royalties. (Olle Andersson, personal communication, 1 September 2006)

The Swedish companies Scapa and Ekens were known for their high-quality beds. Scapa, a producer of mattresses and upholstered furniture, was regarded as an innovative leader (Scapa Inter, 2009), and Ekens was highly renowned for its exclusive beds and innovative designs (Ekens, 2008). To be well ahead of these producers, Olle Andersson engaged in the development of a new product, realizing the idea of the polyfoam mattress. While in the process, he encountered some resistance coming from the experts in the field, and from the evening paper, casting doubts on his idea to pour foam directly on the elastic bottom of a bed. Since the mattress idea was not immediately shared by others and did not conform to established production methods, Andersson was left to endure 'individually constructed reality'. This can be a heavy burden to bear, as Czarniawska-Joerges and Wolff (1991) contend, but those who succeed in socially confirming their inventions can actually be seen as 'worldmakers'. As Andersson admits (personal communication, 1 September 2006), he used to be very persistent, committing himself to trying out things in spite of doubts and resistance. Rather than scanning for opportunities 'out there', the owner-manager constructed opportunities.

Emotions narratively expressed in reference to doubts, resistance, persistency, commitment and stubbornness arguably became constitutive of Andersson's reality. Energized by these emotions, experimenting activities made sense, but from the viewpoints of the doubtful and resistant others, such activities obviously appeared to lack a sense of meaning.

When I take a decision, I pursue it with determination, following it through and facing the consequences. I am a very persistent person. My entire life I have stubbornly committed myself to doing things, trying out things despite facing difficulties and opposition. Even if people sometimes thought I was annoying and unreasonable, I did what I felt was right under the circumstances at hand. I am fairly convinced that if it were not for my persistency, commitment and stubbornness, the business would not have been growing.

Although I completely lacked experience in how to handle plastic material, I bought a machine from Germany for approximately DM40,000. I contacted Stenungsund, in Sweden, to get in touch to supply chemist expertise. Two engineers arrived in Hästveda, giving me advice and assisting me with the production of foam. I provided them with food and accommodation and we had a great time.

I didn't hesitate to carry through the project. I thought of the making of the mattress as very similar to the making of a cake, smoothly smearing the paste on the bottom of the holder and after half an hour realizing that it had risen. I just remember delivering a mattress to a female customer … she called me, harshly pointing out that when she unpacked the mattress it continued to rise for a while …

I poured foam straight on the elastic bottom of the bed although it was simply impossible to do so, according to experts in the field. The evening paper paid a great deal of attention to my ideas and work. Until I had finished the project, I was hard pressed and somewhat harassed by those who didn't believe in my idea. Therefore, it was a long shot on my part when I decided to exhibit the polyfoam mattress at the next trade fair in Stockholm. Of course, my colleagues were present at the fair. They took a close look at the mattress and I noticed that they actually seemed very interested and I must admit that it was really a good thing that it went off all right. (Olle Andersson, personal communication, 1 September 2006)

Andersson adds that the experiments and the development of products were always informed by the philosophy of producing high-quality beds and making a profit. When practiced, the philosophy translated into an endeavor to be further advanced than other bed and mattress producers operating in the region.

If I am not misinformed, I was also the first one to offer products under a trade description. Always, I strived for the highest product standard and to make a healthy profit on the products. I was pretty persistent in my attempts to be well ahead of and further advanced than the other producers located in the region. It is no use trying to produce and sell a product unless one succeeds in producing a better and cheaper product than the competitors. The whole philosophy has been to produce high-quality products on the precondition that calculations were confirmed and that I got what I wanted in terms of profit. This proved to be the right philosophy and, as we all know, we made money and developed the business. (Olle Andersson, personal communication, 1 September 2006)

Hotel furnishing was also an important production area. In 1976, Russian buyers placed an order that by far exceeded the turnover of Hilding Anders. The Hilding Anders beds exhibited at the trade fair in Copenhagen strongly appealed to the Russians but before reaching the trade fair, a series of emotion-related situations emerged. Andersson reveals:

Another production area of our concern was hotel furnishing. I was going to the furniture fair at Bella Center in Denmark. At the ferry for Copenhagen, there was a man who persisted in getting my undivided attention and I tried to sneak away from him; he seemed to be on a spree. I don't drink alcohol, which is why I was not very delighted to make his acquaintance. When I got off the ferry, I hastened to a cab, which I shared with two other people who also were on their way to Bella Center. One of the guys, a Swede, told me that the two of them were going to look at bedroom furniture that should suit a big Russian hotel located in Leningrad.

I paid for the cab and straight away brought my fellow-passengers to the Hilding Anders exhibition stand, assuring them that the Hilding Anders beds were the very best beds and that there was no need to visit the other stands at the fair. Fortunately, the bed design strongly appealed to them so I contacted my marketing manager, who continued talking with them. Usually, I talk too much and sometimes people seem to distrust my words; people just stop and listen to me. I have never been a sales representative: that is why I used to pass on to my marketing manager.

I continued to Cologne, in Germany. When I returned to Hästveda in Sweden I told my wife that we needed to get a hotel room ready immediately to be shown to the Russian buyers who would soon be on their way to us. I hired a builder and together we set up a show room in the factory. Within a week, a hotel room was furnished and fully equipped with carpets and curtains. Then the Russians came and looked, and to our great pleasure they seemed very happy.

My marketing manager Bengt and I went to Russia. Bengt negotiated the deal with the Russians and in the afternoon we met at the hotel. I had brought with me sandwiches. Since there was no table or tray available, I unhooked a door to serve as a tray for the afternoon meal.

The order for hotel furnishing, amounting to SEK12 million, was successfully negotiated by Bengt. At the time, the turnover of Hilding Anders was SEK6 million. Hardly anyone, least of all I, believed in the huge size of the order which, surprisingly enough, exceeded the turnover of the whole company. (Olle Andersson, personal communication, 1 September 2006)

Arguably, international market making (Oviatt and McDougall, 1994) took place through personal contacts with people as well as through the avoidance of contacts. Unexpected meetings and interactions between people construct growth possibilities. The marketing manager Bengt Adolfsson, through extensive travel to Russia, interacting and negotiating with the hotel customers, plays a significant role here. The local newspaper announced that the order received from the big Leningrad hotel with 1,500 rooms almost made Hilding Anders world famous (*Norra Skåne*, 1978). The size of the Russian order is unique in the Swedish furniture industry. In the words of Adolfsson:

This was a breakthrough. Never before had actors in the Swedish furniture industry experienced an order of that size. Indeed it helped strengthen the relatively weak position Hilding Anders had at the time in the retail market for furniture. Spin-off effects of the Russian order allowed for numerous opportunities to provide the Swedish hotel chain SARA with furniture. (Bengt Adolfsson, personal communication, 8 September 2009)

Looking further back, former production manager Bertil Henningsson compares different periods of business activities performed in the name of

Hilding Anders. Henningsson worked with Olle Andersson during two different periods: the first occurred in 1962–71 and the second in 1985–2001:

> In the 1960s, there was much focus on product development and production of bedsteads, bed frames, interior-spring mattresses, bed bases and bedside tables. I was involved in all kinds of activities. Olle and his wife Britta ran the business, and this couple was the driving force of the business.
>
> Over the years, the Hästveda factory increased in size from about 5,000 square meters in the 1960s to about 30,000 in the early 2000s. Clearly, the Russian hotel order made a huge difference. The business expanded considerably after 1976, requiring a larger production area. (Bertil Henningsson, personal communication, 26 June 2007)

Although a number of turning points are implied in Andersson's telling, only three turning points will be highlighted. These three are strategically important, promoting continued expansion of the business.

Turning Points

One turning point concerns the difficult situation that was gradually clarified by the move from Bjärnum to Hästveda, the place nearby where permission was granted to establish a new factory. Apparently, sense was made by reading into present experience the expectations of future expansion. Clearly, the move was a turning point that allowed for the prospects of continued business growth to be part of sense-making. The turning point seems to be infused with a sense of hope and will for the future (Orbuch, 1997). It defines itself in the way Olle Andersson tells of the move.

Another turning point is exposed in connection with Andersson's experiment, development and introduction of a new mattress product, the polyfoam mattress. The good results of the experiment exhibited at the trade fair in Stockholm silenced the voices of the doubtful and resistant. The overcoming of the objections raised at the making of the polyfoam mattress depicts a turning point that entails self-confirmation and conversion from an individually constructed reality to a socially confirmed reality.

The order placed by the Russian buyers for hotel furnishing also amounts to a turning point, the financial consequences of which were extraordinary. Bengt Adolfsson succeeded in negotiating an order that exceeded the turnover of Hilding Anders.

The words of the local newspaper and the words of the son of the founder expose the significant role that machine construction, experiments and development of products played in realizing the expansion plans. Olle Andersson vividly puts us in the time of everyday practice (Hjorth, 2007), illustrating through his words how new opportunities for increases in sales were constructed. While experimenting suggests taking a risk, it brings out some distinguishing features of entrepreneurship, at the heart of which is 'creating, shaping, recognizing, and interpreting unformed opportunities followed by will, ability, desire, competences, responsibilities, and initiative to seize and pursue these opportunities,' as Bratnicki (2005: 19) asserts. In social-constructionist terms, the entrepreneurial Andersson self is seen as the one who constructs opportunities (Chell, 2000), actualizing ideas with willpower and initiative (Czarniawska-Joerges and Wolff, 1991). In addition, distinguishing features of entrepreneurship with regard to the ability to construct a unique opportunity for expanding the Hilding Anders business – as reflected in the Russian order and its spin-off effects – are clearly ascribed to marketing manager Bengt Adolfsson, later on appointed deputy CEO of Hilding Anders.

THE ENTREPRENEURIAL SELF

The bits and pieces narratively communicated by Olle Andersson paint, in connection with theory, an entrepreneurial self who engages in experimenting activities while, at the same time, keenly confirming calculations and meeting expectations of profitability. He streamlines production and puts much effort into renewing production methods and products. He takes risks when making investments and offering the customers a price that is significantly lower than the price the colleagues within the furniture industry offer. A driving force is the hope to do well, supplying the customers with what they want and even exceeding their expectations, expanding the business while manufacturing high-quality products and making a profit. Expansion implies increases in sales volumes and the safeguarding of profitability. There is no growth unless profits are generated, as Andersson emphasizes:

> It is imperative to generate sales in a profitable way. Over the years, we always managed to keep the profit margin at or close to 10 percent. This was a significant goal. We could not grow unless our business generated profitable sales. It is necessary always to keep an eye on how much out of every Swedish Krona of sales we could keep, since increases in our earnings did not necessarily lead to improved profit margin. On occasion, production costs could increase at a greater rate than sales revenues.
>
> When it was time for my daughter and son-in-law to take over the business I told my daughter that the profit margin must be at least 10 percent. (Olle Andersson, personal communication, 1 September 2006)

Olle Andersson might even earn the epithet of a risk-taking adventurer (Casson, 1982). Through experimenting, developing, testing and introducing new products, Andersson constructs growth opportunities rather than discovering them. Here entrepreneurial judgment (Penrose, 1959) plays a significant role, displayed by Andersson's ability to put innovative ideas in practice when using unconventional methods. A persistent, highly committed and stubborn person tried out things in spite of difficulties and opposition. A salient feature of Olle Andersson's entrepreneurial self is also the way he shows trust in relations with business partners, relying on a handshake when entering into an agreement. Trustful relationships between people contributed to a positive ambience in Hilding Anders.

> People used to warn me about the unpleasant things that might happen if I relied completely upon a handshake and a verbal agreement. I was strongly advised that I should sign a document, recording the agreement. As I see it, an agreement made between parties need not be written down. It is a gentlemen's agreement.
>
> I have shown little interest in documents. What is verbally agreed on, the parties keep to, trusting each other. One does not break promises. This has been my guiding principle over time and it still is. It certainly contributed to a positive ambience in Hilding Anders, also invoking in people not directly involved in the business, a positive feel for the business. I don't recall meeting a single person who expressed a negative attitude toward Hilding Anders. Yet today I really feel that people I talk to about Hilding Anders expose a positive attitude. (Olle Andersson, personal communication, 1 September 2006)

Andersson further refers to an emotion-laden meeting that undoubtedly illustrates his concern for people. At the same time, he stresses how his wife inspired other people.

> As we are sitting here in my kitchen, I remember many meetings at this very table with people with whom I used to work before retiring. While having coffee, they tell me that they learned a lot from me. I especially recall a visit paid by a big guy, who many years ago was one of my employees. He had come a bit astray in life and I gave him a new chance by offering him a job at Hilding Anders. The other day he came to my house, entered the kitchen, sat down at the table and drank the coffee I prepared. Then he told me that he was completely 'clean' and that he greatly appreciated the help I gave him back then, thanking me for the lessons he learned. This was fantastic to hear ... and there are many other episodes I take great pleasure in thinking about. My wife Britta was also of great inspiration to other people, giving them good advice in different life situations. (Olle Andersson, personal communication, 1 September 2006)

While portraying what people do together, one can recognize a social interactive characteristic of entrepreneurship. Not driven by self-interest, the owner-manager Olle Andersson helped people, and was involved in a rich variety of activities without bothering about formal titles and functional boundaries. Showing itself in different practices, entrepreneurship expands beyond a person's status as founder and owner-manager (Davidsson, 1991).

Yes, I was the CEO. Besides, I was also the production manager, the truck driver and the boiler man who kept the building warm. But there were no formal titles.

I was the first to enter the building at six o'clock in the morning and most of the time, the last person to leave the building, locking the doors.

It was actually a great advantage to be in the middle of things; not wearing a formal suit, just working together with my workers in the factory. I was always informed about what was going on which meant that I also got valuable insights into matters that bothered people. So I was involved in all kind of activities. (Olle Andersson, personal communication, 1 September 2006)

As witnessed by Claes-Göran Jönsson (personal communication, 13 November 2006), who is involved in the production of beds and mattresses at the Hästveda factory: 'Olle Andersson didn't hesitate to immerse himself in the production on the factory floor. He also realized many innovative ideas while making prototypes and developing new products, especially beds, mattresses and bed furnishing. From my point of view, Olle was a fantastic CEO from whom we learned a lot.'

Tomas Modén, who is also involved in the production of beds and mattresses at the Hästveda factory, recalls:

Visitors could not believe that Olle was the CEO. He didn't like to stay in his office but preferred to spend time working in the factory, also walking around wearing clogs and jeans while checking that everything ran smoothly and that our products continually developed and met high quality standards. (Tomas Modén, personal communication, 13 November 2006)

In 1987, Olle Andersson retired. Bengt Adolfsson assumed the position as CEO. The name of the company changed to Hilding Anders AB (Hilding Anders). Bengt Adolfsson and his wife Ann-Charlotte acquired 100 percent of the equity.

Some colleagues of mine who sold their businesses were not able to let go of it while still being concerned and immersing themselves. As for me, I signed over everything and left discretion to my daughter and son-in-law, without any intention to interfere in matters regarding the business, its operations and future development. I completely agreed with leaving the business to them and did not cause them the inconvenience of struggling to try to make me hand over the key to them. In my opinion, it is necessary to know when to step down, retiring in time. As far as a green plant is concerned, one doesn't hesitate in cutting off old twigs and dead wood . . . there must be room for renewal . . .

There were 50–60 employees when I left. The turnover amounted to SEK1.5–2 million per employee. The focus of the business had been organic growth for generating profit. Later on the focus shifted toward growth through acquisitions.

Before I left, I also got rid of things that littered the factory building and made it look untidy. I used to keep things, even discarded and damaged goods. They were worth saving, I thought. They might be useful when carrying out different experiments for developing new products.

My wife stayed on in the business for a period of time but I left at the age of 58 to engage in work on my farmyard. I bought an excavator and did construction work, laying out roads that were needed for accessing more easily my place, located at the outskirts of Hästveda, and involved in many other activities as a farmer. (Olle Andersson, personal communication, 1 September 2006)

This chapter thus closes by referring to a turning point at which Olle Andersson handed over the baton to his daughter Ann-Charlotte and his son-in-law Bengt Adolfsson. This he did without displaying any hard feelings. He saw it necessary to leave the business at this point in time to 'cut off old twigs and dead wood,' opening up possibilities for renewal. Arguably, retirement occurred 'gracefully', to use a word from Davis and Taguiri (1989: 541). Although Olle Andersson entered a stage of life in which, according to individual life-cycle theory, he would have experienced a feeling of loss, his retirement opened up new and meaningful activities. Not having trouble heading in a new direction and building a life apart from the new owners of the business, he engaged in farming.

5. Involvement in merger activities

The generation shift took place in 1987. Bengt and Ann-Charlotte Adolfsson gained total control by purchasing 100 percent of the Hilding Anders shares from Olle and Britta Andersson. The turnover was SEK62 million at the time. Bengt Adolfsson assumed the position of CEO and Ann-Charlotte continued to work in the office in Hästveda where the headquarters remained until 2001. Several changes in the organizational structure and production were accomplished over the years. Under the ownership of the Adolfsson family, turnover increased steadily while profitability was maintained.

> When we took over the company in 1987 a restructuring of the operations took place. For a considerable period of time, production had focused on bedsteads with the mattress product playing a minor role. On the basis of economic calculations, we decided to revise the production concept. More effort put into mattress production would augur well for the future, we thought. Improving the production concept meant, among other things, an increased degree of automation. Robots were installed, performing complicated series of tasks automatically. As a result of the use of a more sophisticated production technique, a bed was put together within one minute. (Bengt Adolfsson, personal communication, 26 April 2006)

With the new CEO, the focus on the market strengthened, as Tomas Modén, former supervisor and from 2008 production manager, emphasizes:

> When Bengt became the CEO, things changed. When he took over after Olle I was foreman and supervisor. With the new CEO, market-orientation became more important and we attracted new customers. Bengt was able to contact and establish relationships with the big 'dragons'. As a consequence production doubled within a short period of time. (Tomas Modén, personal communication, 13 November 2006)

People also tell of Bengt Adolfsson's unique ability to know how business should be done and how one should achieve high quality in business. Stories are told about how Adolfsson immediately got a feel for what needed to be done just by visiting a factory or a company.

During the period 1990–4, sales quadrupled, amounting to SEK370 million in 1994. The number of employees increased to 225 (Atle, 1999).

LONG-TERM PROSPECTS AND MULTIPLE MOTIVES

Toward the end of the 1990s, due to unforeseen circumstances, a stressful and emotionally charged situation emerged. To remain confident about the longer-term prospect, the CEO saw a necessity to welcome new owners. The situation is narratively framed as a 'terrible state of things' that occurred because some employees were struck by serious illness. There was a compelling need to find a way to deal with this particular situation. Questions were raised about what would happen tomorrow and in the near future. Profitability was exceedingly satisfactory, but it was considered important to strengthen the financial basis of the company further, which is why the CEO suggested bringing in some co-owners. In the face of an uncertain and unpredictable future, a shared ownership made sense.

> It may sound trivial but quite a number of people fell ill. It turned out that many got the serious illness cancer, and in that terrible state of things one worried about the future. Since about 500–600 employees indirectly and directly depended on us, our responsibility was to figure out how to deal with the precarious situation that emerged. When looking to the future we saw no other alternative than to welcome new owners. A shared ownership would grant financial strength in the future, we thought. Our children showed no interest in running the company and, as I see it, family ownership can never be an end in itself. Due to our excellent profitability, we did not lack proposals from prospective buyers. Some were assiduous in their attention. (Bengt Adolfsson, personal communication, 26 April 2006)

Adolfsson addresses the employees' concerns and the dependence on the employees, as in their contribution as stakeholders, is highlighted. When using the pronoun 'we' he clearly regards the employees as family members (Demers, Giroux and Chreim, 2003). The CEO continues by telling of the contacts made with the collective agents Nordic Capital and Atle. Nordic Capital, founded in 1989, is a group of private equity funds that invests in Nordic-based companies that operate in different sectors, providing the companies with ownership, strategic development and operational improvement.

> Nordic Capital provides committed ownership and support to portfolio company management and encourages a hands-on operational approach to problem solving. Nordic Capital's overriding aim is to build enduring partnerships and create long-term value, whether by creating new industrial combinations, pursuing a strategic repositioning or exploring internationalization opportunities. (Nordic Capital, 2007)

Atle, listed on the Stockholm Stock Exchange in 1993, is an investment company that is involved in developing unlisted small and medium-sized companies (Atle, 1999). 'Atle's core expertise is business development which includes the ability to find interesting companies, create acquisition situations and through active and responsible ownership to develop and after a period of time to find new suitable habitats for owned companies' (Atle, 1998: 2).

The investment companies Nordic Capital and Atle shared an interest in the operations and structure of the Swedish furniture industry, says Adolfsson (personal communication, 26 April 2006). Since October 1997, Nordic Capital had owned 60 percent of the equity in Apax, a Swedish manufacturer of beds and upholstered furniture with subsidiaries in Sweden, Denmark and Finland (Atle, 1999). Before the Nordic Capital entrance, Apax was owned by Skandia Investment (23 percent), the Conradsson family (38.5 percent) and the Hultman family (38.5 percent), but in terms of votes it was jointly controlled by the two families Conradsson and Hultman (Case No IV/M.1026 – Nordic Capital/Apax Industri, 6 November 1997). Through Nordic Capital's stake-holding in Apax, Atle indirectly gained 15 percent of the shares in Apax. Consequently, the Hultman family, represented by Anders Hultman, and the Conradsson family, represented by Yngve Conradsson, reduced their holding to 30 percent, and Skandia Investment to 10 percent (Atle, 1998).

In January 1998, Atle acquired 60 percent of the equity in Hilding Anders, leaving the Adolfsson family a share amounting to 40 percent. According to Arne Karlsson (personal communication, 6 November 2009), business area manager at Atle, Hilding Anders was a very interesting investment. Bengt Adolfsson (personal communication, 26 April 2006) emphasizes: 'Arne Karlsson strongly believed in Hilding Anders and seemed determined to maintain the ownership position achieved in Hilding Anders. Now things heated up and it did not take long before we had a representative of Apax on the phone, making a proposal for a merger.'

The then-Apax CEO Anders Hultman recounts:

> During 1997 and 1998, prior to the contact with Hilding Anders, there were several Norwegian bed manufacturers attracting our interest. The whole idea of bringing in Nordic Capital as the main owner was to construct an opportunity for the contribution of additional value, especially concerning the production and marketing of beds. In our pursuit of growth, we found a suitable merger candidate in Hilding Anders. We shared the objective of growing and forming a bigger corporation. So it was natural to combine the two companies. (Anders Hultman, personal communication, 9 November 2009)

Not part of the original idea to open up for co-owners in Hilding Anders, Apax, by coincidence, became a merger candidate, as Adolfsson explains (personal communication, 26 April 2006). Lars Haux, production and purchasing director in Hilding Anders at the time (personal communication, 20 December 2006), adds that 'the furniture industry in Sweden is relatively small and fragmented, consisting of many family-owned firms. The owners and managers of these firms knew each other quite well, business-wise, and could easily check on each other's moves.'

A Crucial Customer Relationship

It was also essential to maintain current sales and even to increase sales to the main customer Ikea. Bengt Adolfsson ascribes to Ikea a crucial role, pointing to the good relationships that were established with the Ikea buyers:

> Ikea, our main customer, has meant a lot to us. In the media, Ikea receives criticism for treating their suppliers very differently but I must admit that our expansion would not have been possible without Ikea. By being involved in both the production of long series and the development of customer value we gained economies of scale.
>
> Ikea's policy is to exchange the buyers regularly. When you have become acquainted with one buyer, it is time to make a change. I am sure I negotiated with at least five or six different buyers. Although the buyer–seller relations changed, I never experienced any kind of misunderstandings. Ikea was a very good customer and all the buyers I met with were excellent. (Bengt Adolfsson, personal communication, 26 April 2006)

A merger between Apax and Hilding Anders would most likely render a more efficient allocation of resources and improvement of logistics for the benefit of Ikea. For a considerable period, Ikea was the single largest customer of both Apax and Hilding Anders. Apax started its operations in 1989 when Scapa Inter AB (Scapa Inter) was bought out from the Stockholm Stock Exchange. The origin of Apax is thus Scapa Inter, founded in 1959 to provide its first customer Ikea with upholstered furniture and sprung beds.

> History tells that when the Scapa business started up, its founder Göte Karlsson knew Ikea's founder and owner Ingvar Kamprad quite well. At that point, Ikea faced some difficulties in finding suppliers since furniture dealers had little interest in doing business with Ikea. One even demonstrated a strong aversion to doing business with any supplier of Ikea. However, Ikea went abroad and found suppliers in Poland. Eventually, Scapa became a supplier of Ikea. This was very much due to the close relationship between Göte Karlsson and Ingvar Kamprad. (Lars Haux, personal communication, 20 December 2006).

Historical notes introduce Göte Karlsson as an innovative leader who put much effort into the development of production methods and design. 'Göte concentrated on innovation in both production methods and design, and his leadership was characterized by youthful enthusiasm and independence for the co-workers in the team' (Scapa Inter, 2009).

Scapa evolved into 'one of the most prominent companies in the Swedish furniture industry,' exporting to the rest of Scandinavia and Europe. During 1997 and 1998, two independent companies were formed: Scapa Inter with a focus on upholstered furniture production, and Scapa Bedding with spring bed production (Scapa Inter, 2009).[10]

Hilding Anders had begun its partnership with Ikea by the end of the 1970s, Lars Haux informs us (personal communication, 20 December 2006). In 1997, Hilding Anders received Ikea's best supplier award (*Norra Skåne*, 1997: 5). Prior to that, Ikea had conferred distinctions upon Hilding Anders at least ten times (Bengt Adolfsson, personal communication, 26 April 2006). The award for best supplier received attention in the local newspaper. A narrative frame of meaning is constituted here in the official recognition of the customer focus of the business.

Ikea following suit meant expansion abroad and a move on to the Polish market. The new constellation Apax-Hilding Anders primarily focused on the Nordic market but was also interested in moving on to markets outside Scandinavia. Lars Haux says, 'We viewed a Polish establishment as a strategic cornerstone that could promote further expansion in Europe while also significantly lowering our production costs. The western part of Poland especially attracted our interest because of the industrial culture, the good infrastructure and the proximity to Germany' (personal communication, 20 December 2006). Haux continues:

> Apax founded a company in Lithuania, in 1997, and through this establishment, we got in touch with PricewaterhouseCoopers who advised us to contact a Polish man who served at the company in Stockholm. We also contacted a representative for Ikea whom we had known for quite some time. He accompanied us to Poland, where he had already established contacts with Ikea's suppliers.
>
> As a result of the business trip to Poland, we strongly felt that it was right to start something new. We bought a piece of land and built a new factory, not very far from Poznan. We started up production in January 2001 with a mixed Swedish and Polish management on site during the first six months.
>
> In a similar way, we arranged for production in Lithuania; by visiting the country, traveling about and making contact with companies there. We talked to people and asked questions in order to learn about their companies. We enquired about what they had accomplished over time, how they worked and why. Our intention was to get a feel for the country, its culture and people. (Lars Haux, personal communication, 20 December 2006)

Lars Haux, production director at the time, was part of Bengt Adolfsson's team that visited Poland, analyzing alternative ways for market expansion. It is also important to add that, prior to the merger, it was in the interest of Hilding Anders to pursue the establishment of a Polish location. Bengt Adolfsson (personal communication, 17 December 2009) reveals that a deal with Ikea concerning a big order paved the way to move into the Polish market.

While recounting how establishments were made in Poland and Lithuania, the Ikea relationship is pictured as important and complex. Ikea's search for suppliers is narratively framed: the historically close relationship between Göte Karlssson and Ingvar Kamprad, and the contacts made between representatives of Apax, Hilding Anders and Ikea. The customer Ikea seems to play a crucial role in the exchange between the merger candidates. Moreover, emotions are narratively framed in reference to phrases such as 'we strongly felt it was right' and 'to get a feel for'. As Isaacs (1998) points out, emotions are offered in the form of 'feeling experiences', providing important information about the significance and meaning of activities.

The emerging opportunity for a merger between Apax and Hilding Anders reflects multiple motives. The creation of a larger unit also relates to market-oriented motives and the need to adjust to changing conditions in an increasingly globalized environment. These motives suggest a basis for justifying the merger and direct the attention to different modes of legitimacy, as will be pointed out next.

Creating a Larger Unit

The Apax and Hilding Anders parties decided to carry out the merger for building up financial strength, meeting the intensified competition in the markets for beds and mattresses, anticipating investors' restructuring moves and following the main customer. There was some fear of a scenario where a big European firm acquired Apax and Hilding Anders and where the two firms lost their discretion over strategic and operative matters. Globalization, associated with the application of sophisticated information techniques and enhanced market transparency, urged on the formation of larger units, according to Lars Haux:

> We discussed the development of the Scandinavian and European bed firms. Intensified competition was noted among the suppliers and the producers of beds and mattresses in Sweden as well as outside Sweden. In other industries, there was a tendency toward creating bigger players to make it possible to meet fierce competition in the market. New ways of gathering and communicating information on customers and competitors, largely due to the application of sophisticated IT, began to influence customer behavior and logistics while also increasing market transparency. Globalization tendencies in the business instigated the formation of larger units and standardization of products and production. (Lars Haux, personal communication, 20 December 2006)

Apax and Hilding Anders, both with a strong position on the Nordic bed and mattress market, produced own brands and private labels that they marketed through a similar customer structure. In 1998, Apax, employing 422 people, showed sales (including upholstered furniture) amounting to SEK588 million (Anders Hultman, personal communication, 9 November 2009).

A Turning Point

Merger discussions were initiated, involving representatives of the investors Nordic Capital, Atle and Scandia investment, and the three families Hultman, Conradsson and Adolfsson. A meeting was held at a hotel near Stockholm's Arlanda airport. Arne Karlsson, representing Atle, the main owner of Hilding Anders, conducted a thorough analysis of the two merger candidates. Based on the analysis, Karlsson identified a series of potential barriers to overcome:

> At the meeting, I raised provocative questions, addressing the issue of how two strong entrepreneurs, Anders Hultman and Bengt Adolfsson, would get along. I considered that it would be problematic for the entrepreneurs to realize synergistic gains, mainly due to differing cultural traditions in the companies. The meeting helped to bring into the open problems that otherwise might have been overlooked and we came up with satisfactory solutions to the problems identified. From my point of view, this meeting was a turning point, leading to the decision to merge Apax and Hilding Anders. (Arne Karlsson, personal communication, 6 November 2009)

Narratively indicated by Karlsson is the idea, originating in a cultural discourse, that actors are not neutral decision-makers but represent different cultures, and that there could be conflicting objectives of integration. Vaara (2002: 229), referring to a cultural discourse, states that central to this discourse is 'the staging of post-merger decision-making as a confrontation between different cultures, nationalities, or sub-cultures.' As opposed to a rationalistic discourse in which the integration is usually not questioned and it is sufficient to point to profitability, strategic position and synergy, a cultural discourse allows for plurivocal and critical interpretations of a merger process.

On 21 October 1998, a formal decision was made to merge Apax and Hilding Anders. According to Bengt Adolfsson the decision was a milestone in the expansion of Hilding Anders (*Dagens Industri*, 2002). The third largest bed and mattress manufacturer in Europe was formed with annual sales amounting to approximately SEK1 billion and earnings before financial income and expenses of SEK110 million (AllBusiness, 1998). The new constellation had more than 500 employees, involved in the production of 700,000 beds annually in Sweden, Finland, Denmark, Norway, Estonia and Lithuania under private labels to furniture retailers such as Ikea, MIO and Europa Möbler, and under own brands that were already well-established in the retail segment: Hilding, Ekens, Scapa Bedding, TibroBädden, Stjärnbädden and ScandiSleep. The owners were Atle 35.6 percent, Nordic Capital 25 percent, Bengt and Ann-Charlotte Adolfsson (Bacapps AB) 18.2 percent, Anders Hultman 7.6 percent, Yngve Conradsson, 7.6 percent and Skandia Investment 5.6 percent (Atle, 1998).

'We thought carefully about the proposal and eventually decided when all our claims were met to carry through a merger with Apax. We ended up with a diminished share of the equity but evidently gained a piece of a bigger cake,' says Bengt Adolfsson (personal communication, 26 April 2006). Despite a reduction in shares in Hilding Anders, Adolfsson enjoyed a strong position in the bed and mattress industry. The investment companies did not find it necessary to interfere in the operations of Hilding Anders. Adolfsson affirms: 'As long as I accomplished things and delivered good results they were satisfied. We never encountered any problems. Fortunately, we were extremely profitable. Hence there was no reason for the investors to intervene.'

Many years of experience and the development of a unique management competence gained the CEO great respect from colleagues and owners. Adolfsson was involved in expanding the Hilding Anders business through numerous international contacts and cross-border transactions. He points to several milestones that indicate a complexity of growth activities, starting with the spectacular Russian order successfully negotiated by Adolfsson in 1976. Described as 'The Big Boost!' worth SEK12 million, it doubled the turnover of Hilding Anders (Hilding Anders, 2009a). The generation shift in 1987 was followed by many other 'successes' associated with both organic growth and acquired growth.

The meeting at the hotel outside Stockholm, combined with the publicly announced decision to merge Apax and Hilding Anders, defines a turning point. The turning point holds a positive image of growth, exhibited by the owners' agreement to list Hilding Anders on the stock market within two years (AllBusiness, 1998). Most likely, the representatives of Nordic Capital, Atle and Skandia Investment, and the Hultman, Conradsson and Adolfsson families were energized by an image of a future in which their expectations of positive synergies were realized and competitive strength generated. By forming such an image in accord with one another, social energy is created (Hjorth, 2007). In the words of Lars Gårdö, managing director of Atle:

It is very pleasing that we have so rapidly succeeded in implementing this transaction. When Atle acquired a 60 percent holding in Hilding Anders in January this year, we stated our plans to create a group which will have the strength required for a continued expansion in Europe. Soon thereafter, we participated in the first acquisition – of the Finnish bed manufacturer, Unituli. (Atle, 1998: 1)

Lars Haux also expressed a feeling of satisfaction with the formation of the new group:

Two family-owned and entrepreneurial firms, each holding a strong focus on customers, formed a new organization, Hilding Anders AB, comprising people with long experience of and knowledge about the business. The merger promised to create a major competitor on the Scandinavian and European bed and mattress markets. The larger size would meet the expectations of the managers and owners and lead to outcomes and positive synergies that reduced the threats of the competitors. There would also be a more solid financial basis for boosting product development, marketing and growth. (Lars Haux, personal communication, 20 December 2006)

The turning point lies in the analysis conducted by Arne Karlsson, the questions raised by him and the result of the exchange of arguments among the parties present at the meeting at the hotel outside Stockholm. It extends to the solutions suggested to the problems brought up by Karlsson at the meeting, the decision made to merge Apax and Hilding Anders and its public announcement. Further, the turning point manifests in feelings of pleasure and also in market-oriented calculative reasons. Entwined with the feelings of satisfaction, the factual tone of Lars Haux and Lars Gårdö reflects market-oriented calculated reasons behind the merger. The merger represents a business opportunity for two high performers within the bed and mattress industry. Clearly, the motive of uncertainty avoidance played a role in the merger between Apax and Hilding Anders. The parties wished to enhance control of their environment. The environment – which refers to the Scandinavian and European bed and mattress markets – imposes constraints on each separate business in terms of limited competition. The parties involved in the merger negotiations chose a level of expected positive gains that was subjected to the uncertainty associated with environmental constraints. Avoidance of uncertainty also implies dealing with organizational interdependence by reducing competitive interdependencies through horizontal integration (Pfeffer, 1972; Thompson, 1967).

With Reference to Catalytic Elements

A focus on strategic dynamics and catalytic elements provides a more complex view of merger and acquisition motives. A constructionist narrative approach, influenced by French structural narratology (see Demers, Giroux and Chreim, 2003), directs attention to the so-called canonical and actantial schemas. Closely related, the two schemas suggest a move beyond a unilateral view of merger and acquisition motives. The canonical schema applied to the Apax-Hilding Anders merger illuminates the strategic consequences of different catalytic elements that helped initiate and drive the merger process.[11] The catalytic elements here are the CEO's way of dealing with the fact that some employees in Hilding Anders got cancer, his welcoming of new owners to Hilding Anders, the telephone call from Apax and following the lead of Ikea to establish plants in Poland and Lithuania. In addition, catalytic elements refer to the investment companies Nordic Capital's and Atle's shared interest in the Swedish furniture industry, Atle's ownership position in Hilding Anders and the actions taken by Arne Karlsson. Karlsson called for a meeting at which the parties discussed how a combination of Apax and Hilding Anders – each represented by a strong entrepreneur – could bring about positive synergies. This meeting clearly paved the way for the decision to merge the two companies.

The actantial schema includes humans, organizations and institutions – the so-called actants – and the roles the actants play. The schema pairs the actants by a binary opposition, conceiving a narrative as a quest. Binary opposition implies identifying a subject and an object with reference to a destinator and a destinatee. Drawing on Demers, Giroux and Chreim (2003), the quest for value is triggered by the board of directors, comprising representatives of the investment companies and the Adolfsson, Conradsson and Hultman families who add value for the shareholders, the employees and the customers. The board then acts as the destinator while combining financial resources and carrying out projects to coordinate operations, forming a larger and more valuable and competitive object – the destinatee. In recognition of the close relationship and kinship bonds among some of the members of the board of directors, the shareholders and the top managers, the binary opposition somewhat loses its explanatory power, however. The subject–object relationship characterizing the destinator–destinatee is undermined by the fact that the role of the destinator coincides with the role of the destinatee. When a family member is involved in strategic issues as owner, board member, and in daily operations there is a considerable overlap of different roles, as Nordqvist (2005) emphasizes.

Confirming the Legality

The Commission of the European Communities confirmed the legality of the merger in February 1999. The Commission story tells us that Apax Intressenter, the holding company with 100 percent share in Apax Industri (Apax), acquired all shares in Hilding Anders Holding (HAH), owned by Atle and Bacapps AB (Bacapps; Bengt and Ann-Charlotte Adolfsson), and issued new shares to Atle and Bacapps. Apax Intressenter then owned 100 percent of both Apax and HAH. The new board was composed of six members, representing Atle, Nordic Capital, Skandia Investment, Bacapps and the previous management of Apax, that is, the Hultman and Conradsson families.

Narratively, a merger, referred to as a 'marriage', leads to 'a brief foray into the civic world where the legality of the marriage is confirmed by courts and regulators' (Demers, Giroux and Chreim, 2003: 234). Apax and Hilding Anders, holding a strong market position respectively, formed a constellation that from an international point of view was unique in the furniture industry. The combination of the two businesses did not change the character of the business. The relevant product market was still the market for beds, which mainly included box-spring beds but also polyfoam mattress beds and sofa beds. Through the merger, Apax and HAH would have a combined market share of 30 percent of the Nordic market. They were not in direct competition with the box-spring beds produced by Dux and Hästens, who market and sell their products through other distribution channels. If Dux and Hästens were excluded from the market, Apax and HAH would obtain 50 percent of the Nordic market (Case No IV/M.1357 – Nordic Capital/Hilding Anders, 2 April 1999).

As stated in the documents, submitted with the notification by the Commission of the European Communities, Apax and Hilding Anders were obliged to maintain their current sales to Ikea. The relationship with Ikea was depicted as subcontracting.

The single largest customer of both Apax and HAH is Ikea, which accounts for [<30%] and [<40%] of their respective total sales. The importance for the parties of maintaining their current sales to Ikea and other large customers is clearly set out in the documents submitted with the notification. Ikea, which is active on a world-wide basis, is several times larger than even a combined Apax/HAH. It is also a sophisticated customer, whose relationship to Apax and HAH can be described as subcontracting. As such, all of Apax and HAH's sales to this customer are made according to specifications set by Ikea and sold under the latter's own brand names. In addition to Ikea, the parties will also face a number of other relatively large furniture retail customers, such as Jysk and Europa Möbler. Also these customers account for important parts of the parties' total sales and sell the products in question under their own brand names. These large customers have not expressed any serious concerns about the proposed concentration. (Case No IV/M.1357 – Nordic Capital/Hilding Anders, 2 April 1999: 6)

The volumes offered Ikea were strongly increased thanks to effective work with post-merger integration, Lars Haux points out (personal communication, 20 December 2006): 'As a bigger player and purchaser, contracts with the suppliers were renegotiated for the benefits of our customers. The new constellation was capable of allocating resources more effectively, improving logistics and meeting the customers' requirements and needs.'

By joining forces, Apax and Hilding Anders intended to bolster financial consolidation, development and growth. The merger activities offered a bright future. The bed and mattress industry and markets are evident in these activities, designating a calculative rational response to environmental uncertainty. They bring to the fore the Weberian logic of rationality (Demers, Giroux and Chreim, 2003), which refers here to instrumental rational action oriented to a clearly formulated goal amd a set of clearly formulated values (Weber, 1947). The merger activities further build on the foundation of legitimacy in line with the legal aspects pronounced by the official representatives of the Commission of the European Communities.

The firms, the families and the legal claims indicate different modes of legitimating the merger activities. Following Demers, Giroux and Chreim (2003), these modes correspond to the merchant, the domestic and the civic 'city' (or 'world'). The merchant city relies on the financial-oriented arguments behind the merger between Apax and Hilding Anders; the domestic city expresses family tradition and loyalty; the civic city builds on the interest of official representatives. Here the merchant and domestic cities conjoin. No sharp limits mark the boundaries of the two cities since the families were the owners of the firms. However, as owners they mainly advocated financial matters. 'Family traditions' did not play a significant role (Anders Hultman, personal communication, 9 November 2009).

Expectations of Continued Growth

The merger took almost a year, Bengt Adolfsson informs us:

> In the course of the process we dealt with the issue of who would be best suited for leading the company. The new constellation called for a separation between board activities and operative activities. Dual command on the operative level would cause many problems, we thought. Once we reached the decision that Anders Hultman, the former President and CEO of Apax, should take on the responsibility as Chairman of the Board of Directors, I assumed the position as President and CEO. (Bengt Adolfsson, personal communication, 26 April 2006)

The new group needed to continue growing through acquisitions while improving efficiency and capitalizing on innovations, says Adolfsson:

> The first target stage for the new Group is to have sales within two years which permanently exceed SEK1 billion, with a profitability of 8–12 percent. Within five years, we will be the largest manufacturer in Northern Europe of beds with an interior-spring mattress and one of the largest producers in the world. In order to succeed in that process, continued structural transactions, innovations and increased efficiency will be required. This transation should be seen in the light of that strategy. In the new Group, we will also continue to prioritize a high rate of innovation.
> A further step in that direction is a recently carried-out acquisition of the development company Newtec. The transaction is strategic as the former Hilding Anders has developed its own production lines together with Newtec in recent years. The technology has led to the fact that Hilding Anders has a very high productivity. (Atle, 1998: 1–2)

Adolfsson adds:

> We don't aim at a specific market share. We don't think in terms of market size. Instead it is essential to show profitability on the markets where we operate, and be among the largest producers in these markets.
> We focus on improving our production concepts. We try also to improve logistics

chains in terms of efficiency and effectiveness but refrain from making changes in production. Each subsidiary knows their respective market and customers best. The bed and mattress business is local. Production must be close to sales otherwise the transport costs will be huge. The customers' tastes differ a lot, which is why it is necessary to be close to the customer, offering the customer the specific product and brand the customer wants. (*Dagens Industri*, 2002)

With four new subsidiaries, Bengt Adolfsson was obliged to discuss various matters with the heads of the subsidiaries, being prepared to debate contentious issues and criticism whenever they arose.

Now there were four new subsidiaries, one in Denmark, two in Sweden and one in Finland. Prior to the merger, Hilding Anders bought the factories of Ekens and Stjärnbädden in Sweden. So I discussed different matters with six managers. The whole 'gang' went to Spain for a conference for three or four days, joining to outline the strategy. The board of directors felt a bit worried when bringing together people that shortly before the merger represented our competitors and were used to check on our moves. Of course, one feared the consequences of the conference. Fortunately, we got on very well. Although different opinions were voiced at the conference, we had no disagreements. When returning to Sweden we felt a team with the members of the team closely knitted together. Competitors? Oh, no, we were never competing against each other. From day one, we were already a team.

I formed a top management team that comprised people from Apax and Hilding Anders. Both sides were represented. We reached an agreement that granted the subsidiaries some autonomy in their operations. To begin with, the maintenance of an independent position was important. Thereafter, we focused on coordinating purchasing and other activities across the boundaries of the subsidiaries in order to realize positive synergies. I started traveling abroad like a 'madman', visiting the subsidiaries and the factories to check up on things while having the opportunity to exert some influence over how things were done. On my business trips I met with the heads of the subsidiaries. We spent a couple of days analyzing the business plan and other business-related matters, discussing how to move ahead. Technicians and purchasers were involved too, following up on the business plan.

I was very content that coordination ran smoothly. Actually, everything worked out just fine. (Bengt Adolfsson, personal communication, 26 April 2006)

Adolfsson (personal communication, 8 September 2009) adds that the deputy CEO, Danish Poul Erik Rasmussen, played an important role in the integration of the two businesses.

Adolfsson narratively characterizes relations between the managers representing the subsidiaries of Hilding Anders as compatible. Former competitors started working together, constituting a team that addressed the issue of coordination and, it appears, they were infused with positive emotions relating to the state of contentment and to the experience of being a well-knitted team. People related to each other in new ways, creating social energy (Hjorth, 2007), which is illustrated by the pleasure taken in working together and the interest in coordinating some activities across the boundaries of the subsidiaries. Arguably, compatibility between the managers representing the different subsidiaries is negotiated and relationally constructed. Compatibility is realized through the managers' interactions and positive emotions, and provides a sense of the coordination of activities. Sense made through talk-in-interaction and face-to-face relations aims at mutual understanding (Rovio-Johansson, 2007) of the members of the 'gang'. A mutual understanding clearly facilitated the onward post-merger integration.

Expectations associated with the merger justified activities for carrying out a variety of projects to coordinate operations across organizational units. By reading into the present their expectations of future development and growth, the parties arguably constructed a frame for sense-making. Connected with these expectations was temporary experience that drew on a future-oriented frame, allowing the prospect to be a significant part of sense-making (Wright, 2006).

> Staff in Apax and Hilding Anders designed and carried out a number of projects in order to coordinate the operations of the different units of the new constellation. Changes accomplished during the first half year after the merger mainly focused on improvements in logistics, standardization of material as well as of some products and product components. Product development was also subject to change but required a more long-term-oriented approach.
>
> We learned a lot from each other and about each other's production, systems and operations. It was necessary to make changes across the boundaries of the subsidiaries in working methods, IT systems, financial systems and in the report system that built on data about markets and products. It was important to grant the subsidiaries some autonomy in their operations. The intensive post-merger work encompassed a wide variety of activities. It is worth emphasizing too that with future expansion in sight, there were no lay-offs.
>
> I was responsible for production but also for purchasing and logistics in Hilding Anders. I worked intensively with the post-merger integration. In addition to this, I engaged in the establishment in Poland. (Lars Haux, personal communication, 20 December 2006)

Anders Hultman (personal communication, 9 November 2009), the chairman at the time, adds that the Poland establishment originally derived from a project developed by Apax. It is also important to note that a deal between Hilding Anders and Ikea concerning a big order paved the way for Hilding Anders to establish itself in the Polish market before the merger with Apax (Bengt Adolfsson, personal communication, 17 December 2009).

The CEO Bengt Adolfsson (personal communication, 26 April 2006) expressed great satisfaction with the merger and the way in which it was managed and consolidated. Two years after the merger he noted that the objectives had been met and that a solid basis for continued growth had been laid. Earlier research on mergers and acquisitions points out that the expectations of the shareholders and managers are not always realized. Lower productivity, higher market-related risk and a higher degree of variance in performance often accompany mergers and acquisitions (Bergh, 1997; Cardel Gertsen, Søderberg and Torp, 1998; Dahlgren and Witt, 1988; Jemison and Sitkin, 1986; Ravenscraft and Scherer, 1987; Schmidt and Fowler, 1990). Some scholars claim that related horizontal mergers and acquisitions exhibit superior financial performance, whereas others show that gains to target firm share-holders in unrelated vertical or conglomerate mergers and acquisitions are higher compared to those in the related ones (Datta, 1991). Considerable diversity in the findings of studies focusing on performance then give little support for a strategic fit and synergistic benefits as determinants of perfor-mance. A more crucial issue is, according to Datta, organizational fit, which refers to compatibility in the styles of the acquiring and acquired firm manage-ments and how the use of existing capabilities are made more effective through the post-acquisition integration of operations. Major differences in management styles can prove to be serious impediments in the integration phase, leading to reduced productivity and poor performance (Buono and Bowditch, 1989). Apparently, compatible management styles facilitated the post-merger integration of operations in Apax-Hilding Anders. Agreements between individuals justified coordinated action in the form of the new constellation named Hilding Anders. Two strong entrepreneurs, Anders Hultman and Bengt Adolfsson, joined forces.

Hilding Anders became the largest manufacturer of beds in Scandinavia. 'Success' relates here to the way the CEO describes the consequences of the merger. Earlier studies on mergers and acquisitions illuminate a number of factors for success (Kitching, 1967) and methods by which success is measured, but devotes little interest to the social construction in narratives of success (Vaara, 2002). Accounting and financial specialists use different meth-ods for assessing success, as Hunt (1990) informs us. Accounting specialists relate success to the return on the investment several years after the legal closure. Financial specialists evaluate the impact of the merger and acquisition on the equity price of both buyer and seller shares at the time of the bid. However, a behavior-oriented evaluation of what may or may not lead to success is also needed, claims Hunt. A more complex assessment method accounts for behavioral processes that refer to firms' targeting, bidding, nego-tiating and implementation of a merger strategy. It is imperative, according to Hunt, to recognize what expectations the buyer and seller have and in partic-ular to pay attention to the tone of the negotiating parties. His study gives precedence to the influence of the mere tone on subsequent processes. A hostile tone polarizes the negotiation process whereas a friendly tone allows for an open and unhurried debate among the negotiators.

As pointed out by Bengt Adolfsson (personal communication, 26 April 2006), the special we-feeling emerging among people representing different organizational units and functions of the new constellation facilitated the coordination of activities. Promoted by the entrepreneurial spirit that characterized both Apax and Hilding Anders, the we-feeling undoubtedly indicates a friendly tone among the merging parties. Although a factual and impersonal tone is often used with reference to financial, strategic and legal matters (Demers, Giroux and Chreim, 2003), it is pertinent to note that intuition and emotion can play a significant role in merger activities. As Lars Haux reveals:

> There were people in both Apax and Hilding Anders who were courageous enough to take decisions rapidly and to follow them through persistently without engaging in comprehensive investigations and analyses. They disliked long decision channels and accordingly refrained from building hierarchical levels that would slow down decision-making. An entrepreneurial spirit characterized the firms. Knowledgeable, skillful and experienced people contributed to that spirit. People were good listeners and sensitive to changes in the market. Also, intuition and feelings played a major role. (Lars Haux, personal communication, 20 December 2006)

The new millennium started with continued expansion in terms of turnover and market shares. In 2001, Hilding Anders increased sales from SEK1 billion to SEK3 billion. Despite turbulence in the currency and raw material markets, during 2001, Hilding Anders made a profit. With continued growth in sight, new requirements followed. A decision was made to move the headquarters to Helsingborg. Thereafter, the Adolfsson family, currently living in Hästveda, moved to Helsingborg.

> The headquarters remained in Hästveda up until the move to Helsingborg in 2001, a point in time at which we reached a turnover of SEK1 million. With the growth of the company followed new requirements of how to obtain the necessary qualifications for taking part in the intensified competition on the international bed market. Growth was based on export but also on acquisitions of European companies.
> Nine people worked at the headquarters in Helsingborg and there was no need to delegate authority via decentralization of decision-making. A limited number of people engaged in planning and strategic decision-making. Thus we were close enough to gain insights into real-life situations that could be dealt with in an efficient and flexible way. Today, about 30 people work at the headquarters, which moved to Malmö in 2004. (Bengt Adolfsson, personal communication, 26 April 2006)

Over the years that followed, to continue expanding the brand portfolio, Hilding Anders people were involved in several acquisitions of bed manufacturers and brands, as the next chapter reveals.

6. Building a brand portfolio

Hilding Anders' business concept includes manufacturing and marketing beds, mattresses and associated products under own brands and private labels. The private labels in combination with the own brands, which maintains a mix of power brands and local brands, constitute the brand portfolio. A firm's brand portfolio is a 'resource base', according to Varadarajan, DeFanti and Busch (2006), that in response to differences between markets could be composed of a number of local, national and global brands developed internally but also acquired by the firm in various country markets. The power brands are well-known brands that have expanded in international markets whereas local brands, also called local jewels, refer to the ones continually adapted to the local consumers and retailers (Hilding Anders, 2008a). Private labels are often denoted as retail-owned brands or store-brands (Staahl Gabrielsen and Sørgard, 2007). 'A typical private label is Ikea, which always has been an important "leg" for the corporation,' remarks Lars Haux (personal communication, 20 December 2006). Thus, there are two segments, the brand segment and the private label segment, with different dynamics and different stories.

> In the brand segment, products are normally developed, manufactured and sold under the manufacturer's own label. In the private label segment, the products are specified by the customer, manufactured by an external producer and sold, for instance, by a furniture chain under its own brand. (Hilding Anders, 2004c: 10)

By definition brand is: 'all the expectations and associations evoked from experience with a company or its offerings. Logos, taglines, advertising jingles, spokespeople or packaging are merely the representation of the brand. The actual brand is how customers think and feel about what the business, product or service does' (Petromilli, Morrison and Million, 2002: 23).

What makes a brand a brand is 'personality', the presence of which imparts utility and value to the customer, as Christopher (1996) indicates. Personality refers to the human characteristics of a brand, such as sincerity, wholesomeness, reliability, cheerfulness and success, Keller (2002) clarifies. Taking a wider perspective, Blombäck (2005) includes in a brand a company's creation and management that make the customers notice, understand and believe that the company's offer is better suited for them than that presented by a competitor. With a focus on industrial marketing and marketing communication, she analyzes the role of corporate brands and branding in a subcontractor context. She points out that the customers will not consider a purchase unless they perceive value, deriving from the company's offer and from many other factors connected with the relationship customers have with their supplier. Just as Harrington (2007) purports, it is insufficient to add value without accounting for the reciprocal nature of 'adding' and 'extracting'. Extracting refers to the processes through which a company benefits by adding value to the customer and presupposes access to and efficient use of tangible and intangible resources.

> Adding value focuses on the customer, with value added in terms of producing and delivering products to the market at one end of a continuum to building customer loyalty through continually meeting and exceeding consumers' expectations at the other end. Extracting value focuses on the company with the intent to appropriate value back to the company through profits at one end to the value extracting continuum moving toward the building of reputation at the other end. (Harrington, 2007: 123)

The reciprocity of adding and extracting value requires a manager to be aware that the brand image plays a decisive role and that the image a single customer has of the company and the brand affects what the customer recognizes, remembers, becomes interested in and is attracted to. In this context, the power of impressions, emotions and gut feelings cannot be underestimated, Blombäck (2005) contends. Customer value is strongly tied to emotions. Harrington (2007: 128) suggests that 'one must go through emotion meeting the consumer's heart, while accepting that triggering cognition alone is insufficient. The question for brand and product managers then becomes, what levers are most efficacious in triggering and engaging the emotion facet of the relationship with consumers.'

In the wake of the Apax-Hilding Anders merger, a crucial issue was how to develop present domestic and internationals brands and to continue expanding the brand portfolio by adding value through acquisitions and launching of new brands. Here value builds on a complex set of factors that account for feeling expressions and customers' emotional connections with a brand. As pointed out in this chapter, value is influenced by long-term relationships with customers, product quality, the efforts Hilding Anders people put into sustaining a balance between the brand segment and the private label segment, and the central support given to local branding. Branding concerns how a brand is employed across the products of a firm (Keller, 2002).

Under the management of Anders Pålsson – from January 2003 the CEO of Hilding Anders – and Bengt Adolfsson, chairman of the Hilding Anders board during 2003, plans for continuous expansion were made and actual expansion of the brand portfolio took place. Acquisitions of brands further propelled Hilding Anders into the European and the Asian bed and mattress markets. As Pålsson declares: 'Our overall goal is to become one of the world's leading bed and mattress manufacturers, and we will reach that goal through organic growth and strategic acquisitions. For that reason we will act to enhance our position further in Europe and in Asia' (Hilding Anders, 2007c).

Since each brand operates somewhat independently, Hilding Anders employs what can be described as the house of brand architecture. The house of brand architecture, as opposed to the branded house architecture, which employs a single (master) brand to span a range of offerings, expects the sum of performance of the brands to be greater than if the brands are managed under a single master brand (Petromilli, Morrison and Million, 2002). The focal point for the subsidiaries constituting Hilding Anders is obviously a multibrand (Chailan, 2008) growth strategy that makes up the house of brand architecture.

The house of brand architecture is informed by an understanding of the fragmented bed and mattress markets for serving multiple customer segments and matching various customer interests. The European bed industry is fragmented with production carried out by small local companies. Cultural differences and local ties mean that each region requires a distinctive product. Turnable mattresses on bedsteads are the norm in many countries, whereas in other countries divans with storage drawers or sprung mattresses with wooden frames are preferred. Anders Pålsson describes the bed market as 'very local':

> But the bed market is very local. It is mostly in the Nordic countries that we sleep on a thin top mattress on top of an interior-spring mattress. In Britain, many people sleep on divans with drawers built into the bed. In southern Europe, people like a slatted base while only one percent of India's population sleeps in a bed at all. In China, which is the fastest growing bed market right now, hard beds are popular and divans beds are bestsellers in the higher price ranges. (Malmö Trade and Industry, 2008)

CONTINUOUS GROWTH

Preparations and plans openly mention hopes for future growth. Establishments and acquisitions realize these hopes, encouraging Hilding Anders people to carry out operations to nurture relationships with customers, keeping up a position in a specific market, supplementing price segments, developing brand products and entering into a new market for broadening and consolidating the brand portfolio while, at the same time, trying to minimize business risk. Activities linked with these operations reveal route followers which help to reinforce and back up the corporate-level strategy. The route followers are strategic in character, conveying the notion that brand as value creator plays a key role in generating competitive advantage over competitors (Ponsonby-Mccabe and Boyle, 2006), spurring continuous growth.

The overarching profit-driven, focused-growth strategy of Hilding Anders entails the objectives of growing organically and through acquisitions, reaching a fifty–fifty balance between own brands and private labels, as Anders Pålsson explains (*Hilding Anders News*, 2004a, No. 2). The notion of balance and the endeavor to sustain an even balance between the brand segment and the private label segment present no particular turning points. Rather, activities spark off and realize moves, from the perspective of the Hilding Anders managers, in a future-oriented direction that pushes for enhanced customer focus and growth. Embodying route followers, these activities are fully in line with current strategic objectives of Hilding Anders:

> to secure and enhance its leading position in Europe and Asia and to strengthen its position on the world market. Hilding Anders should also be one of the leaders in each and every individual market the company operates in – whether it will be in terms of sales, profitability or product development.
>
> By carrying out operations in a number of different geographic markets and in a number of different price segments, business risk will be minimised. (Hilding Anders, 2008c)

A brand plays a strategic role, constructing opportunities for expansion through its entrance into a new market and price segment. If expansion takes place through acquisition of a brand one must take into account special practices for targeting, due diligence, valuation, a portfolio strategy and a post-merger management process, Kumar and Hansted Blomqvist (2004) assert. Nevertheless, this chapter only touches upon some of these acquisition practices. My main intention is to point to and expose one key aspect of growth: the strategic route-following aspect. This aspect mainly refers to activities that managers in favor of an acquisition-based strategy share and participate in. While presenting a number of brands brought to the Hilding Anders portfolio, the chapter moreover gives indications of qualities and values associated with a brand and accordingly with the route follower described.

The exposition of route followers takes as its starting point the Swedish brands Hilding and Ekens, and the Danish company Carl Thögersen (the company name does not correspond to a brand). It continues by directing attention to acquisitions and launching of brands in many other European countries during the period 2001–8. In chronological order, the chapter refers to the following acquisitions: 1991, Ekens; 1998, Unituli; 2001, Carl Thögersen, Bico, Crown Bedding, Wifor, Slumberland, Billerbeck and Pullman; 2002, Dunlopillo; 2004, Jensen and André-Renault; 2005, Hespo;

2006, Somilar; 2007, Perfecta, Tropico, Eastborn, Timbo and Myer's; 2008, Happy and Bedding.

Further, this chapter points out that Hilding Anders managers operate in Asian countries and have significant plans for expansion in China and India. Acquisitions of brands refer to small and medium-sized companies, many of which are family owned. Most often, the name of the company corresponds to the name of the brand it offers. This places the corporate brand at the center. In brand management, one general trend is to focus on the corporate brand, representing the name of a company (Blombäck, 2005). Since customer actions are guided by an increased ethical and environmental awareness, the focus has shifted toward the corporate brand that can be used as a supplement and support to a product brand, Blombäck explains. An emphasis on corporate brand requires actions to be taken at the company level to make visible and clearly communicate what the company is doing and what it stands for. By just mentioning a company's name, the customer will have an immediate impression and expectations of the company. Nonetheless, it is not just having a name that is important, Rotfeld (2008) explains. A focus on the company name should not distract interest from the value of the corporate brand and its image.

> In these days of product placement and viral marketing, companies of all types focus on brand awareness and an extensive effort to put their name out there (wherever 'out there' might be). But it is not just having a name that is important, but the image that the name conveys to consumers. (Rotfeld, 2008: 122)

Hilding, Ekens and Carl Thögersen

At the beginning of 2000, the most well-known brands were Hilding, positioned in the mid-range price segment, and Ekens, representing the premium price segment. Price premium reflects the willingness of the customer to pay for a certain brand and a brand's ability to command a higher price than the competitors (Anselmsson, Johansson and Persson, 2007). Hilding traces its roots to 1939, when Hilding Andersson started up a business in Bjärnum, a municipality located in the southern Swedish province of Skåne.[12] With the move in 1961 to Hästveda, in the proximity of Bjärnum, the business continued to develop and grow under the ownership and management of the son Olle Andersson. Keeping the production of beds and mattresses in Hästveda, also under the ownership and management of Bengt Adolfsson (the son-in-law who succeeded Olle Andersson), the Hilding brand was strengthened. In 2002, the Hilding production moved to the subsidiary Scapa, located in Rydaholm in the Småland province, north of Skåne. In these circumstances one might have thought that the Hilding brand, representing a local jewel, would weaken and bring the risk of brand dilution. In Hästveda, the production continued to focus on the customer-owned private label Ikea, which earlier on had been moved from Rydaholm to Hästveda.

Hästveda, where the Hilding brand had for so long evolved, was associated with a feeling of family that was clearly weakened with the transfer of the Hilding production of beds and mattresses to another geographical place, as Tomas Modén, former supervisor, and from 2008 production manager, admits. But the recent move of the Ikea production to Poland gave room for the Hilding production to return to Hästveda. A special feeling of having one's own brand was evoked, Modén emphasizes:

> Under the ownership and management of Olle and Bengt, there was a much closer contact between the owner-managers and the employees; a sense of family developed, coupled with the Hilding brand and the production here. So when the production of Hilding moved to Scapa we realized that something important was missing. Now the Hilding product has returned to Hästveda. The Ikea production moves to Hilding Polska and this makes room to bring the Hilding brand back to Hästveda. It is a very special feeling to have one's own brand. It knits together people working at the Hästveda factory. (Tomas Modén, personal communication, 13 November 2006)

Ekens, joining the Hilding Anders Group in 1991, started manufacturing beds in 1953 in Tollarp, situated in the Swedish province of Skåne. The Ekens brand, building on the qualities of unique and individual comfort, innovative solutions and exclusive design, is positioned in the premium segment of the market (Ekens, 2008).

Primarily, Scandinavian furniture stores and chains market the Hilding and Ekens brands. At the annual Swedish furniture fair in Stockholm, Hilding attracted these marketers' interest in the new collection,[13] the Midnight Blues, that was launched in 2001. The very same year Ekens also launched a new collection. Strongly appreciated by the customers, the new Ekens beds brought about increased sales volumes and improved profits. More recently the independent Swedish institute Testfakta evaluated beds on the comfort and durability dimensions in the price range of SEK6,000 to SEK22,000. In the test, which included high-quality beds such as Hästens, Dux and Ekens beds, Ekens came out with the highest rate on comfort and durability (Hilding Anders, 2008i).

To strengthen the Hilding and Ekens brands further, the Dr Sleep school was established, offering courses for training and supporting retailers. Dr Sleep feels the pulse of sales conditions, urging the retailers to keep it at a healthy level to meet the specific needs, wishes and expectations of each individual customer, developing long-term relationships.

Retailers used to be invited to the factory and given a tour and the opportunity for some socializing, as Poul Erik Rasmussen, business area director during the years 2003–6, relates. Interest in the factory tour decreased over time, though, and the idea then arose to establish the Dr Sleep school. Swedish and Danish salespersons reaped the benefits of training at the school with Olle Carlsson in Sweden and Dan Meinertz Petersen[14] in Denmark as the Dr Sleep teachers and ambassadors (*Hilding Anders News*, 2004a, No. 2).

The focus of the school is twofold: to understand and guide the customer toward the right solution; and to understand customer experiences and questions regarding sleep and sleeping quality. The courses taught thus stress personal service to help the retailers find confidence in the sales situation and act as the customer's professional and competent guide, Olle Carlsson says. A bed is not merely a physical product. In the sales situation, one must also communicate the intangible qualities of a bed.

> It is essential to get the customer to explain their needs, sleeping habits and wishes, and then use this information to suggest which bed or beds would best suit that customer. The next step is to get the customer to try the bed out. A bed is not a product that you can demonstrate and sell based on facts. A bed should be tried out and should feel comfortable. I usually use imagery in my training courses and ask those participating how they think a sportsperson chooses running shoes, an angler a fishing reel or a golfer a driver. They keep on trying and testing. Everyone can learn how to open the mind of a potential bed buyer, so that he or she can test their way forward and discover advantages and differences between beds. This process will convince the customer in their choice of bed, while the salesperson acts as the professional and competent guide. And that's what we are hoping to accomplish with Dr Sleep. (Olle Carlsson, *Hilding Anders News*, 2004a, No. 2: 16)

To enhance presence in the Nordic market, the Danish company Carl Thögersen was brought to Hilding Anders in 2001. The Thögersen family had founded the company in 1946 with a focus on antique furniture, highly aware of the fact that there are two central aspects of a successful business: namely cost and productivity. The company is located in the north of Denmark, in the town of Hurup Thy, known for its high work ethics. The employees are seen as hard working and loyal colleagues who always try to do their best for the company.

> Productivity was emphasized from the beginning and with the local mentality it was completely natural that one could not expect a wage until one had done a proper day's work. It is, without doubt, this inspired attitude among our employees, their motivation to carry on and do things in the best possible way that is the key to our success. Without a doubt. (Poul Erik Rasmussen, *Hilding Anders News*, 2004a, No. 3: 8)

Over the years, the mattress production developed and the business expanded. Carl Thögersen grew at the same pace as its largest customer Jysk, which it supplies with a private label program, says Knud Larsen, vice managing director at Carl Thögersen (*Hilding Anders News*, 2004a, No. 3).

Route Followers

With regard to the Hilding and Ekens brands, route followers define themselves in a variety of customer-oriented and growth-related activities. Imprinted by occurrences from long ago, the route followers speak of the former owner-mangers' activities, the launching of the new collections and of Dr Sleep feeling the pulse of sales conditions. Growth-related moves are influenced by the customers' needs, sleeping habits and wishes. The route followers build on information generated annually at the furniture fair in Stockholm and at the training sessions the Dr Sleep school offers the retailers. In accordance with the overriding strategic growth aims of Hilding Anders it makes sense to engage in these activities, specified and organized in the arenas of fair and school. Sense-making is accordingly influenced by the belief and expectations in the twofold focus of the school held by the business area director, the managing director, the teachers and the ambassadors.

Another route follower refers to Danish Carl Thögersen, promising continued growth in the Nordic market. The company represents values associated with high work ethics and long-lasting relationships with customers. It directs attention to the geographical place in Denmark where the Thögersen family built up the business, highly aware that a key to success is the employees' motivation to do things in the best possible way and simultaneously take into account cost and productivity.

Swiss, Belgian and French Brands in View

In the close wake of the Apax-Hilding Anders merger, with the Swiss, Belgian and French brands in view, the companies Bico, Crown Bedding and Wifor were brought to Hilding Anders.

Swiss Bico was founded in 1861 by Meinrad Birchler. In 1988, the Birchler family sold the company to the Varlora Group, a Swiss holding company. Eleven years later the Valora Group was integrated into the Sparte Slumberland Group. Since 2001 Bico has been a part of Hilding Anders (Hilding Anders, 2008b). Today, Bico is one of the most established brands in Switzerland, with a product line of mattresses, insert frames, bed systems and accessories comprising all levels of products up to the premium range. Bico is a leading brand in healthy sleeping comfort with advanced technical systems. 'High quality standards, consistent innovation management and special services are the reason for BICO regularly taking first place in polls concerning image values such as "confidence, quality, price/performance, future-orientation, innovation"' (Bico, 2008: 1).

Belgian Crown Bedding, acquired by Hilding Anders in 2001, started off in 1910 by manufacturing metal springs for the furniture, mattress and car industry. Over time, new techniques were developed. Production concentrated increasingly on beds, quilt and pillow products, serving wholesalers, department stores, mail-order houses and large retailers, but also hotels and holiday villages. The company strives to fulfill 'fully the needs of the customer regarding comfort, health, security and aesthetics' in the markets of the Benelux, France and Germany (Crown Bedding, 2008: 1).

French Wifor today offers a broad range of bed and mattress products (Hilding Anders, 2008b). The business started its operations with only one sewing machine in the 1960s, putting into practice the idea of transforming polyester foam by manufacturing tops of seats. In 1991, Wifor merged into the Valora Group, which became integrated in 1999 with the Sparte Slumberland Group. Since 2001, Wifor has belonged to Hilding Anders (Wifor, 2008).

Route Followers

With the focus extending beyond the boundaries of the Nordic countries, two route followers clearly emerge with the Swiss Bico and the Belgian Crown Bedding, promoting further growth. The emphasis on healthy sleeping comfort and high-tech bed systems in Bico proposes a route follower entwined with values such as quality, price/performance, future-orientation and innovation. This route follower announces a leading brand that infuses customer relations with satisfaction and confidence. For Crown Bedding, the route follower realizes comfort, health, security and aesthetics in customer relationships.

Notwithstanding the limited information provided in this chapter on the Wifor brand and activities associated with the development of Wifor bed and mattress products, the outlines of a third route follower can be drawn. Together the three route followers enable continued growth in the European markets consistent with the strategy of Hilding Anders.

The route followers exposed here, especially those related to the Bico and the Crown Bedding brands, elevate brand values that impart tangible and intangible utilities to the customer in the form of beds that provide healthy sleeping comfort. Advanced technology used in the Bico concepts and the techniques applied to the Crown Bedding products add value in terms of personality. Personality refers to the brand's uniqueness (Christopher, 1996) and originates in technical characteristics of the bed products that differentiate them from other brands. This of course assumes that the target customer recognizes the offers made by Bico or Crown Bedding as more attractive than those presented by a competitor.

Jensen

Through the acquisition in 2004 of Norwegian Jensen Møbler (Jensen), located in Svelvik, Norway, Hilding Anders increased its presence on the Nordic market. By acquiring Jensen, a premium brand name was added to the brand portfolio. A strong position in the mid-range segment was already assured through the Hilding brand but further acquisitions were needed in the premium segment as a supplement to the existing premium brand, Ekens. According to Christer Persson, business development director of Hilding Anders:

> This acquisition has given us the premium brand name that is interesting in terms of volume, which we didn't previously have in the Nordic countries. Jensen is not just a company with a highly renowned name on the market, it also fits in perfectly and supplements our brand portfolio in a very pleasant way. (*Hilding Anders News*, 2004a, No. 2: 8)

In 2004, Jensen was owned by Norwegian Sektorgruppen AS (95 percent) and the Jensen family (5 percent). Apart from the Nordic countries, Jensen operates in Poland, Germany, the UK, Spain and the Netherlands.

Profitability had to be improved in Jensen. This was to be done under the guidance of the 'Program 100 days' (P100), which stipulated that before 100 days elapsed, the Nordic activities should be coordinated to realize positive synergies and to promote better production opportunities for Jensen. The managing director of Jensen welcomed Hilding Anders as the new owner of Jensen. Being incorporated into Hilding Anders promised 'tremendous opportunities' for development and improvement.

> We now have an industrial European owner that is highly active in this business and also has considerable experience and know-how in this field. When it comes to product development, internationalisation and purchasing – three obvious examples – this new ownership offers Jensen some entirely new and tremendous opportunities. It's also naturally important for us to continue developing and anchoring our position as a manufacturer of *premium brands* in the Hilding Anders family and to proffer *our* experience and knowledge. (Jan Trygve Jensen, *Hilding Anders News*, 2004a, No. 2: 12).

An informal two-day meeting with the management team of Jensen was held at Hilding Anders headquarters in Malmö.[15] A number of workshops that focused on issues related to purchasing, finance and production laid the basis for P100. The acquisition, which also included the joint venture company Padvaiskas that operated in Lithuania, ran smoothly and took a relatively short time, following the standard model. This model includes meeting with the owners and management team, carrying out due diligence, reaching an agreement, signing the contract and getting approved by the competition authority, as Christer Persson clarifies (*Hilding Anders News*, 2004a, No. 2). Although a demanding process, it is important, according to Jan Trygve Jensen, to continue business as usual:

We have now launched a number of product development projects and are in the midst of a fairly intensive marketing phase. It's absolutely essential that everyone at Jensen continues working with the same high ambitions and the same focus as before. But I can see that this solid foundation, together with the synergies and cooperation that we are now striving to establish, promises an exciting and very positive future for Jensen in Svelvik, in Scandinavia and on the international arena. (*Hilding Anders News*, 2004a, No. 2: 12)

The acquisition of Jensen also brought great pleasure to Anders Pålsson, the CEO of Hilding Anders. He expresses this feeling:

There was really only one company that interested us in the Nordic countries, and that was Jensen. We are tremendously pleased that we managed to incorporate Jensen into our family and we strongly believe that Jensen will become a fine member of the Group. We perceive excellent opportunities for achieving, together with Jan Trygve Jensen and his team, the results we are aiming for. We also want to furnish Jensen with further instruments and strength factors, and at the same time we and our existing companies want to learn from Jensen and their ideas too.

It is obvious now that we are growing again. (*Hilding Anders News*, 2004a, No. 2: 9)

Pålsson addresses Jensen, Jan Trygve Jensen and his team as a constitutive member of the Hilding Anders Group. Using the noun 'family' he clearly conceives of the Hilding Anders Group as a family and Jensen a family member. Moreover he refers to a future of 'excellent opportunities' to realize expected results and to opportunities to learn from Jensen, evoking within himself a feeling of satisfaction with the prospects of growth.

Jensen, founded in 1947 by Arne K. Jensen (the father of Jan Trygve Jensen) was built on pure craftsmanship. The first mattress that was delivered was made out of horsehair and cotton. Over the years, innovations were accomplished, resulting in products that today are based on more sophisticated technology and material (Hilding Anders, 2008b).

Employees have taken a strong pride in the craft, with skills 'passed down' to them from their parents working in Jensen. Comfort, design and performance are core values that always have been part of the philosophy underpinning the business activities there. Constituting the Jensen brand, the core values are realized by four product groups: turnable mattresses, box-spring mattresses with frames, continental mattresses and adjustable beds. The product groups represent the grades: comfort, royal, ambassadør and supreme, Jan Trygve Jensen says (*Hilding Anders News*, 2004a, No. 2).

A Route Follower

A route follower emerges through the acquisition of Jensen, a much-needed supplement to the brand portfolio in the premium brand segment of Hilding

Anders. The acquired brand then plays a supporting strategic role, contributing to the existing strategic brands in the portfolio. A supporting role ascribes to the Jensen brand the ability to help fight off competitors and to infuse existing brands with new quality. In addition, the Jensen brand can serve as a stepping-stone for an existing brand to enter a new market (Kumar and Hansted Blomqvist, 2004).

Through the acquisition of Jensen, positive synergies are realized between Jensen and Hilding Anders, generating competitive advantage and enabling growth in the Nordic market. Pertinent to the route follower are also qualities linked to Jan Trygve Jensen's craftsmanship and to the comfort, royal, ambassadør and supreme grades attributed to the different product groups. The values constituting the brand – comfort, design and performance – are integrated with these qualities. Narratively framed, the values subscribe to a dynamic character, lived and tied to practice (Urde, 2001) ever since Jan Trygve Jensen founded and built up the Jensen business and the brand name.

Slumberland and Dunlopillo

In parallel with the expansion taking place in mid-2000s in the Nordic market, the consolidation of Hilding Anders UK added value to the Hilding Anders brand portfolio. The acquisitions of the companies Slumberland and Dunlopillo laid the basis for the UK business, which in 2004 consisted of three business units: Slumberland, Dunlopillo and the private label business for Ikea – each covering a specific price segment.

Slumberland, acquired in 2001, was founded in 1919. Owing much to the invention, in 1964, of the unique spring system Posture Springing, Slumberland grew into one of the largest bed and mattress manufacturers in the UK (Slumberland, 2008). Investment in research and quality assurance granted the company several awards. 'In addition to the two royal warrants granted by H.M. the Queen and H.M. the Queen Mother and due to high standards of quality the company has been awarded the prestigious "Guild Mark" from the worshipful company of Furniture Makers' (Hilding Anders, 2008b: 1).

The acquisition of Slumberland Holding in Switzerland took about one year to complete, says Lars Haux, business area director internal supply during the years 2003–5:

> To expand our market we acquired, in 2001, Slumberland Holding AG, one of Europe's biggest bed and mattress manufacturers, located in Switzerland. We knew that Slumberland was for sales. It was a huge company and it took almost a year of negotiations before consummating a deal. This was mainly because certain parts of Slumberland were of less value to us. To bring about synergistic gains, we looked at the company's customer structure and how it fitted with the structure of Hilding

Anders. Through the acquisition, turnover increased from SEK1,000 million to SEK3,000 million. (Lars Haux, personal communication, 20 December 2006)

Bengt Adolfsson, then Hilding Anders CEO, expressed great satisfaction with the acquisition of Slumberland, one of the largest bed and mattress manufacturers in Europe, with factories in Great Britain, the Netherlands, Switzerland, France, Germany and Austria. Because of the acquisition, the Hilding Anders business expanded considerably geographically and brought very strong national brands to the portfolio.

> We are extremely pleased that we have succeeded in acquiring certain parts of the Slumberland Group. The companies that will now be part of our Group are among the most profitable in Europe and as the Scandinavian Hilding Anders companies are also very profitable, this will make our new group a very strong entity. We also have a number of customers who are planning to expand outside Scandinavia or have already done so. We hope our new organization will make it possible for us to develop with them. (Bengt Adolfsson, Atle, 2001)

In 2002, Hilding Anders acquired Dunlopillo in the UK and Ireland. Dunlopillo offers the deluxe latex mattress in the upper to premium price segment. The blending of natural latex, tapped from the trunks of mature rubber trees, with synthetic latex resulted in deluxe latex foam that was used in the production of mattresses. A Mr E.A. Murphy led the research team that invented Dunlopillo latex foam. By 1929, the team had already conducted latex experiments in a corner of the Fort Dunlop building in the UK. After the Second World War, sales of latex foam mattresses and pillows for retailers and contract markets steadily increased. Even the Houses of Parliament in London used latex in all upholstery (Dunlopillo, 2008).

Slumberland and Dunlopillo are well recognized in the British market. Over the years it has been essential, according to Stephen Luddington, managing director of Hilding Anders UK (2004–7), to strengthen these brands by building up a marketing mix that gives Hilding Anders UK a more distinct profile. Here a narrative frame of meaning develops that directs attention to the importance of chiseling out and highlighting the particular features of the brands. 'Both Slumberland and Dunlopillo are well-known, strong brand names on the British market. ... It's now time for us to wake them up with a new, proactive branding and marketing strategy,' says Luddington (*Hilding Anders News*, 2004a, No. 1: 10). The intention to 'wake them up' makes sense in a presumed context of what is not talked about (Feldman et al., 2004), a context which is demonstrated in signs of dormancy and a reactive branding and marketing strategy.

A more proactive branding and marketing strategy implied a makeover of the marketing and sales organization through merging two brand name teams that used to work separately. Through the appointment of a key account executive and a retail director, customer relations received more attention. The British bed market is highly fragmented, according to Luddington, with sales channeled through a large proportion of independent retailers, at least 120 bedding multiple retailers, and department stores such as Harrods, John Lewis, House of Fraser, Selfridges and Fenwick. In realizing the strategy and revitalizing the Slumberland and Dunlopillo brands, the managers expended much effort on the marketing mix, with sales training for the retailers' store staff. To understand better what the customers wanted in terms of design, color and mattress material, customer attitude surveys were conducted. According to Luddington: 'This will give us a better picture of how our brand names are perceived and what the needs of today's bed-users are. Getting to know the market and our competitors better will enable us to optimize our marketing mix' (*Hilding Anders News*, 2004a, No. 1: 11).

An official marketing and sales organization builds on efficient production. Vertically integrated stages of operations, streamlined production and a standardized range of products contribute to enhanced design competitiveness and improved profitability.

> We have come a long way in this process and in the case of, for example, our divans (a unique bed on the British market with drawers in the base), which are a major product for both Slumberland and Dunlopillo, we will be able to reduce the range without losing any of our design competitiveness in the shops. Initiatives like that lead to better profitability. (Stephen Luddington, *Hilding Anders News*, 2004a, No. 1: 11)

In studies of brands, a most critical issue is the adding of value through unique 'design competitiveness'. As Tollington (1998) asserts, the goods and services linked to a specific brand must be clearly differentiated from those of competitors. The high quality associated with the Slumberland and Dunlopillo brands marks a value that renders it worth continuing to work with these brands, acknowledges Morris Cummings, representing the retailer Fenwick. Fenwick is a UK department store chain owned by generations of the Fenwick family, and with long-lasting relationships with Slumberland and Dunlopillo. Morris Cummings, head of purchasing for furniture and beds at Fenwick, has been involved in developing these brands for more than 20 years:

> We have three major brands of beds in our bed department, two of which are Slumberland and Dunlopillo. Strong brand names are incredibly important for a department store since they give sales a definite, extra push. Dunlopillo and Slumberland both offer top quality and are great-value choices in their respective process classes. (*Hilding Anders News*, 2004a, No. 1: 15)

In September 2007, a Slumberland bed factory was closed down and production moved to another site in the UK. The *Rochdale Observer* described this as devastating for a number of employees and their families. Wilkinson (2007) wrote that the Slumberland closure would cost 260 jobs and that only a limited portion of the workforce could be offered employment at another place in the UK.

Route Followers

With reference to the acquisitions of Slumberland and Dunlopillo, route followers are narratively framed that promote growth activities associated with the development of a marketing mix and a proactive branding and marketing strategy. The route follower that interlinks with the Slumberland brand has a certain royal flavor; investment in research and quality assurance contributed to prestigious royal awards. The route follower emerges from hard work done by Hilding Anders personnel to bring about positive synergies when integrating Slumberland with Hilding Anders. The acquisition of Dunlopillo makes explicit a route follower that addresses a past connected with a successful experiment that helped Dunlopillo grow and reach the premium price segment.

The two route followers reflect strong brand names. Here 'strong' denotes positive and unique associations that help the customers differentiate the brand from other available brands (Dawar, 2004). A strong brand makes the customer willing to pay a price premium to receive the unique features (Aaker, 1991).

The route followers are further shown in activities of vertical integration of operation stages and standardization of products, the halting of losses, and the relocation of production to bring about increased competitiveness and profitability. It should also be noted that the Slumberland route follower reflects feelings of worry and dissatisfaction developed among the employees in Slumberland in connection with the closing-down of a bed factory, which meant that many people lost their jobs.

Pullman and André Renault

To continue the expansion in the European market, the Dutch company Pullman was incorporated in Hilding Anders in 2001. The name Pullman denotes the best-known and most distinctive brand for beds in the Dutch market, as Frank van de Ven, former managing director, points out. The strong brand position is mainly due to close relationships with retailers and customers, consistency in keeping to a particular price segment and to the support given by the Hilding Anders Group management, admits van de Ven.

> Thanks to its close and tight relationships with its retailers and a very alert eye on the watch for new trends and tendencies, Pullman has been able to defend its position most successfully as the best-known and most distinct brand name for beds in the Netherlands. We haven't managed to do this just by defending our brand name, we have also resisted the temptation to move into other segments. We have a unique name on the market because we have been so consistent. Moreover, backed up by leading product development in the business, top level service and good, close relationships with our customers, it is to be hoped that our success will continue right on the track. (*Hilding Anders News*, 2004a, No. 1: 19)

A narrative frame of meaning develops, infused with feelings associated with hopes for continued success. It places at the center a distinct brand leveraged by product development and top-level service for adding customer value.

Associated with the Pullman brand is high quality and lasting luxury and comfort. The development of this brand has taken consistent work that goes back to the 1800s, when the American industrial capitalist and cabinetmaker George Mortimer Pullman (1831–97) constructed the first hotel on wheels. The railway cars, put into service between Chicago and eastern points in the United States, provided travelers with a level of comfort never before experienced. Turkel describes it:

> The hotel car had two drawing rooms each furnished with a sofa and two large easy chairs that converted to two double and two single berths at night. Each hotel car had a large kitchen which prepared fine food that compared favorably with the best restaurants of the day. The wonderfully compact eight-foot square kitchen contained a specially-designed three-tiered range which permitted baking, broiling and boiling. Every inch of space was carefully designed for storage of kitchen equipment and supplies along with storage space for meats, vegetables, wines and condiments. From this kitchen, the cooks were able to produce 250 meals per day. (Turkel, 2006: 2)

Turkel (2006) characterizes Mr Pullman as a master of public relations. The cabinetmaker engaged in a variety of activities to attract the attention to the Pullman name. He used the word 'palace' to describe the cars, invited kings and queens to use his personal car and published dozens of self-praising newspapers.

The Pullman name was additionally used for hotels and a luxurious car model manufactured by Mercedes, Frank van de Ven tells us. In 1938, the Dutch company Corona obtained the right to use the Pullman name for its mattresses. When exploiting the strengths of the brand, the company patented the spring mattress for making a comfortable bed that was in 'a class of its own.'

> The challenge was also for these products to exploit the strength of the Pullman brand name and build up a range of products that represented top quality, luxury and, not least of all, unsurpassed comfort. They had to satisfy all the demands that

were expected of the Pullman brand name. Pullman had also developed and patented its own unique system of spiral springs that made for a lovely, comfortable bed in a class of its own. It was the spring system that became associated with the Pullman brand name and has since then, represented a bed of absolutely the very best quality. (Frank van de Ven, *Hilding Anders News*, 2004a, No. 1: 18)

Frank van de Ven further informs us that the Pullman brand name was reinforced during the last decade. This was mainly due to the company keeping a focus on a small clear-cut premium price segment, providing the retailers with support and engaging in persistent and long-term advertising and promotion. From the perspective of van de Ven, this is 'exactly like the Pullman carriages when they captured the attention of railway enthusiasts more than a century ago' (*Hilding Anders News*, 2004a, No. 1: 19).

The brand name serves as a quality cue (Jiang, 2004) that represents a variety of associations (Aaker, 1991; Keller, 1993). Consistency in keeping to a premium price segment enables retailers and customers to learn about the relationship between the brand name and the quality of the bed and mattress products. While treating the brand name as a proxy for quality attributes it can be used to eliminate other alternatives (Jiang, 2004).

In 2004, French André-Renault was acquired. Bengt Adolfsson had left the position as chairman of Hilding Anders. Brian Dickie, representing the new owner Investcorp,[16] joined the board of directors as chairman (Hilding Anders, 2006a). André-Renault, previously a family-owned company, focuses on luxury bedding and bed linen. The Renault family placed the emphasis on technical expertise for raising 'the name of André Renault to No. 1 in the world of luxury bedding and bed linen' (Hilding Anders, 2008b: 1).

Route Followers

A route follower is narratively framed which relates to the acquisition of the Dutch company Pullman and the development of the Pullman brand. It accounts for activities performed over many years for leveraging the brand, realizing what the American cabinetmaker George Mortimer Pullman and the company Corona did in the past. The Pullman name captured attention in various ways. The hotel on wheels with drawing rooms and a kitchen preparing fine food offered the railway travelers back in the 1800s a comfort 'never experienced before.' By making the past come alive in the present, retrospect is made part of this route follower. At the same time, it incorporates prospect, which in the light of the past reads hopes for the future into the present. Reinforced by the present, the Pullman brand catches the attention in a way that is pretty similar to the way the luxury railway carriages caught attention a century ago.

The route follower asserts the intention of the managing director at Pullman to strengthen the present and future market position while satisfying the demands of the customers. Continued success appears to be equivalent to continued growth, which requires keeping on the track for a small clear-cut premium segment. Clearly, a close relationship between customers and retailers help maintain a strong brand position intimately linked with the high quality and lasting luxury and comfort of the Pullman brand. Value is added through specialization in activities in a defined price segment (Christopher, 1996).

The limited information on André-Renault indicates a route follower that helps strengthen Hilding Anders' presence in the French market. It brings technical expertise to the fore and the endeavor of the previous owner-family to develop a name that stands out as a luxury bedding brand.

PURSUING 'A RATHER AGGRESSIVE GROWTH STRATEGY'

Further expansion of the brand portfolio, which took place during 2005–8, exhibits route followers that in chronological order moves geographically through Croatia, Spain, the Czech Republic, the Netherlands, France, the UK, Russia, Asian countries, Italy, Switzerland and Germany. Pursing a 'rather aggressive strategy' – the words of the CEO of Hilding Anders, Anders Pålsson – 11 acquisitions were completed during that period, contributing a number of new brands to the Hilding Anders portfolio. When carrying out more than one acquisition, the competencies of the people experiencing acquisitions develop and lead to a growing ease in undertaking and completing acquisition processes, as Salvato, Lassini and Wiklund (2006) observe. Yet, even if the targets are quite similar, the lessons learned from relying on the Program 100 days and a standard model might be difficult to apply in some situations. Salvato, Lassini and Wiklund raise a warning flag about being too confident about the applicability of lessons learned. Due to heterogeneous growth paths, a flexible approach is preferred over a standardized acquisition mode.

> … the lessons learned involved ways of conducting the deal: how to carry out negotiations; the degree of flexibility in meeting the needs of the seller; the decision to take risks that go beyond those already implied in the standard contract . …. Rarely do the lessons learned involve formal rules. More often they offer principles of flexibility learned from experience. (Salvato, Lassini and Wiklund, 2006: 262)

Hilding Anders people are involved in acquisitions that imply meetings and negotiations with people coming from various countries. It could then be necessary in some situations to move beyond a standardized mode to rely on principles that are more flexible. The acquisition of a Czech brand presumably differs from the acquisition of shares in an Asian company, which might require special sensitivity to different cultural conditions.

Adding New Brands

The bed and mattress producer Hespo became a part of Hilding Anders in 2005. The company was founded in 1979 by Stjepan and Maria Hresc and their partner Josip Gecic with a focus on the recycling business. At the beginning of the 1990s, the company turned to bed and mattress production. Since then, the business has grown and placed itself as 'the clear market leader' in Croatia. 'High quality, value for money in all price segments and close relationship with retailers are some of the company's keys to success' (Hilding Anders, 2008b: 1).

The acquisition of Spanish Somilar took place in 2006, in line with Hilding Anders' growth strategy to strengthen the position in southern Europe. Somilar, founded in 1985, is a well-respected bed and mattress manufacturer that had grown substantially in recent years. It operates with the brands Somilar, Technoplus and Dorsuit. 'Spain is among the top five markets in Europe, and has been a prioritized target market for Hilding Anders to enter and by the acquisition of the Somilar Group we will further strengthen our position as the market leader in Europe,' Anders Pålsson notes (Hilding Anders, 2006b).

In May 2007, the Croatian company Perfecta was brought to Hilding Anders. The main reason behind the acquisition was to find a suitable complement to the sleeping products of the Croatian company Hespo and attain a leading position in the Croatian market. Anders Pålsson explains:

> When we acquired Hespo in 2005 our aim was to establish a presence in the Croatian market. The acquisition of Perfecta makes us the leading manufacturer in Croatia, which is in line with our expansion strategy. With two of the leading brands on the Croatian market in our portfolio we will be able to create profitable concepts. The acquisition of Perfecta is a continuation of a rather aggressive growth strategy. (AllBusiness, 2007: 1)

Perfecta was founded in 1992 and has increased its mattress sales ever since. Production plant and furniture stores specialize in sleeping products. Known for its brand Perfecta Dreams, the company positions itself in the medium and premium segments (Hilding Anders, 2008b). Through investments in the computerization of the entire production process and in machines for mattress testing, Perfecta complies with European standards and is able to adjust quickly to the customers' needs and desires (Perfecta, 2008). With an increased environmental awareness, nature is a great source of inspiration in the production process.

> Nature is the main inspiration. Motivated by a belief that production and environmental awareness must go hand in hand, the production process involves natural fabrics of cellulose fibers for they have exquisite anti-allergic and anti-bacterial effect (repelling mite and dust), fabrics with carbon fibers which release the body of the accumulated negative energy, fabrics treated with Aloe Vera which favorably stimulate regeneration of new skin cells, and many other materials that create natural healthy sleeping environment. (Perfecta Dreams, 2008: 1)

Next, in June 2007, to strengthen the position in the market of the Czech Republic, the company Tropico was acquired. As Anders Pålsson claims:

> One of our goals is to become an even stronger participant in the region around Czech Republic. The acquisition of Tropico is a step on the way. We are now the clear market leader in all price segments in Czech Republic and we see significant opportunities to enhance our position further in the surrounding markets Slovakia, Austria and Germany. (Hilding Anders, 2007d)

Since its establishment in 2000, Tropico has evolved into the Czech market leader in the economy and medium segments, selling beds and mattresses under the brand Tropico Plus (Tropico, 2008).

In July 2007, to strengthen the Benelux markets further, Hilding Anders acquired the Dutch company Eastborn. Since its establishment in 1959, the focus has been on product development and the design of brands such as Sand, Master and Lund. Through the division Marine Eastborn it supplies the cruise industry with mattresses, bedspreads, curtains and quilts. As a producer of beds and mattresses in the upper price segment, Eastborn supplements Dutch Pullman's products in the premium segment (*BedTimes Bulletin*, 2007; Eastborn Marine, 2009).

> The Dutch market is important for Hilding Anders as it also affects the Benelux area and provides opportunities in the nearby German market. The addition of Eastborn to our group enables us to perform coordinated domestic and important brand portfolio strategies in these markets. With our increased capacity, we will also be able to serve our private-label customers to an even greater extent.
> Hilding Anders intends to grow into one of the world's leading bed and mattress manufacturers. By acquiring Eastborn and thereby enhancing our position in the Benelux markets we are acting according to that strategy. (Anders Pålsson, Hilding Anders, 2007e)

Another acquisition completed in July 2007 was that of the French bed producer Timbo. The company, founded in 1983, evolved into the main manufacturer of bed frames in all price segments. It supplements the bedding companies André-Renault and Wifor operating in the French market.

The following month, Slumberland and Dunlopillo were joined by the company Myer's Comfortable Beds (Myer's) in the UK. In order to strengthen the position in the UK, the biggest market in Europe, and supplement the bed brands represented by Slumberland and Dunlopillo, Hilding Anders bought all shares in Myer's, a family-owned bedding company well-known for the brand Myer's and the premium brand Staples. Founded by Horatio Myer, the company has a long tradition in manufacturing beds and related products from iron bedsteads to divan beds. In 1986, Myer's acquired the company Staples, which received the warrant to produce and supply beds to the royal family. Anders Pålsson regarded the acquisition of Myer's as a way to make Hilding Anders particularly strong in the premium segment in the UK: 'As the U.K. is the biggest market in Europe, it lies in our interest to expand our business in this area. It is particularly satisfying to acquire a company such as Myer's, given the company's reputation and history, which is not entirely unlike our own' (*Business Wire*, 2007b: 4).

With the inclusion of the Myer's and Staples brands, building on long tradition in manufacturing as reflected by the royal warrant, value was added to the Hilding Anders portfolio.

Into the Russian Market

As part of the 'rather aggressive' growth strategy, Hilding Anders moved in to the Russian market. To launch the Scandinavian bed brands and become the leading supplier of the hotel contract business in Russia, Hilding Anders formed, through its Finnish subsidiary Unituli Oy (Unituli), a sales organization in St Petersburg: Unituli OOO. In 2006, Unituli was selected as a supplier of beds for Grand Comfort and Baltic Star Hotel in Russia. Anders Pålsson thought that this event had to be great timing since Unituli was about to initiate its efforts in the Russian market. Unituli OOO opened in November 2007 (Hilding Anders, 2007f).

Unituli is a Finnish bed producer, founded in 1989, and bought by Hilding Anders in 1998. The then-Hilding Anders CEO Bengt Adolfsson says: 'Through the acquisition of Unituli we developed a local platform for providing Ikea and other customers in Finland with our products. The Finnish company also had contact with the Russians. The Finnish–Russian network diplays big potential for the development of Unituli and Hilding Anders' (*Norra Skåne*, 1998).

The primary focus of Unituli is the contract manufacturing of private label products (95 percent) to meet the needs of the largest furniture chains in Finland. In addition, Unituli sells Hilding Anders' own-brand products Ekens and Koz, says Mats Östergård, managing director of Unituli (personal communication, 21 February 2007). Despite a declining market with increases in the price of raw material, Hilding Anders continued to grow in 2008 through acquisitions and investments in factory and a sales organization.

Acquisitions and Investments in 2008

Hilding Anders expanded its business in Asia. On 14 November 2006, the Hong Kong-based Integrated Distribution Services Group Limited (the IDS Group) announced that it was about to divest 40 percent of its shares in Slumberland Asia Pacific (SLAP) to Hilding Anders, which currently held 20 percent interest. The IDS Group focuses on serving brand owners of consumer and health products who wish to penetrate the Asian markets. Anders Pålsson reveals that the agreement included 'an option to eventually acquire the remaining 40% and thus absorb the company as a wholly-owned subsidiary of the Hilding Anders Group' (*BedTimes Bulletin*, 2007: 1).

From the perspective of Mr Ben Chang, CEO of the IDS Group, long-term aggressive growth and geographic expansion of SLAP is important. Through the transaction with Hilding Anders that was completed by July 2008, SLAP positions itself as Asia's leading bed and mattress company, providing Hilding Anders with the opportunity to introduce its own brands to Asian customers. SLAP has brand rights in 22 countries in Asia and a portfolio of brands of mattresses and bed-related products targeting mid- to upper-income consumers (IDS, 2006). It currently operates five manufacturing plants, two in China and one plant in Thailand, Malaysia and Indonesia. Apart from these countries, Hilding Anders today distributes mattresses and bed-related products in Hong Kong and Singapore, and exports to Sri Lanka, India and the Philippines.

Referring to the expansion plans in 2008, Anders Pålsson reveals:

> During the spring, the opening of our new Bangkok factory took place. The event was very successful and resonated well with both important customers and Thai media. The increased capacity will be needed, as the Group has significant plans for expansion in Asia. New production units in China are forthcoming, as well as continued expansion of the retail network. In the longer term, the Indian market is also very interesting for Hilding Anders. (Hilding Anders, 2008d)

During 2008 there were also opportunities for Hilding Anders to reinforce its position on the European markets further. In June 2008, a new sales organization opened in Frankfurt, Germany, to launch the tailormade product concepts Curem, Marinotto, Nordvig and Nottena. The time was right for a renewed appearance in the German market, under the name of Hilding Anders Deutschland GmbH (Hilding Anders, 2008e). Since the beginning of the 2000s, Hilding Anders had been able to follow closely the developments in the German market, especially through the Billerbeck unit in Germany, which was a part of Hilding Anders during the years 2001–3. Billerbeck, established in 1921, manufactures high-quality quilts and pillows. In connection with the acquisition of Slumberland in 2001, Hilding Anders became the owner of Billerbeck with units in Germany, Switzerland and Hungary (Hilding Anders, 2003a). Hilding Anders sold the subsidiary Billerbeck Group in 2003, the main reason for which was that it no longer matched Hilding Anders' core product mix of beds and mattresses.

The next acquisitions were Swiss Happy and Italian Bedding.

Two strategic acquisitions have been carried out during the first half year of 2008. It is very pleasing that the Group, after several years of trying, now has managed to enter the Italian market. The acquisition of Bedding Srl means that the Group can tick off another 'white space market'. Bedding manufactures beds in the premium segment and also runs a small network of retail stores in northern Italy. The other acquisition of Happy AG further strengthens Hilding Anders' position in Switzerland. Happy manufactures products in the medium segment, which supplement the Group's premium Swiss brand Bico. With two new companies and brand in our portfolio, Hilding Anders' position in Europe is even further reinforced. (Anders Pålsson, Hilding Anders, 2008d)

Happy, originally a family-owned Swiss company, was established in 1985. Its brand Happy Systems, positioned in the medium segment, serves as a supplement to the existing Swiss brand Bico, which sells products in the premium segment and engages in the hotel contract business (Hilding Anders, 2008f). Through the acquisition of Happy in March 2008, Hilding Anders became the market leader in Switzerland, which implied a strengthened position in central Europe (Hilding Anders, 2008b).

The entry onto the Italian market was a breakthrough for Hilding Anders, says Anders Pålsson. By acquiring the company Bedding in June 2008, Hilding Anders was able to access a prestigious market in the bed industry where the demand for premium products is expected to increase steadily. Bedding enables enhanced collaboration with customers in the European markets and makes it possible for Hilding Anders to bring onto the Italian market some of the own brands. Italy, one of the largest markets in Europe, is a trendsetter in the design and form of beds and mattresses (Hilding Anders, 2008b, 2008g).

Route Followers

The acquisitions and launching of brands during 2005–8 suggest a number of route followers. Hespo and Perfecta Dreams in Croatia, Somilar in Spain, Tropico Plus in the Czech Republic, Eastborn in the Netherlands, Timbo in France and Myer's and Staples in the UK are brands accounting for activities embodying route followers. Consistent with the growth strategy of Hilding

Anders, they construct opportunities to expand in the European bed and mattress markets. Moreover, in Russia, the launching of the Scandinavian bed brands through the establishment of a sales organization brings out a route follower. Also the move into the Asian market, with the agreement with SLAP increasing Hilding Anders' shareholding from 40 percent to 60 percent in SLAP, makes a route follower explicit.

Further route followers extend through the acquisition of Italian Bedding, ticking off a 'white space market', and through the acquisition of Happy with the brand Happy Systems supplementing the Swiss Bico premium segment of the portfolio. In addition to this, interlinked with the overarching growth strategy, route followers appear in activities associated with the opening of a factory in Thailand and the establishment of a sales organization in Germany. It seems that certain markets and geographical places are more attractive than others. Just as a corporate brand and a product brand incur value, a geographical place incurs value, as Roulac (2007) acknowledges. St Petersburg, Bangkok and Frankfurt – or other places that Hilding Anders people find attractive – could be assigned a 'place brand'. The place brand component of the value increases as certain places become more attractive and command higher prices, Roulac points out.

The plans to start up new production in China held hopes for future growth and, when implemented, these plans transformed into a route follower that arguably helped strengthen the position of Hilding Anders in the world market. Yet more brands are to be acquired in the years to come. By means of acquisition, opportunities are constructed for Hilding Anders people to cooperate more closely with customers in different market regions in Europe and in Asia. The customer structure, products and brands of the acquisition partners supplement the line of Hilding Anders. Expansion through acquisitions 'is in line with our overall goal of becoming one of the world's largest bed and mattress manufacturers,' confirms Anders Pålsson.

TO BUILD A BRAND PORTFOLIO

How the acquired brand fits into and associates with the brand portfolio of Hilding Anders is a critical issue. In accordance with Petromilli, Morrison and Million (2002) organizational and management activities need to focus on the relationships between the brands and across the portfolio to realize returns that exceed the sum of individual returns.

> Where much of an organization's brand-building efforts once focused on acquiring, launching, or aggressively extending brands to expand the brand and business portfolio, today's focus is on trying to get the most from existing brands through better

organizing and managing brands and brand inter-relationships within the existing portfolio (Petromilli, Morrison and Million, 2002: 22).

The brand portfolio concept entails examining links between brands and combining brands to meet the overriding strategic objectives of securing and enhancing Hilding Anders' leading position in Europe and in Asia and to strengthen its position on the world market. As Chailan (2008) asserts, brand combination within a portfolio is a key factor for a company that wants to develop and grow:

> The brand portfolio concept is a core concern for most world business leaders and companies ... companies are not only focusing on brand management, but also on defining the number of brands required to reach their goals. In addition, they are examining the links between brands within the company and the organisation of these links. Brand combination within a portfolio is a key factor for many companies' development, growth and risk management. (Chailan, 2008: 255)

Pia Rasmussen, managing director of Hilding and Ekens during the period 2001–4 and responsible for branding coordination 2004–6, says that the acquisitions of new brands, and the development and reinforcement of existing brands are strategies that add value to Hilding Anders and its owners (*Hilding Anders News*, 2004a, No. 1). A driving force behind the acquisitions is the potential brand supplement to the existing portfolio. Referring to Petromilli, Morrison and Million (2002: 26), the issue is then to identify 'what stream of related new products could help drive growth and redefine the brand's role within the overall brand portfolio.' Although a risky task to undertake, acquisition is often the only option for capitalizing on new value-creation opportunities. If the migration of the brand through the post-acquisition process is managed well, the brand is strengthened. This implies the integration of all customer contact points, that is, 'all the contacts where the brand and customer interact during the purchase cycle, whether through communications like advertising, the cashier at the retail store, or the customer service call center' (Kumar and Hansted Blomqvist, 2004: 25).

Active brand name teams in a multibrand company such as Hilding Anders play a significant role then. As Rasmussen tells us, there are teams familiar with the uniqueness of each brand as well as with the relationships between them. The teams engage in product and brand development, launching new brand products and with cross-fertilization and coordination of brands to achieve synergistic gains.

> The strategies very clearly state the *plans of action* for product development, product launches, new markets, sales and distribution network development and many other factors. Of course, each brand determines its own positioning, sales and marketing efforts, but since we have so many successful brands in our Group, we

also have a great source of *best practice* guidelines. Moreover, even if our brands are independent and unique, there are still a lot of synergies we can benefit from. (Pia Rasmussen, *Hilding Anders News*, 2004a, No. 2: 14–15)

Through the cross-fertilization and coordination of brands, one avoids the risk of exposure that is related to one single brand. Identifying opportunities for investments across brands is a less risky branding strategy than managing brands and investing in brands individually. When applying the theory of portfolio management, derived from the financial field, one notices the risk link to the brand (Petromilli, Morrison and Million, 2002). Portfolio theory suggests that the investor maximizes return and minimizes risk. If it is not possible to reach a point at which return is maximized and risk is minimized it may nevertheless be possible to over time increase return and reduce risk. The brand portfolio must clarify the specific needs that brands should satisfy, assessing the economic attractiveness of meeting these needs and analyzing how the brands fit together. It may also be necessary to reposition some brands, retaining and improving underperformers and divesting those that have lost their relevance. But when continually faced with heavy pressure to grow and adjusting to fragmented customer needs, marketers often expand rather than prune their brand offerings, as Carlotti, Coe and Perrey (2004) point out.

Managers using a coordinated approach seem not to hesitate in phasing out brands that no longer help secure and strengthen the core business. In 2003, the Billerbeck Group was sold (Hilding Anders, 2003a). With an enhanced focus on branded bed and mattress products and a need to synchronize stronger brands, quilt and pillow products offered by Billerbeck lost their relevance. As Carlotti, Coe and Perrey (2004: 1) argue: 'If marketers are to thrive, they must resist the compulsion to launch new and protect old brands and instead shepherd fewer, stronger ones in a more synchronized way.' By streamlining and consolidating the portfolio and thereby eliminating nonstrategic brands, savings can be made in marketing, material and distribution (Petromilli, Morrison and Million, 2002). Returns can surprisingly increase when business risk linked to a certain brand is reduced.

To identify and construct potential opportunity to increase the value of the brand portfolio, it is necessary to look at the Hilding Anders brand portfolio as a whole. One must watch the balance between the private label segment and the brand segment[17] while being aware that through the involvement of larger and fewer customers, the private-label segment entails a higher commercial risk than the own-brand segment. Moreover, building the brand portfolio implies taking into account both local and central branding. Predicated on the vision of the local company, market demands and the management's concerns, local branding is a well-structured process in Hilding Anders. In support of central branding, the local branding process translates into specific goals and action plans for the company that operates in the local market. Pia Rasmussen explains:

> Everything depends on the vision the local company has for its brand and the demands made by the local market. Working from this basis, the companies have to formulate their objectives and then break them down into strategies that lead specifically to different plans of action. This makes branding a systematic and well-structured process. We are a resource that the local companies can use as they require in this all-important process. (*Hilding Anders News*, 2004a, No. 1: 19)

Through achieving a certain balance between the brand segment and the private-label segment and through the development of local branding, supported by central branding, customer value is enhanced. The wider concept of customer value must embody brand value and include 'total cost of ownership' (Christopher, 1996: 58). Total cost of ownership, rather than price, delineates a most critical element in a customer's purchase decision and refers to, for instance, inventory carrying, maintenance, running and disposal. A marketer such as Hilding Anders who seeks to deliver superior customer value while, at the same time, assessing the economic attractiveness of meeting the specific needs of the shareholders, defines and communicates a value proposition that accounts for the dimensions of value and cost.

> Value is perceptual but comprises the customers' understanding of what they are getting compared to what they are giving. In other words the functionality of the product and any emotional or intangible value plus the hard, tangible benefits must be set against the total cost of ownership.
>   The task of marketing, therefore, has to be expressed in terms of the creation and delivery of customer value. (Christopher, 1996: 65)

When faced with the challenge of integrating a new brand into the portfolio as a result of an acquisition, the Hilding Anders managers arguably address the questions proposed by Petromilli, Morrison and Million (2002). One of these questions concerns whether the brand – in its relation to the other brands in the portfolio – adds value to the customers. The other questions ask how the acquired brand supports the overall strategy and whether the brand strengthens the company's presence in a market or allows entrance into a new market. In line with Blombäck's (2005) argument, one takes into consideration that brand value derives from several factors not only connected with the customers' perceptions, experiences and expectations of a brand. Brand value also relates to how the people representing the company make the customers notice, understand and believe that the company's offer is better suited for them than is that of a competitor. Implied in this is a value proposition that basically accounts for the reciprocal character of customer value (Harrington, 2007), directing attention to the tangible and intangible resources and processes through which Hilding Anders benefits by adding value to the customers.

From the perspective of the Hilding Anders management, high quality, service and innovation are key words that should be synonymous to the brand in the brand portfolio. They are predicated on the vision to 'give the world a good night's sleep' while caring about a brand's uniqueness and interrelationship with other brands.

> As one of the world's leading bed and mattress manufacturers, key words such as high quality, service and innovation should be synonymous to our brand. The job to improve ourselves has been intense and has now shown results in an independent study. It encourages us to continue our efforts even more, and brings us further toward our strive to 'give the world a good night's sleep', which is Hilding Anders' vision for the future. (Anders Pålsson, Hilding Anders, 2008i)

A strong brand provides trust for the customer. Trust is based on the customer's belief that the brand has specific qualities that meet the wishes and requirements of the customer (Delgado-Ballester and Munuera-Alemán, 2005). If it lacks the support of the customers, the strongest brand cannot achieve its full potential (Christopher, 1996). The work with improving operational efficiency through standardizing administrative systems, coordinating purchasing procedures and minimizing costs might very well propose a move toward an enhanced 'customer intimacy'. A customer-intimate company stresses flexibility and responsiveness in the business processes and empowers people to work closely with the customers, making sure that the customers get what they want as Treacy and Wiersema (1993) emphasize.

In parallel with the growth activities associated with the building of the brand portfolio, new owners entered the scene, prompting an enhanced focus on productivity and profitability, as the next chapter describes.

7. Hilding Anders for sale

In 2001, two investment companies, Nordic Capital and Ratos, held a major share of the Hilding Anders equity. As well as providing investment opportunity to stock market players on the Nordic market, both aimed at maximizing shareholder value over time through developing primarily unlisted companies (Nordic Capital Ratos, 2003). In May 2001, Ratos and the British private equity company 3i acquired Atle, dividing the Atle holdings between them (Arne Karlsson, CEO of Ratos, personal communication, 6 November 2009). That meant that the three biggest owners of Hilding Anders were Nordic Capital with 32 percent, Ratos owning 27 percent and Bacapps AB (Bacapps; the Adolfsson family) still controlling 18 percent of the equity.

> External owners Ratos and Nordic Capital both acquired their interest in Hilding Anders during the expansion period of the past five years. The Ratos stake of 27% originated when Atle AB, under its Business Area Manager Arne Karlsson, invested in the company in 1998. The holding was transferred to Ratos in the buyout of Atle in May 2001. Nordic Capital's stake of 32% originates from its 1997 investment in Apax Intressenter AB which merged with Hilding Anders in 1999. (Investcorp, 2003b)

Growth accelerated because more capital was raised by Nordic Capital and Ratos and through a new share offer and a bank loan. Within the year 2001, 12 companies were bought. CEO Bengt Adolfsson recounts:

> We chose to share the ownership with others. ... Since then, the firm has grown continuously, both organically and through acquisitions in Europe. Today, Hilding Anders consists of 23 companies in 14 countries. Twelve companies were bought last year with the help of money from the owners, a new share offer on SEK450 million, and from bank loans. A milestone in that expansion was the merger with the bed and mattress manufacturer Apax in Småland, Sweden. (*Dagens Industri*, 2002)

For about two years, Ratos held a stake in Hilding Anders. From 1999, Ratos was a listed private equity company with the vision to be the best owner company in the Nordic region. Its business concept is:

> To generate, over time, the highest possible return through the professional, active and responsible exercise of its ownership role in a number of selected companies and investment situations, where Ratos provides stock market players with a unique

investment opportunity. Added value is created in connection with acquisition, development and divestment of companies. (Ratos, 2008)

Arne Karlsson, CEO of Ratos, discussed with the representatives of the other owners the issue of offering the Hilding Anders shares on the public market. Listing the shares on the Stockholm Stock Exchange had been under consideration ever since the investment companies became major owners. According to the original plans, going public was planned for the fall 2002 but due to increased signs of deteriorating conditions in the economy and bad stock market prediction, these plans were postponed. Maintaining the view of worsening conditions in the economy, industry experts saw two threats: a substantial decrease in customers' willingness to pay for bed products, and the market reaching a state of maturity (*Dagens Industri*, 2002). Nevertheless, maturity is hardly a characteristic feature of the Hilding Anders' bed and mattress market, Adolfsson asserts:

> We cannot imagine a mature market. Beds must be changed every 10 or 15 years, and thanks to the mix of beds in the low, middle and premium price segments, Hilding Anders is not as sensitive to ups and downs of the economic climate as a bed and mattress producer that represents just one price segment. (*Dagens Industri*, 2002)

Coordination and growth of the merged Apax-Hilding Anders group were prioritized. Bengt Adolfsson adds:

> It should not be an introduction on the stock exchange for the pure sake of an introduction. At the turn of the year, an organization should be prepared for listing Hilding Anders. An introduction is a part of a long-term plan but there is no need for listing the company only for the need of money. Besides, unforeseen circumstances might once again delay the plans. (*Dagens Industri*, 2002)

The preparations made by the owners of Hilding Anders were aimed at listing the company in fall 2002. Intensive work, including the recruitment of a new CEO, was carried out to pave the way for possible stock exchange listing. According to Bengt Adolfssson, who was about to leave the position as CEO of Hilding Anders and from 2003 assume the position of chairman of the board: 'This is a suitable time to make changes in the company's management while the fact that I will remain as chairman of the board will provide continuity' (Ratos, 2002). In January 2003, Anders Pålsson, currently head of the service business area at Sydkraft, took over the position as CEO of Hilding Anders.

The following year, the headquarters, comprising about 15 people, moved from Helsingborg to Malmö, which was considered a more attractive place to be based, being closer to Copenhagen in Denmark. 'As Europe's largest

bedding manufacturer we need a central location close to the continent,'
Anders Pålsson emphasized (Hilding Anders, 2004b).

> Being close to Copenhagen Airport is, of course, one important reason. We travel a
> lot within the group, to our subsidiaries and to our customers, who, like us, are
> spread all over Europe and Asia. Another argument in favor of Malmö is that
> recruitment is easier here.
>
> From a head office point of view, Malmö is a good geographical location to be
> based. Apart from its proximity to Copenhagen Airport, it is noticeable that Malmö
> has developed into a dynamic city which attracts major events such as the America's
> Cup and international horse competitions at Ribban. And this trend will only
> increase with two new arenas acting as meeting places.
>
> Malmö is also a good city for those who want to run a business. Many new trades
> and industries are developing within the commercial sector. Collaboration with
> Malmö University and Lund University is constructive. We have benefited from this
> through market surveys and lectures. (Anders Pålsson, Malmö Trade and Industry,
> 2008)

As indicated above, the main actor is the investment company.
Conceptualized as a collective agent, it provides opportunity for the collective
agent Hilding Anders by raising capital, preparing for an introduction of the
shares on the stock market. Driven by the financial logic, coherent with a rationalistic discourse (Vaara, 2002), the investment company pursues a value-
maximizing growth strategy. Operating under the assumption of value
maximizing means that 'earnings are objectively determined to reveal the true
position of the business to its owners and the capital market' (Findlay and
Whitmore, 1974: 46).

The move of the Hilding Anders headquarters seems to have been an
important part of the plans to go public. Narrative bits and pieces directing
attention to collective agents do not reveal, however, any differences in opinions and beliefs that might have been expressed among individuals included in
the collective agents about the potential performance of Hilding Anders and
about the move from Helsingborg to Malmö.

As illustrated next, the collective agent Investcorp played a crucial role.
With limited access to individual-specific material, there appear to be coincident meanings among the collective agents about the new ownership exercised
by Investcorp. Both Nordic Capital and Ratos regarded the Investcorp
purchase of Hilding Anders as a satisfactory exit route.

INVESTCORP – THE NEW OWNER

Nordic Capital and Ratos offered Hilding Anders for sale in May 2003.
Bidders were invited and, after a second-round sale process ending in August,

the sellers granted exclusivity to Investcorp to complete due diligence (Bollen, 2007). Arne Karlsson (personal communication, 6 November 2009), representing Ratos, underlines: 'We would have continued exercising our ownership role in Hilding Anders. We considered Hilding Anders a most valuable investment. But the other owners' representatives held out the prospect of a change in ownership. So we made the decision to exit Hilding Anders.' On 7 December 2003, Investcorp announced that an agreement had been signed to acquire 100 percent of the Hilding Anders shares (AME Info, 2003). Investcorp paid Nordic Capital and Ratos 410 million (Bollen, 2007). The main intention of the new owner was to strengthen and consolidate Hilding Anders' position as the leading European manufacturer of beds.

Investcorp, established in 1982, is a global private equity company based in the Kingdom of Bahrain with offices in New York and London. In terms of total assets and equity capital, Investcorp has grown considerably since its start, as Nemir A. Kirdar, executive chairman and CEO of Investcorp, informs us: 'The achievements of the past 26 years speak for themselves. Investcorp has grown 95 times in terms of its total assets and 25 times in its equity capital. It has transacted investments with approximately $41 billion generating top quartile returns to its clients' (Investcorp, 2008).

According to Kirdar the mission of Investcorp is:

> To create a working environment that demands integrity and stimulates entrepreneurial spirit, together with a deep sense of responsibility to the firm, its shareholders and its clients. To achieve market recognitions of the firm's reliability, professionalism and accountability in all the products and services it offers. To ensure the firm's long-term growth and consistent profitability through careful yet imaginative risk and resource management. To be global in our outlook, organization and operating structure for maximum competitive advantage. (Investcorp, 2003b)

Investcorp contacted Hilding Anders. Bengt Adolfsson (personal communication, 26 April 2006) explains: 'Through my co-owners Nordic Capital and Atle, later on Ratos, I knew the rules of the game. The business concept is "exit" and I was fully aware of that. I would also like to add that Investcorp paid us well – of course, this is a factor to take into account.'

At the time of the Investcorp acquisition, bed and mattress products were sold under own brands including Ekens and Hilding in the Nordic region, Bico in Switzerland, Dunlopillo and Slumberland in the UK and Ireland, and Pullman in the Netherlands. Private labels were sold to the pan-European furniture chains Ikea, Mio, Europa Möbler and Jysk. Over the previous five years, Hilding Anders had multiplied its revenues eightfold. In 2002, Hilding Anders had about 2,200 employees, involved in generating sales of SEK3,656 million (Investcorp, 2003a). Salman Abbasi, managing director and general manager of the Bahrain office of Investcorp, was impressed by Hilding Anders' position, its management team and production expertise (AME Info, 2003). Investcorp managing director Yves Alexandre also felt confident about completing the acquisition of Hilding Anders: 'We were also impressed by its management team and product expertise. We plan to support Hilding Anders in developing both its branded and private label products and in strengthening its relationships with existing customers, as the company grows and consolidates its position across Europe' (Investcorp, 2003a).

Investcorp's private equity team continually searches for investment opportunities in mid-size companies with 'capable managers, prominent positions in their industries, a strong track record and potential for growth' (Investcorp, 2003a). Hilding Anders was an interesting choice for Investcorp: 'Hilding Anders' portfolio of strong brands, together with our clear focus on growth, our healthy financial status and well-functioning operational activities, made us an interesting choice for Investcorp' (Hilding Anders, 2004c: 16).

From the viewpoints of the two biggest former owners, the Investcorp purchase of Hilding Anders turned out to be a satisfactory exit route. In the words of Arne Karlsson, CEO of Ratos: 'We believe this provides both the best way forward for Hilding Anders, in supporting its consolidation and European expansion plans, and the most desirable exit route for the Investors' (Investcorp, 2003a). 'Negotiations conducted with Investcorp resulted in a solution that created good prospects for the company to focus on continued expansion, entailing an enhanced exit situation for the owners in terms of value,' added Karlsson (Nordic Capital Ratos, 2003).

While exiting Hilding Anders, Morgan Olsson, partner at Nordic Capital, complimented the management of Hilding Anders for its entrepreneurial energy and solid expertise: 'The management of Hilding Anders is characterized by entrepreneurial energy and solid expertise. It has been a privilege to have joined them in establishing Hilding Anders as the leading European bed manufacturer' (Nordic Capital, press release, 24 November 2003). Arne Karlsson, referring to Bengt Adolfsson, who was about to leave the position as the CEO of Hilding Anders, adds:

> Bengt is a fascinating entrepreneur. I have known him for quite some time. He belongs to a small group of entrepreneurs who exhibit the exceptional ability to grow in the role as CEO. As the business grew in terms of increases in turnover, and whether the turnover amounted to SEK62 million or reached the level of nearly SEK4 billion, Bengt performed well. He was an excellent all-round CEO. His leadership style can be described as tough and fair, to put it briefly. Throughout the years, I met Bengt several times and discussed with him various business matters, realizing that he constantly develops his competence. I must admit that he is the most driven CEO I ever met, and as a former business area manager at Atle and presently CEO of Ratos, I have had the opportunity to interact with several CEOs. (Arne Karlsson, personal communication, 6 November 2009)

Bengt Adolfsson expressed a feeling of satisfaction with the new owner-ship:

> I have worked for the Hilding Anders Group since 1975. And about 15 years ago my wife and I became the principal owners when we took over the business from my father-in-law, Olle Andersson. I'm comforted that Hilding Anders' new owner possesses a broad network of international contacts and has high ambi-tions for the company's continued growth. (Nordic Capital Ratos, 2003)

Bengt Adolfsson metaphorically traveled a long and exciting journey; a journey that he seems to have greatly enjoyed. Over 15 years, he partici-pated and shared in continuous growth and development accompanied by increases in profitability.

> This journey, in terms of turnover expanding from about SEK62 million to nearly SEK4,000 million within a period of 15 years, held much excitement and fun. Behind those figures are numerous meetings with people. I traveled a lot, meeting with people in many different countries. When I left Hilding Anders, I think we had 23 factories spread through in 14 countries.
>
> Although plans played an important role when doing business, it was also a game of chance. You use an opportunity without making plans. While relying on your gut feeling you hope that things will happen in the way you wish them to. But we always kept an eye on profitability. Profitability is a key word. Increases in revenues are worth nothing unless profitability accompanies them. Because of the expansion, the number of employees increased as well but, at the same time, we were aware of the need for rationalization.
>
> Growth means development. Sustainable and profitable growth of the business closely relates to the research and development that has taken place in coopera-tion with experts, customers and retailers. For several years, Hilding Anders cooperated with sleep researchers at Sahlgrenska University Hospital in Gothenburg, Sweden, with the development of the concept bed, the intelligent bed, in order to improve the quality of sleep. The bed is intelligent in the sense that it registers breathing, heart frequency and the body temperature of the sleep-ing person and is able to respond to these signals by adjusting its firmness and temperature. (Bengt Adolfsson, personal communication, 26 April 2006)

The closure of the deal was subject to the approval of the European competition authority in Brussels, which meant that the Commission of the European Communities examined the acquisition. As a result, the operation through which Investcorp, by way of purchase of shares, acquired control of the whole of Hilding Anders was found compatible with the common market and with the European Economic Area (EEA) agreement (Case No. COMP/M.3315 – Investcorp Group/Hilding Anders AB, 17 December 2003).

Under the ownership of Investcorp, the new CEO Anders Pålsson took up the challenge to continue strengthening and consolidating Hilding Anders:

In the past year, I have had the privilege of quickly getting to grips with Hilding Anders activities and becoming acquainted with staff, customer and suppliers. Being able to work together with all these people for an even stronger Hilding Anders is a fantastic challenge. The change in ownership will not entail any direct operational changes in the business. 'Business as usual.' (Hilding Anders, 2003b)

Based on its experience from the earlier investment in Simmons Bedding Company, from 1996 to 1998 the second-largest bed manufacturer in the United States, Investcorp's ownership instilled confidence in the CEO of Hilding Anders. Investcorp would encourage continued capital strength and growth, he thought.

This will enable us to continue along the path on which we started, so successfully, with Ratos and Nordic Capital. Investcorp has relevant industry experience through its successful ownership of the US bedding manufacturer, the Simmons Company, and a track record of supportive ownership. So, with Investcorp on board, we are very confident about the future for this company, its customers and employees. (Anders Pålson, Investcorp, 2003a)

From the point of view of Yves Alexandre, managing director of Investcorp, Hilding Anders was an attractive investment. He explains:

The investment process confirmed the company's key attributes that made it an attractive opportunity. These key attributes included an impressive CEO (Anders Pålsson) who had joined the company in January of 2003, bringing with him experience in consolidating manufacturing operations and serving large fast-moving consumer goods (FMCG accounts). Built through acquisitions, the group was not yet integrated and enjoyed only limited coordination of purchasing/manufacturing
…
    This is a sector that fits the leveraged buy-out model well. It is stable, though slow growing. The market is replacement-driven. The demographics are in its favor. And people are spending more on their beds as their purchasing power increases. (Yves Alexandre, cited in Bollen, 2007: 2)

The increased demands for beds owe much to the health trend, says Anders Pålsson:

For a long time now, kitchens and bathrooms have been the focus of attention for those who enjoy décor and furnishing. Now it's the turn of the bedroom. This is also partly to do with a health trend. People are again being made aware of how important sleep is to good health.
    Beds made entirely from natural materials are also in greater demand. These days, it is possible to make beds entirely of environmentally-friendly materials. (*Malmö Trade and Industry*, 2008)

The Investcorp team identified savings and improvements in Hilding Anders. Yves Alexandre relates:

> We put a big team on the case: Bain for market analysis, Russell Reynolds to assess and confirm management's skills, McKinsey to conduct an operational review and validate the upside with identified purchasing savings and production improvements, PricewaterhouseCoopers for due diligence, as well as Citigroup and Credit Suisse on the advisory and financing side. (Yves Alexandre, cited in Bollen, 2007: 2)

Zenon Nie, former CEO of Simmons Bedding Company, also assisted in the implementation of Investcorp's strategy for Hilding Anders. In connection with Investcorp's prior investment in Simmons, Investcorp established a relationship with the CEO of Hilding Anders (Bollen, 2007). In the ensuing period, due diligence rendered extensive work in different areas, Anders Pålsson points out. With change being a part of daily life, change work also continued after completion of due diligence.

> A large part of 2003 was devoted to carrying out *due diligence* and other matters relating to the change of ownership. The operational work on the part of the group executive board in matters relating to productivity development and purchasing strategy, for example, was given much lower priority than would normally have been the case. However, now that the ownership structure has been decided, we are returning to several central issues that concern the process of change with which a company of our size is constantly occupied.
>
> Changes can sometimes cause a certain element of distress. Our customers, consumers and other interested parties place new demands on us that mean we have to be continually working with modifications and revisions. But change is part of everyday life and if we always do our best to meet these changing demands, *and at the same time* work as a team to become better at what we do, we will then have a positive future ahead of us. We have to realize that we are not on a long, straight road, but one with curves and bumps. Let's make the most and the best of our journey together. (Anders Pålsson, *Hilding Anders News*, 2004a, No. 1: 2)

It was particularly important to carry out the 'Program 100 days' (P100), a central part of the change process. Before 100 days elapsed, the project groups appointed for areas such as purchasing, production, accounting and finance were obliged to come up with a final report on the changes made.

> This is a central part of our process of change and throws the spotlight on several areas of special strategic significance – production efficiency, purchasing strategy and IT, to name a few. Each individual programme is run by specially appointed project groups that, before one hundred days have passed since Investcorp's acquisition, must have presented a report of their goals, strategic and general plans of action for their programmes. (Anders Pålsson, *Hilding Anders News*, 2004a, No. 1: 2)

Collective agents are narratively framed, engaged in different activities, but representative persons of these agents do also make themselves heard. The major change in the ownership structure of Hilding Anders entails intensive work with a focus centering specifically on production efficiency, purchasing strategy and IT. This work might have induced distress among the employees. By emphasizing teamwork, the CEO Anders Pålsson refers to collective sense- and meaning-making to reduce distress, reminding the employees that change is part of daily life and that they all need to do their best even if the road ahead is curved and bumpy.

Tied to the process of individual identity generation and maintenance, sense-making reflects an individual's interpretation and understanding of a phenomenon (Brown, Stacey and Nandhakumar, 2008). In interaction with others, an individual searches for plausibility and coherence. Past experience and expectations provide material for plausibility and coherence (Weick, 1995). Hilding Anders employees are urged to embark on a journey together and to engage in teamwork but there is no guarantee that sense and meaning are shared. According to Van Maanen (1979), shared meaning is difficult to attain. People's ego-defenses introduce discrepant narrative sense-making of organizational participants (Brown, Stacey and Nandhakumar, 2008).

To Increase Efficiency in Purchasing

The accomplishment of the goals set for the different areas required resource allocation, project group formation and action planning. Christer Persson, business development director, recounts that one of the long-term projects included in the P100 concentrated on the purchasing system. To increase effi- ciency in purchasing one needed to realize and consolidate positive synergies between the many companies acquired and brought to Hilding Anders in recent years. Persson says: 'We are now concentrating on achieving greater profitability and paving the way for offensive growth by having a more effi- cient purchasing system, better productivity and, not least, an optimization of our resources. Both organically in our existing companies and through new acquisitions' (*Hilding Anders News*, 2004a, No. 1: 7).

Because of the transition to a centralized purchasing agreement, the number of suppliers decreased. Anders Pålsson says:

> You may be wondering why we should now have central purchasing when several companies have good routines in that area and are also showing excellent results. The answer is: Altogether, we purchase material for almost SEK2 billion, we have thousands of different components and around 300 suppliers. If we can save 5% with a group-wide purchasing agreement, and that is probably a relatively modest estimate, then we can save almost SEK90 million for the group's companies. Each year. (*Hilding Anders News*, 2004a, No. 1: 2–3)

Due diligence work afforded an increased awareness of potential savings inherent in central purchasing. In realizing the potential, Rutger Jönsson, purchasing director, saw that it was necessary to expand the network for purchasing, covering the parent company and the production subsidiaries. A coordinated negotiation and competent partner would make a difference when meeting with the suppliers, Jönsson thought. 'The crucial point in negotiation is of course that we always negotiate with one person, have one interface to each supplier. The person might be one of our material managers, but could also be staff from the central purchasing function here' (*Hilding Anders News*, 2004a, No. 1: 12).

Relating to the centralization of activities, Rikard Eriksson, production development manager of Tibrobädden, a subsidiary of Hilding Anders, says:

> Tibrobädden, originally a part of Apax, was brought to the new Hilding Anders through the merger between Apax and Hilding Anders in 1999. We were still able to exert great discretion in performing our operations. After 2003, new restrictions came up, which most likely had to do with the shift in ownership in Hilding Anders … and I must admit that Gunnar did not completely agree with these … he found it difficult to act in accordance with the directives that put more restrictions on business activities. Gunnar was our managing director until 2005 … my father, who started up the Tibrobädden business in 1987.
>
> There has been a tendency toward centralized coordination of different activities. Earlier on, the choice of suppliers was our own, but nowadays this is not the case. The number of suppliers providing us with material has decreased. When it comes to production, we need to increase efficiency through identifying 'best practice'. Of course, we have made tremendous savings through centralizing these activities. In 2005, production here in Tibrobädden was closed down and moved to Hilding in Hästveda and to Scapa in Alvesta. This required great effort on our part. Not only did we transfer the computer system, but also physically moved all equipment, emptying the factory. Today we focus entirely on product development, concentrating on the customers of Hilding Anders. When you talk about 'growth', there are two things I would like to emphasize. On the one hand, it is about growing through your existing customers by the means of product development. By centering the focus on product development, you create demand for a product rather than take the traditional position of fulfilling demand. In the old days, the customer contacted us asking for a specific product. This is still the case but increasingly new products are developed and presented to the customers. On the other hand, growth occurs through acquisitions of companies and brands. (Rikard Eriksson, personal communication, 14 November 2006)

Activities associated with logistics and material supply are closely linked to activities performed in the strategic area of central purchasing. A group-wide purchasing agreement lowers time-to-market and build-up inventory costs, which means shortened lead times, from order to final handling of the material as well as a reduction in the number of components, as the purchasing director Rutger Jönsson notes. With the help of the consultancy firm McKinsey, rationalization of purchasing proceeded in a satisfactory way, according to Anders Pålsson (*Hilding Anders News*, 2004a, No. 1).

Underlying the work with centralized purchasing is a calculative rationality. It is revealed in resource allocation, project group formation and action planning to reach specific goals and, further, in production optimization, to which attention turns next.

To Help Optimizing Production

Productivity is a key word. To meet the requirements of the market, it was necessary to optimize the entire production process of Hilding Anders and adapt it in the best way, as Lars Haux, business area director internal supply during the years 2003–5, explains. By looking into how the different units of the organization utilized production capacity, measures were developed to help optimize production.

> We have a sales curve that peaks from July/August to November and then levels out to be followed by a slight upward swing in January and February. By looking at how we utilize the capacity within the Group as a whole, it is easier for us to see how surplus capacity at one place can compensate for a lack of capacity at another. (Lars Haux, *Hilding Anders News*, 2004a, No. 1: 8)

To give each subsidiary access to efficient tools for planning, measuring and managing their businesses, the Movex system of common platform IT projects was implemented. These projects fostered the use of the same language and the same parameters and measurements throughout the group. Ove Hansson, IT manager 2004–8, remarks: 'When it comes to measuring and calculations, which we are doing all the time, for sales, manufactured units, disposal percentages, we all go about it in completely different ways. We use different standards of measurement, we measure in different ways and some companies more than others' (*Hilding Anders News*, 2004a, No. 2: 6).

A range of issues linked to a company's policy, strategy and overall goals shared narratively legitimizes actions and working styles, as Reissner (2005) maintains. A common language means that Hilding Anders people will recognize and agree on the need for new working methods and high-performance production plants to improve productivity and magnify the customer focus. This prompts the development of a coherent picture to explain the difference between activities of former and present future-oriented activities. The IT manager is just one of those giving voice to the efforts that have to be made to gain an increased appreciation from the customers.

The shift to the Movex system enabled increased transparency in processes and operations, giving the subsidiaries and the headquarters the possibility of comparing financial results, productivity, developments and delivery performance. The introduction of a uniform standard for measurements did away with time-consuming work of collecting information in Excel spreadsheets, and automated the internal order processing between subsidiaries with customer relationships, Ove Hansson explains:

Once the entire system is in place, it will be possible to follow, for example, order intakes and invoicing each week from a central quarter. But most important of all, it is the companies themselves that will benefit greatly, as the system will enable them to control and optimize their operations in a completely different way than they can today …

The overriding goal for those projects is that we will visualize our processes and operations in a clear and practicable way. User-friendliness is a highly suitable term to use in this context. (*Hilding Anders News*, 2004a, No. 2: 7)

To help optimize production, another crucial question concerned standard-ization of components and products, the responsibility for which lies at the group management level. Market strategy and product mix is the responsibil-ity of each subsidiary. However, it was essential that the group management and the subsidiaries provided coordination and ongoing communication, as Jonas Jerklind, the production director, reports. They also took into account the requirements of each local market when reducing the variety of bed types, measurements and materials that the acquisitions brought to Hilding Anders (*Hilding Anders News*, 2004a, No. 2).

As it appears, a calculative rational way of acting is reached by actions taken in connection with the development of efficient tools for planning, measuring, standardizing, optimizing and managing. Productivity work is premised on the assumptions that managers and project teams agree on and are motivated to realize the owner's expectations of a more integrated group that is capable of increasing the growth rate in European markets while providing better profitability, improved productivity and a magnified customer focus. The Hilding Anders managers participate and share in the optimization of production and coordination of operations of the subsidiaries. They seem to agree on the need to meet the requirements of the new owner and the market. There is little indication of differences in individual understanding (Brown, Stacey and Nandhakumar, 2008) of these requirements or of the expression of emotions. When directing the attention to sense-making one becomes concerned with the preservation of the individual self. It can be argued that through a process of sense-making, Hilding Anders people enact a reality that consists of activities strongly associated with a calculative rationality.

The Pilot Project

A pilot project was carried out at the factory in Hästveda, Sweden, where the new Ikea collection was manufactured. Although the Hästveda plant already operated well, the aim 'was to make it even better' (Anders Pålsson, *Hilding Anders News*, 2004a, No. 1: 3). In cooperation with the consultancy firm McKinsey, the improvements that were hoped for regarded 'reduced stocks, greater floor space in the factory, increased machine capacity, improved labor efficiency and shorter delivery time' (Jonas Jerklind, *Hilding Anders News*, 2004a, No. 1: 9). The pilot plant was considered to help create a learning organization, inspire the heads of production of the other units of Hilding Anders to import the methods of the plant to improve productivity in their own areas.

Once we have achieved the various goals for the pilot plant at Hästveda and seen an improvement in profitability we won't have completed an important task, we will be starting it. That's because Hästveda will then become the model that the other factories can follow. Before we can 'export' these practical solutions, we have to create a burning interest among the heads of production at the other units, so that they in turn bring about improvements in their own production processes, based on the standards and methods of the pilot plant. (Jonas Jerklind, *Hilding Anders News*, 2004a, No. 1: 9)

Two subsidiaries, Hilding Anders UK in Great Britain and Scapa Bedding in Sweden, immediately applied the pilot plant methods and reported improvements (*Hilding Anders News*, 2004a, No. 1). By fall 2004, the subsidiary Bico in Switzerland implemented the pilot plant project. The Swiss project was named Matterhorn, with the expectation that it would achieve 'a new, higher vantage point of the productivity "cliff face" and leave chasing competitors a safe distance behind' (*Hilding Anders News*, 2004a, No. 3: 19). Within a week, the team working with the project had formed a new production structure.

The work with the pilot project in Hästveda proved to be more demanding than expected, reveals Anders Pålsson, which is why an evaluation of their own work as well as of McKinsey's work was conducted. A learning organization could not be realized until productivity improved in all production plants (*Hilding Anders News*, 2004a, No. 2). Besides, the time aspect was crucial, as Jonas Jerklind adds:

We calculate that each Pilot Plant project takes approximately 4 months, and at that pace, the project, seen from an organization wide perspective, takes a long time. Therefore it is important that we are also working on other fronts, in parallel with this, to achieve faster, better optimization of our total production apparatus. (*Hilding Anders News*, 2004a, No. 3: 18)

To speed up work in productivity improvements, more detailed planning was needed for different parts of the production process. Inspired by production models used in the Japanese car industry, a number of productivity drivers were identified, including active production leadership from foreman to managing director, central and local key indicators to establish status and define areas of improvement, and visualization of goals and results (*Hilding Anders News*, 2004a, No. 3).

To reach the goals for 2005, Anders Pålsson felt it was necessary to increase productivity further since several subsidiaries still kept too large a stock of components and finished products which required extra capital investment. Productivity, measured by the number of beds per man-hour, had to exceed any increase in wages, the CEO confirmed (*Hilding Anders News*, 2004a, No. 3).

The plants act as learning spaces for Hilding Anders by reducing stocks, increasing floor space in a factory, increasing machine capacity, improving labor efficiency and shortening delivery time. While seeking to improve productivity throughout Hilding Anders, learning in one plant becomes a source of changes affecting other plants. The organization learns as its participants change and adapt to their environment (Argyris and Schön, 1978; Dodgson, 1991; Easterby-Smith, 1997; Senge, 1990). Directed toward socialization, the relationship between the collective organizational level and the individual level becomes problematic, however. Drawing on Rhodes (1996), the question arises of how the management of Hilding Anders and the consultancy group encourage socialization, and how a plant becomes a force of socialization and contributes to social conformity.

Hilding Anders as social reality consists of activities in which diverse groups of people participate and share. Considering their operations performed in the name of the subsidiaries located in different countries, creating a learning organization necessarily implies a multicultural learning practice. As indicated earlier, local adaptation is essential,[18] entailing the avoidance of a homogenization of meanings and people's identities into a single type narrative (Lämsä and Sintonen, 2006). Employing a narrative approach, each individual learner becomes a viable source of information through which we can access individual and intersubjectively shared meaning (Rhodes, 1996). This contrasts with an organizational learning approach that emphasizes a wholesale change to an organization and its culture, as Rhodes notes.

Rather than assuming that there is one reality as expressed by a monovocal learning organization, we must allow room for individual learners, their interactions, interpretations and understanding. As Lämsä and Sintonen (2006: 112) contend: 'Learning is understood as the process of using a prior interpretation to construct a new or revised interpretation of meaning.' Learning takes place in social negotiation among individuals (Berger and Luckmann, 1966).

Positive Effects on Earnings

The area of control of accounting and finance was also subject to change. The new owner Investcorp requested a stronger focus on forecasting, reporting routines and working capital. Savings made through the central purchasing agreement and increased productivity infused optimism for the future, according to Anders Larsson, chief financial officer 2002–5. Revision of existing reports took place to include sales and earnings for each major customer on a monthly basis (*Hilding Anders News*, 2004a, No. 1).

Effective logistics, lowered time-to-market, and build-up-inventory costs helped reduce working capital, which, in turn, contributed to positive effects on earnings. Key performance indicators (KPI), with regard to goals for average sale price, earnings before interest, taxes, depreciation and amortization (EBIDTA), working capital and cash flow, guided the different functions of the Hilding Anders Group. As Anders Larsson emphasizes: 'A reduction in our inventories through more efficient logistics and production methods and a reduction in trade debtors and optimum utilization of our credit from suppliers are important components in this equation. Consignment inventory can be *one* road toward greater savings in the flow of goods' (*Hilding Anders News*, 2004a, No. 1: 14).

By fall 2004, growth in terms of increased sales and profits exceeded expectations with the EBITDA indicators exhibiting satisfactory results for the entire group. Because of the upturn in the world economy and positive reactions on the share market, the CEO felt that conditions continued to look good for realizing the Hilding Anders strategy. Hilding Anders grew substantially more than the market average. To promote further strong organic growth, it was necessary to put even more effort into productivity work and product development. In addition, one needed to take particular care of the relationship with the principal customer Ikea in order to secure being its first choice. Anders Pålsson concludes:

> ... we must sharpen up our act further with regard to our customer IKEA. Sometimes customer relations can get stuck in a rut, nothing is more devastating. Humility, commitment and a constant desire to improve our relationship must be our lodestar. A competitive price range, especially with all zealous competitors in mind, is necessary to maintain our position as 'IKEA preferred supplier'. (*Hilding Anders News*, 2004a, No. 3: 3)

Predicated on the vision 'to be the customer's first choice, the most profitable player in the bedding business and the creator of values for our owners and employees' (*Hilding Anders News*, 2004a, No. 2: 2), strategic activities concentrated on customer relations, improvement in productivity, cost reduction, rationalization of purchasing and product development. Moreover, a price policy was formulated. Because of the drastic increases in the price of steel of between 20 and 35 percent, unparalleled for 50 years, prices for interior-spring mattress systems increased (*Hilding Anders News*, 2004a, No. 2). In addition, increased oil prices were noticed, which was why it was urgent that these increases were passed onwards. The oil price of over $50 a barrel affected the price of raw materials for steel, foam and polyester. Due to increases in raw material costs, the price of the new high-quality bed was raised. From the perspective of Anders Pålsson, Hilding Anders had ideal conditions to raise this price: 'because, in comparison to other competitors who only supply standard products, we are continually launching new bed models with new characteristics and advantages. It is always easier to pass on price increases in a more highly regarded product' (*Hilding Anders News*, 2004a, No. 3: 2).

To integrate the companies of the Hilding Anders Group and their production systems further while simultaneously finding cost-reducing measures, the SHAPE program was formed. SHAPE stands for Strengthening Hilding Anders Performance Excellence. Rutger Jönsson, the purchasing director, explains that SHAPE works with 'a more penetrating and professional combination of certain central areas of Program 100 Days, which was initiated by Investcorp when it took over the Group' (*Hilding Anders News*, 2004a, No. 2: 18).

With respect to purchasing, by fall 2004 the SHAPE program had already contributed to more close-knit teamwork under the guidance of a group-wide agenda. A professional purchasing organization with a profit-driven strategy worked with the integration of newly acquired businesses. By placing the main responsibility for the purchasing activities of the group onto one person, transparency and clarity were achieved throughout the entire purchasing process (*Hilding Anders News*, 2004a, No. 2).

To facilitate integration of the different companies constituting Hilding Anders further it was necessary to arrange for an exchange of experience among the company heads and to allow room for discussion on crisis issues. Investcorp organized a conference in October 2004. Results from international studies were also presented at the conference, providing the participants with insights into more global matters. Anders Pålsson reports:

> It is, however, particularly important to look to the future, not only from a business point of view but with the entire world in mind. The energy crisis, the successive devaluation of the dollar and the increasing global average age were issues discussed during the conference and are examples of the areas that will affect the development of Hilding Anders, in positive and negative ways. (*Hilding Anders News*, 2004a, No. 3: 2)

Carried by the calculative rationality, growth-oriented activities refer here to more effort put into productivity work and development. Productivity work presumably makes sense when guided by financial measures with a focus on cost reduction, average sale price, earnings before interest, taxes, depreciation, amortization, working capital and cash flow, which admittedly attach the collective agents Investcorp and Hilding Anders to desired results. It can be argued that the making sense is collectively pooled (Walsh and Ungson, 1991).

Turning Point and Route Follower

Bits and pieces provided by collective agents and their representatives narratively frame a turning point that relates to the new ownership by Investcorp, which differently contextualizes Hilding Anders practitioners' activities, promoting an enhanced focus on productivity and growth in the European markets. Nordic Capital, Ratos and the Adolfsson family sold their shares. Based on Investcorp's mission, a context was formed in which people reorganized themselves, implying that some people left Hilding Anders.

The turning point suggests an end to the interlinked owner-management position held by Bengt Adolfsson. It thus resides in activities associated with the Adolfsson family leaving Hilding Anders, the CEO Bengt Adolfsson succeeded by the new CEO Anders Pålsson, and the plans to introduce the Hilding Anders shares on the stock market. The global investment group Investcorp, based in the Kingdom of Bahrain, gained total control by way of purchasing all the Hilding Anders shares. The turning point indicates that the physical distance between the owner and Hilding Anders is substantial.

The Investcorp-related turning point entails following the strategic route set out by the management of Investcorp. A route follower extends, encompassing a wide range of activities oriented toward offensive growth. Offensive growth implies rationalization work that leads to increases in profitability and improvements in productivity in different areas across the subsidiaries of Hilding Anders. More specifically, the route follower refers to centralized purchasing work, the implementation of the Movex system for fostering a common language and increasing transparency in processes and operations, and the reduction of working capital. The route follower holds productivity drivers to speed up work with productivity improvements. The turning point unfolds a route follower that further exposes growth-oriented activities such as centralization of routines, standardization of components and products, resource allocation, shortened lead times, lowered costs, consolidation of the acquired companies and an increased customer focus. Underlying the route-following activities is accordingly a financial logic that brings the calculative rationality to the fore.

On 26 October 2006, the investment company Candover signed a deal to acquire 100 percent of the Hilding Anders shares from Investcorp. The section that follows also reveals that two investment banks Credit Suisse and Citigroup assisted Investcorp in preparing for its exit and that Candover took part in a 'full-blown auction'. Through its scope and market-leading status in the European bed and mattress market, Hilding Anders attracted the interest of a number of prospective buyers.

CANDOVER – THE NEW OWNER

Turning to Credit Suisse and Citigroup, Investcorp prepared for exit.

> During Investcorp's ownership, Hilding Anders transformed itself from a confederation of 20 separate companies to an integrated European group, generating significant organic revenue and growth in earnings before interest, taxes, depreciation and amortization (EBITDA) whilst successfully integrating four add-on acquisitions. … The companies acquired were Jensen Möbler in Norway, Renault in France, Somilar of Spain, and Hespo in Croatia. … The company executed an operational transformation that included the establishment of a strong central purchasing organisation. … Management also oversaw the build-out of an integrated European manufacturing network by closing five plants in high cost countries including England and increasing production capacity in low-cost Eastern European countries. In addition, the roll-out of a lean manufacturing programme yielded improved production efficiency. (Bollen, 2007: 2)

The objective set to reduce the waiting time between the customer's order and delivery was also met. Yves Alexandre, managing director of Investcorp, points out: 'I set an objective, to cut the time to get your bed down to one week from four. That caused a revolution, and changed the way the company thought about manufacturing' (cited in Bollen, 2007: 2–3).

Acting alongside Credit Suisse, Citigroup positioned itself as the lead bank that actively took part throughout Investcorp's acquisition and ownership of Hilding Anders. Before Candover signed the deal on 26 October to purchase all Hilding Anders shares from Investcorp, Citigroup and Credit Suisse received great interest from several other potential buyers of Hilding Anders. Jonathan Rowland, managing director and co-head of the European financial entrepreneurs group at Citigroup, refers to 'a full-blown auction run'. Candover, investing in the Nordic region, was strongly attracted to Hilding Anders and willing to pay 'top dollar' (cited in Bollen, 2007). Rowland relates:

> We have a long established and very close institutional relationship with Investcorp, and maintained a very active dialogue with Investcorp on Hilding Anders from the moment they owned it. We were the lead bank when it bought, refinanced and sold the business. We developed an intimate awareness during Investcorp's ownership – which is something we try to do with all our financial sponsor clients – thereby positioning ourselves as a logical bank to appoint on exit. Moreover, acting alongside Credit Suisse we made a stapled finance package available to would-be buyers, but in the event Candover used its own financing, provided by HSBC. There was a full-blown auction run, and there was always a good likelihood it would go to another private equity buyer because of the short list of potential trade buyers. Candover have been very active in the Nordic region, and were very keen on this particular asset. One option for Investcorp would have been to recapitalize again and keep it, but the stars were in conjunction and it was the right time to move on. (Jonathan Rowland, cited in Bollen, 2007: 1)

Jonathan Rowland continues by describing the process that resulted in a final offer by Candover to acquire Hilding Anders:

> We and Credit Suisse worked together to go round the interested parties, splitting the list of potential buyers between us, maximising the geographic reach and relationships of both banks. There was a lot of interest in the first round, partly thanks to the scale of the company, placing it firmly in the sweet spot for a number of private equity firms, partly thanks to the company's market-leading status. The whole process was crammed into a matter of weeks rather than spread across months. The process commenced at the start of September and final offers were due on October 24, with the deal being signed on October 26. The level of interest was gratifying, but not surprising. It had been in the Investcorp portfolio for some time, and was performing well, and people knew that, meaning Investcorp received a number of proactive approaches about it. (Jonathan Rowland, cited in Bollen, 2007: 1)

On 30 October 2006 Investcorp announced that a contract had been signed to sell Hilding Anders for approximately 1 billion (*Arab News*, 2006). Quite impressed by Hilding Anders and its growth under the ownership of Investcorp, Owen Wilson,[19] investment manager at Candover, said:

> We look for three things in an investment: a very strong management team, growth prospects, and a market-leading position. Hilding Anders had all three. Just look at how the management team have taken a loose confederation of businesses and made them into a more integrated European business that is the market leader across Europe. They really do know what they're doing. Under Investcorp's ownership, the company grew by 7% a year organically as it increased market share across Europe. We expect that to continue. It made four acquisitions under Investcorp, and we are looking to accelerate that rate. It is a great acquisition story. (Owen Wright, cited in Bollen, 2007: 3)

The British investment company Candover became the owner with 100 percent holding of Hilding Anders. John Arney, managing director at Candover, further explains why Candover was attracted to Hilding Anders:

> Hilding Anders demonstrated many qualities which immediately attracted us to the business. Led by Anders Pålsson, it has an excellent management team with a clear strategic vision, established brands, strong cash flows and outperformance in a growth market. We have identified a unique opportunity to work alongside management and expand the footprint of the business. (AltAssets, 2006)

Anders Pålsson comments on the deal with Candover:

> Candover has built a first-class reputation in the Nordic region. We are very proud that Candover is backing us to execute our next phase of growth. The business is in great shape and has performed well under private equity ownership. We are confident that we can continue to deliver organic and acquisitive growth, with the backing and support of our new owner. (*Investigate*, 26 October 2006)

Candover, established in 1980, with offices located in London, Paris, Düsseldorf and Milan, and a local adviser in Madrid is a provider of private equity for larger European buyouts. It specializes in 'finding and backing management with the vision and experience to deliver outstanding growth.' A typical Candover deal is 'large complicated and demands imagination and experience to spot and seize the opportunity' (Candover, 2008: 1). In 2006, Hilding Anders had approximately 4,000 employees involved in generating sales of SEK5.6 billion through 30 subsidiaries operating in 23 European and 9 Asian markets (Hilding Anders, 2007a).

The proposed transaction was not considered as leading to any competition concerns. There were no horizontal overlaps or vertical relationships between the activities of Hilding Anders and Candover. Their strategies were compatible. The European competition authority approved of the acquisition by Candover (Case COMP/M.4468 – Candover Partners/Hilding Anders, 22 November 2006).

With the new owner on board, Hilding Anders was obliged to continue strengthening its position in the European bed and mattress markets and also in the Asian markets. Hilding Anders' immediate priorities were therefore to secure an acquisition in Spain, which would further facilitate expansion in the Far East and westward (Invest in Sweden Agency, 2006).

> Candover, our new owner, wants us to go even further. From now on, our sight is firmly fixed at becoming the world's largest bed and mattress manufacturer. This means that Hilding Anders will continue to grow not only in Europe, but also in Asia where we already have a large market share through our subsidiary Slumberland Asia Pacific. Adding to that, we are of course looking at possible acquisitions in other continents as well. (Anders Pålsson, Hilding Anders, 2007b)

As a consequence of the ownership change, a new board of directors in Hilding Anders was formed with three representatives for Candover. In October 2008, Fredrik Arp left his position as CEO of Volvo Cars in Sweden and took over as chairman of the Hilding Anders board. Looking forward to his new position, Arp said: 'Hilding Anders is an interesting and successful group with many interesting opportunities before it. I look forward to heading the work of the board in its endeavors' (Hilding Anders, 2008h). Pålsson, welcoming the new chairman, said:

> Our intention is to become the world's leading bed and mattress manufacturer, and that is why we are adjusting the structure of the board of directors and engaging external competence. Fredrik Arp has genuine experience from operating large companies as well as excellent competence regarding industrial business. Together with our new owner we look forward to the work that is now about to begin. (*Business Wire*, 2007a)

In 2008, the performance of Hilding Anders displayed growth in terms of sales amounting to SEK7,059 billion (Hilding Anders, 2009c).

Narrative bits and pieces give us information about exchanges between the collective agents Credit Suisse, Citigroup, Investcorp, Candover and Hilding Anders. The more integrated Hilding Anders, which during Investcorp's ownership grew organically by 7 percent a year through expanding its market share in Europe, actually constructs a context which provides these agents with hunches for future growth. Arguably, sense is collectively pooled (Walsh and Ungson, 1991), meaning that the representatives of the banks, the investment companies and Hilding Anders do all read into the present a future that promises expansion of the Hilding Anders business. The collective level generates here a coincident sense and meaning. It is particularly interesting to note that the managing director of Candover voices the expectations that Hilding Anders should gain a world-leading market status. In realizing these expectations, Hilding Anders needs to follow a strategic route that accelerates the rate of acquisitions also in Asia.

On the individual level, from the point of view of Claes-Göran Jönsson, supervisor at the Hästveda factory in Sweden, expansion is, however, less recognizable in the performance of certain activities:

> I was employed in 1978, starting out at the factory floor, as one used to say back then. ...
>
> Today I work with the production of bed frames. In my position as supervisor, I check and make sure that bed frame manufacturing is done efficiently and meets the customers' needs and requirements. Over the years, the degree of technical complexity in production has increased. This means that I nowadays mostly observe how the computerized machines operate and am not much engaged in manual work. The product is still the bed frame. Although the business continually expands, I don't really recognize any changes occurring in the production of the bed frames. Even the merger with Apax in 1999 didn't affect my work. I still concentrate on bed frames. Of course, I notice that the business expands through the increased number of employees. (Claes-Göran Jönsson, personal communication, 13 November 2006)

Turning Point and Route Follower

The new ownership by Candover suggests a turning point, which once again contextualizes Hilding Anders practitioners' activities differently, prompting enhanced focus on productivity and growth. The geographical context for acquisition activities and performance also widens. With reference to Tomas Modén, production manager at the Hästveda factory, there seems then to be little opportunity provided for the establishment of more close contacts between the owners, managers and employees. Modén relates to a feeling of 'being a pawn in a game' and continues:

One felt more important in the position one had earlier on, at least I think so. With an increasing number of hierarchical levels one doesn't get the opportunity to establish a more personal relationship with the CEO. He cannot be present among us, walking around and learning about our work and challenges that we face in our daily work. I get the impression that financial matters play a more significant role today than how people actually work. (Tomas Modén, personal communication, 13 November 2006)

Tomas Modén's colleague Claes-Göran Jönsson agrees:

Yes, I agree with Tomas; one becomes a 'pawn in a game' ... since the company has grown so big. Of course it is satisfying that the company grows and generates profit and it should be noted that there have been no layoffs, and motivation among workers has not decreased. The competition is intensifying and to reduce costs, production is closed down in one place and moved to another place abroad. It is undeniably positive that we are increasing our market share abroad and that we have a very good reputation as the biggest bed and mattress producer. Nevertheless, as individuals we are inclined to direct attention to what is close to us, the reality we experience at a particular geographical place and do not focus very much on what occurs in Poland, Spain or in Asia. We tend to care about our smaller world and evidently we devote our energy to keep the Hästveda factory running. We have concentrated harder on productivity and the development of working methods. (Claes-Göran Jönsson, personal communication, 13 November 2006)

The turning point instigates a move in a direction that accelerates the rate of acquisitions, primarily in the Asian markets. The European competition authority confirmed compatibility between Candover's and Hilding Anders' strategies, which indicates that activities performed by Hilding Anders people embody a route follower that expands on the owner's growth intentions.

Following the new ownership, the board of directors was restructured with a new chairman and members representing Candover. These people together with the CEO of Hilding Anders provide a frame of reference for making sense prospectively of the owner's higher expectations of growth. As sense-maker, the board allows for a route following interpretation and understanding that accordingly directs attention to an imagined time and space (Lämsä and Sintonen, 1996) where Hilding Anders positions itself as the world leading bed and mattress producer. Sense-making generally conveys the idea of retrospect (Starbuck and Milliken, 1988; Weick, 1995) since cues, which refer to familiar structures people apply to develop a larger sense of what occurs, are usually extracted on the basis of previous actions and of things that already happened. But cues could also be prospectively framed (Wright, 2006) and sense-making extended beyond the past and made meaningful in a larger future-oriented context (Boland, 1984) as indicated here.

NEVER ENDING

Business growth manifests also in the never-ending research and development work, predicated on the vision 'to give the world a good night's sleep' (Hilding Anders, 2010a). The bedding concept is based on the consumer's needs for 'good sleeping comfort, health and safety requirements, attractive design, financial capabilities, a positive and unique sleep-experience' (Hilding Anders, 2010b). Research and development are activities performed by Hilding Anders people in cooperation with customers, suppliers and universities continually to improve the quality of sleep, to make people feel better when they are awake.

8. Pattern, plot and narrative rationality

The study of business growth, presented through a variety of stories referring to the son of the founder, a merger, brand portfolio-building and to the sale of Hilding Anders, integrates theoretical-philosophical and methodological concerns. Based on a participatory narrative approach, it opens up the possibility of ongoing interactions between the empirical-oriented material and different theoretical concepts, grounded in narrative as well as in nonnarrative studies of growth, bringing together theory and practice. Embracing Gadamerian lived experience and belongingness to the world, this approach elevates intersubjectivity and relationality, allowing for the development of performative knowledge. The need for more performatively defined knowledge, Hjorth emphasizes:

> Social studies of science have concluded that all science is situated knowledge and it follows that we need an approach and a language that will allow for a more performatively defined knowledge. A narrative approach, and narrative forms of knowledge, holds much promise in this sense. It is in such forms that knowledge has been carried forth. Narratives have always functioned as storehouse of practices and reflections thereon. (Hjorth, 2006: 712–13)

A synoptic account, as opposed to a performative account, approaches growth as an accomplished event, describing the causal antecedents and consequences of this event (Tsoukas and Chia, 2002). Although the present study offers little direct acquaintance with fluidity and indivisibility of business growers' reality, it provides some material on their interactions and activities and the change entailed. By turning our attention to business growth as exposed through dialogues with practitioners and written material, we can at least get some glimpses of its dynamic complexity. As opposed to a synoptic account, a performative account offers insights into change as emergent and grounded in human activity.

'Participatory' relates not only to diversity as regards gender, age, religion and ethnicity (Lämsä and Sintonen, 2006) but also to a theoretical diversity. Interpretation and understanding of business growth emanate from the empirical–theoretical interlaced discussion in this book. In its becoming, the business growth narrative draws on existing ideas presented in narrative studies that place at the center the interacting narrating human beings. Spoken and written fragments also direct attention to the firm, which – conceptualized as a collective agent – interacts with other collective agents. The intercollectively emerging context calls for nonnarrative firm-related theory. In other words, the business growth narrative consists of action and interaction, which presupposes a dialogue between the narrating individuals involved in different kinds of growth activities and the researcher and author of the book. The provision of oral and written stories promotes action whereas counteraction grants the switching of the researcher's role from a listener to an interpreter, who in successive encounters with practitioners continually comments on and interweaves theoretical threads with the stories. The exposition of turning points, route followers and plots thus occurs in the interface between theory and practice.

As pointed out next, the study mediates sense and meaning about growth in reference to 'plots'. Plots, making up the business growth narrative, closely relate to 'pattern' but are more consistent with the narrative approach. While engaging fragmentation and multidimensionality, more than one plot is presented. By definition, a pattern is 'a regular or logical form, order, or arrangements of parts' (Allen, 1990: 873). By focusing on plots, the study is left open to flexibility, reflected in the bits and pieces narratively imparted by the practitioners. Not being trapped in a coherent pattern such as growth stages, the business growth narrative as post-story (Boje, 2000) flows with many voices and many plots.

A BUSINESS GROWTH NARRATIVE EMERGES

Plot interconnects the turning points exposed through the stories provided by the son of the founder of the Hilding Anders business about growth-oriented activities (Chapter 4) and the catalytic elements that amount to a turning point, promoting growth in association with the merger between Apax and Hilding Anders (Chapter 5). Moreover, the plot links together the route followers apparent in activities performed by the practitioners to build the Hilding Anders brand portfolio (Chapter 6), and the turning points and route followers highlighted through the changes in ownership (Chapter 7). A business growth narrative emerges, presenting itself through the plots delineated below.

The Son of the Founder Plot

Interwoven with the theoretical threads I repeatedly provide throughout Chapter 4, the son of the founder plot emerges, ascribing a central position to Olle Andersson, the son of the founder. By interconnecting turning points, it flows with fragments of Andersson's lived experience, stressing his engagement in growth-oriented activities associated with bed and mattress production and products. The plot draws on the dialogues with Olle Andersson that revolved around the rocking chair, the bedstead, the interior-spring mattress, the bed base, the polyfoam mattress and hotel furnishing. The dialogues also brought to the fore how Andersson cared about the employees and the close relationship between husband and wife.

The son of the founder plot is manifested in economic calculations concerned with sales, production costs, revenue per employee and profit. Moreover, it exposes a positive attitude toward growth and belief in growth, which Wiklund, Davidsson and Delmar (2003) see as essential for a manager pursuing growth. The plot announces emotions, expressed through the positive ambience among people associated with the Hilding Anders business, the continued work, the feelings of being confident about future growth and the hopes for continued profit-driven growth. This indicates Andersson's awareness of positive and negative emotions that, according to Brundin, Patzelt and Shepherd (2007), affect the employees' willingness to act entrepreneurially. Arguably, the employees act entrepreneurially when engaging in the development of bed products that meet and even exceed the requirements and needs of the customers. Andersson praised his wife Britta and the other women especially.

The plot further winds through different conjunctures that ground turning points in conflict-laden and emotionally charged sets of activities with reference to the rescue in the 1940s from a situation which could have had disastrous consequences for the business, and to disagreements between father and son. Turning points also reflect the streamlining of production, the move to another geographical place, experimenting, development and the introduction of a new mattress product.

The plot admittedly draws on a self that takes on different disguises along the way. What is a self? If you want to know 'what the self *really* is, you're making a category mistake' argues Dennett (1992: 7). When using a hermeneutical narrative approach we are liable to discover more than one character in a person. Narrative allows the narrator to talk about self. It is an important and powerful vehicle for expressing 'who I think I am' or 'who I think you are', as Markham Shaw (1997: 317) contends. We can learn something about Olle Andersson's business life and we might learn more about Andersson than he explicitly tells by reading in things about him by implication and extrapolation. This signals that indeterminacy will always be a fundamental property of self, which, according to Dennett (1992), distinguishes self from a 'real' object or a theoretical entity.

The plot echoes a past that speaks at present through the voice of the son of the founder of the Hilding Anders business, opening up the potential for intersubjectivity to influence the conception of self. The self-concept of the useful child is formed from the view of the narrating 81-year-old man, who reaches from the here and now to the far away and then space and time when referring to growth-oriented activities associated with a furniture business that started up in 1939. 'Here', 'now' and 'then' are deictic expressions and refer to the spatiotemporal setting of the utterance of Olle Andersson. An expression is deictic because the determination of the reference depends on who says what, where and when, as Herman (1995) explains.

The 81-year-old man (in 2009) remembers being involved in the business already at an early age. The voice of the son of the founder serves also as a channel through which the executive, the experimenting, persevering and the highly committed man comes alive. The useful child self translates into the independent owner-manager and entrepreneurial self who decides what investment to make and what production technology to apply, substantially lowering production costs and making money. The self becomes open to alteration while being receptive to the possibilities of the future (Crites, 1986). The entrepreneurial self develops and acts through social relationships as son, husband, father, father-in-law, co-worker, owner-manager, production manager, truck driver, boiler man and colleague. In the criss-crossing of social relationships Olle Andersson relates to the 'competitors' within the bed and mattress industry as 'colleagues'.

The entrepreneurial self, combining ownership and management, lives business growth through engaging in a variety of activities, committed to practicing the philosophy of always producing high-quality beds and mattresses while making a profit. Entrepreneurship is then not confined to a person's status of being or not being the founder or the owner-manager, as Davidsson (1991) argues. Entrepreneurship is a social activity (Downing, 2005; Øyhus, 2003) embedded in human interactions and relationships.

The son of the founder plot gives rise also to another entrepreneurial self, the son-in-law Bengt Adolfsson, who in interactions with others constructs and realizes extraordinary growth opportunites, as reflected in the Russian order and its spin-off effects. Adolfsson, assuming the position as CEO of Hilding Anders in 1987, is increasingly involved in growth activities associated with significant changes, as the Apax-Hilding Anders merger plot indicates.

The Apax-Hilding Anders Merger Plot

Narrative bits and pieces provided by people involved in the Apax-Hilding Anders merger (Chapter 5) form a plot that includes the merchant, domestic and civic cities when legitimating the claims of the owners, the families and the Commission of the European Community. The plot accounts for multiple motives. Often conceptualized as a goal in the merger and acquisition literature, a motive unilaterally governs merger and acquisition activities without taking into consideration how a motive forms through social interplay and how it is narratively announced. Rather, motives are listed in the forms of categories (Napier, 1989; Steiner, 1975) and taxonomies (Walter and Barney, 1990). Steiner depicts two categories of motives, namely for and against a merger. Napier categorizes merger and acquisition motives as value maximizing and nonvalue maximizing. Walter and Barney present a taxonomy consisting of a number of motives, related to growth, synergy, market power, market share and efficiency. They further explore the relative importance of managerial motives behind horizontal, vertical, concentric and conglomerate mergers and acquisitions types when setting the stage for a contingency framework. The notion of a strategic fit between a company's strengths and the growth rate of its market is rooted in the contingency framework. At the core is an understanding of the relatedness of the company and the economic value created, with no room provided for motives expressed and formed by narrating individuals. Customer-oriented motives are not included in the lists, categories and taxonomies of motives. Neither are relationships between families and family members considered. The calculative quality of individuals' contacts and interactions seem to attract more attention. Although previous studies of mergers and acquisitions emphasize the human aspect (Buono and Bowditch, 1989; Cartwright and Cooper, 1990; Haspeslagh and Jemison, 1991; Jemison and Sitkin, 1986; Lindell and Melin, 1991; Nahavandi and Malekzadeh, 1988), the customer side and the family side are largely ignored.

Research rarely dedicates interest to how owners, managers and other people involved in merger activities relate to each other and talk about these activities (Demers, Giroux and Chreim, 2003). Motives and interactions might go well beyond the categorizing and taxonomizing of merger and acquisition motives. Motives appear and are legitimized in language, and become known in the ongoing social interplay and because of the interplay (Haspeslagh and Jemison, 1991; Jemison and Sitkin, 1986; Weick, 1979). When shifting the focus toward strategic dynamics with reference to catalytic elements, the motive conception extends.

The Apax-Hilding Anders merger plot is driven by catalytic elements amounting to a turning point that includes the decision to merge Apax and Hilding Anders. Through merging, one expected financial strength and other synergistic gains related to operations, systems and products to be realized while fulfilling the customers' needs and requirements. With reference to the significant actor Bengt Adolfsson, the plot emphasizes the issue of sustaining good relationships with the principal customer Ikea. Catalytic elements refer to Adolfsson handling the situation of employees falling ill, his welcoming of new owners to Hilding Anders, and moreover, the moves taken within the Swedish furniture industry by the investment companies Nordic Capital and Atle, and the Apax telephone call initiating merger discussions. Atle's ownership position in Hilding Anders and the actions taken by Arne Karlsson, representing Atle, clearly paved the way for the decision to merge Apax and Hilding Anders. Moreover, the confirmation of the legality of the merger by the Commission of the European Communities suggests a catalytic element. Officially approved, the merger became an 'established fact' (Demers, Giroux and Chreim, 2003) of the strategic direction outlined by the representatives of Hilding Anders in conscience with the representatives of Apax.

The merger between Apax and Hilding Anders makes sense as a calculative rational response to experienced environmental changes, elevating the Weberian logic of instrumental rationality. At the same time, the plot indicates that sense is made with reference to the need of Hilding Anders to build financial strength by reducing uncertainty linked with the precarious emotion-laden situation of employees suffering from cancer. It further shows that emotions come to the fore when pronounced in relation to content, intuition, a 'we-feeling' in close association with the entrepreneurial spirit, then experience of getting along well, consensual agreements and feeling experiences exposed in the utterances of 'we strongly felt' and 'to get a feel for.'

Both human and collective actants, in accordance with the actantial schema,[20] form the merging plot that lends the self-concept a more complex structure. The plot draws on the human voices of the owner selves, the CEO selves and the many manager selves, providing glimpses of their lived experience but also on the 'voices' of the collective actants joining forces. Hilding Anders is a collective actant that 'speaks' with the collective actant Apax. They play the roles assigned to them by the owners, the CEOs and the managers. When merged, Apax-Hilding Anders acts as a bigger customer-centered player and purchaser, and, further, as an efficient resource coordinator, logistics improver, financial consolidator, business developer and growth promoter. Predicated on the idea of world-openness, it can be argued that individual and collective selves, making up the Apax-Hilding Anders merger plot, take active parts in enacting reality.

Based on the narrative approach, embracing the idea of world-openness, there is no environment 'out there' subjected to an objective analysis. With a focus on what practitioners are involved in, and what they experience and expect from an imagined future, it makes sense to engage in the merger. Practitioners participate and share in merging activities. These activities help construct the environment (Weick, 1995). By taking into account customer, market and product, cues are enacted that generate a point of reference (Porac, Thomas and Baden-Fuller, 1989; Smircich and Morgan, 1982) against which the merger forms. The decision to combine Apax and Hilding Anders is anchored in sense-making. Sense-making pertains to the question of how practitioners interactively construct what they construct when enacting reality.

The Apax-Hilding Anders merger plot gives way to the brand portfolio-building plot.

The Brand Portfolio-building Plot

The brand portfolio-building plot extends, connecting the route followers revealed in Chapter 7. It reflects the proliferation of brands and branded bed and mattress products. Narrative fragments based on spoken as well as written text – constituting the route followers and the plot – display a chronological narrative structure that answers to the question of what happened next, limited to a period of approximately 20 years. These fragments bring into focus Hilding Anders as a collective agent that approaches, negotiates with and acquires other collective agents located in different countries. The agents continuously expand their customer base, products and services (Sexton and Seale, 1997) in order to secure and maintain a competitive position (Claver, Andreu and Quer, 2006). Their choice to grow implies staying ahead of competition, improving market orientation (Golann, 2006) and discovering new sources of value for the customers (Kim and Mauborgne, 1997). A multi-firm capability perspective emerges concerned with the identification of and response to partnering opportunities (Moore, Autry and Macy, 2007) with regard to potentially valuable brands. Hilding Anders engages in international market making that requires skills at both geographical and activity coordination (Oviatt and McDougall, 1994). With a focus on the 2000s, the plot tells of growth in reference to entrances in new markets through an increasing number of acquisitions of brands and establishment of factories and sales organizations.

Mainly confined to official narrative descriptions of acquisitions and establishments, the brand portfolio-building plot announces growth opportunities with limited indication of competing accounts and culturally-bound assumptions of the actors involved. Not much is revealed about tensions and conflicts in the historical development of a brand and in connection with the acquisitions taking place. The exposed route followers rationally center their focus on the brand portfolio, its architecture and expansion. Even if the closing down of a factory in the UK is a devastating activity, and the disposal of the Billerbeck Group might have rendered tensions and conflicts among people involved, these events do not propose a deviation from the Hilding Anders overall strategy. The profit-driven, focused growth strategy outlined by the managers is still followed, serving the purposes of the managers for whom preparations and plans for expansion, and acquisitions of brands undoubtedly make sense, while advancing the strategy agenda of continuous growth with the intention of becoming one of the world's leading bed and mattress producers.

Although culturally value-laden and historically imprinted, the brand portfolio-building plot is foremost considerate of brand interrelationships. It does not account for how people belonging to different cultural traditions in the process of communication interpret what is going on. It seems that the route followers, constituting the plot, rather peacefully extend in time and space. They promote change through interaction and activity but mainly with regard to a company as a collective agent, overshadowing conflicts and emotions that might emerge among individuals. The plot simply denotes that the acquired brands, representing different price segments and product qualities, support and supplement one another and are associated with the existing brands in the portfolio. The plot sets off by illustrating the launching and acquisitions of brands in Sweden, Denmark, Switzerland, Belgium and France. Looking for more brands that meet the strategic objectives and closely relate to the core business of beds and mattresses in Hilding Anders, the plot sweeps through Norway, the UK, Ireland, the Netherlands, Croatia, Spain, the Czech Republic, Asian countries, Italy and Germany while adding value to the brand portfolio regardless of cultural differences. In addition, the plot interconnects route followers relating chronologically to the establishment of a sales organization in St Petersburg, a new factory in Bangkok and a sales organization in Frankfurt. The acquisition partners operate in European and Asian markets where the customers' specific requirements of a product have to be met. The bed and mattress market is 'very local', as the CEO of Hilding Anders explains. This suggests acceptance of variety in cultural traditions, permitting different degrees of integration (Nahvandi and Malekzadeh, 1988) between the acquired companies and Hilding Anders. Building a brand portfolio suggests a more heterogeneous world of practice in terms of workforce diversity. Sensitivity to the different characteristics of each brand enables interplay between different perspectives of people involved in marketing and developing the brands. While not assuming a melting-pot approach the challenge is to allow for many local views on brand and branding issues.

The brand portfolio-building plot sheds some light on the idiosyncratic nature of the route followers. Idiosyncrasy emanates from the skills 'passed down' from generations, a particular work ethic, qualities and production techniques developed over generations. This makes it difficult for competitors to replicate the brand portfolio concept and the house of brand architecture of Hilding Anders. Idiosyncrasy is a powerful generator for causal ambiguity, Chailan (2008) points out. It hinders potential imitators from knowing what to imitate and how to do it. 'Causal ambiguity refers to an uncertainty pertaining to reasons for performance differences between companies' (2008: 260). The fact that the Hilding Anders brand portfolio is composed of a number of brands and also of company-specific processes that interrelate and continuously develop the brands contributes to causal ambiguity.

Stories that people tell about the development of a business and its products and brands further contribute to idiosyncrasy. The affective values of such stories can help connect customers to a company and build long-term relationships (Harrington, 2007). Emotions felt and expressed by the customers are difficult to imitate and challenge by competitors. 'What goes straight to the heart' (Mahajan and Wind, 2002: 38) can create 'an internal reality' within the customer which is difficult to reason with once generated, confirms Harrington (2007). Fragments of historical development in companies and brands referred to in the chapter are indicative of emotions.

While looked at in relation to the Hilding Anders strategy, activities associated with acquisitions, development and launch of brands suggest route followers sensitive to a variety of qualities and values. A narrative frame of meaning exists in brand names as proxies for quality and value attributes, reflecting what one can be proud of in ongoing exchanges that involve Hilding Anders representatives, customers, retailers, acquisition partners and others.

The brand portfolio-building plot allows for an extension of the brand value concept. Not only is what makes a brand its 'personality' at the center. Brand value is also embodied within the broader concept of customer value (Blombäck, 2005; Christopher, 1996; Harrington, 2007). Part of a network of Hilding Anders representatives, customers, retailers, acquisitions partners and others, the brand portfolio-building plot elicits a value proposition that embraces the reciprocity of adding and extracting value in the Swedish market but also across national borders, in European and Asian markets. In this sense, the plot accounts for the processes through which Hilding Anders people, including the owners, gain benefits by adding value to the customers, offering branded bed and mattress products that make the customers feel the quality comfort while giving them a good night's sleep.

In parallel with the growth activities associated with the building of the brand portfolio, owner changes took place, enhancing the focus on productivity and profitability as the next plot illustrates.

The Investcorp and Candover Ownership Plot

Studies demonstrate that corporate governance and type of ownership affect strategy but also that divergent and conflicting views exist (Le Breton-Miller and Miller, 2008). By analyzing owner-manager agency costs, it is argued that managers can use their superior information to exploit small shareholders while pursuing a value-maximizing growth strategy (Jensen and Meckling, 1976). The assumption in the field of finance is that the manager should act to maximize the wealth of current shareholders. In most agency relationships, the principal and the agent incur monitoring and bonding costs, nonpecuniary as well as pecuniary costs, as Alchian and Demsetz (1972) inform us. An agency problem refers to a manager's desire to increase the market share, expand the business and build an empire. If managers are able to substitute their own interests for those of the shareholders, an agency problem arises resulting in agency costs. Rather than maximizing shareholder wealth, managerial wealth is maximized at the expense of shareholder wealth. Although higher restrictions, under such circumstances, are likely to be imposed on the managers, they will still be the financial decision-makers of a company and will probably continue to introduce personal interests through their decisions, Findley and Whitmore (1974) assert. Studies of family business ownership conclude that major family owners favor utility maximization that limits firm performance (Bertrand and Schoar, 2006) whereas other studies claim that family businesses outperform publicly traded companies (Andersson and Reeb, 2003).

Rather than centering on ownership configurations, owner-manager agency costs, conflicting views in the literature on ownership, and being involved in the ongoing debate on the effects of concentrated ownership, my focus is on growth-oriented activities and their inherent moves with regard to turning points and route followers. By combining the Investcorp turning point and route follower with the Candover turning point and route follower displayed in Chapter 7, the Investcorp and Candover ownership plot emerges. The plot relates to ownership that has an enhanced focus on profitability, productivity and growth. Investcorp requires a stronger focus on 'greater profitability' and 'offensive growth' in the European bed and mattress markets, while Candover demands accelerating the rate of acquisitions in order to speed up growth outside Europe. The Investcorp route follower is thus successively modified in the sense that it at a later point in time reinforces the focus on growth through acquisitions. It evolves into the Candover route follower, a directional change which is set by the predetermined aim of Hilding Anders to become a world-leading bed and mattress producer.

Hilding Anders people apparently internalize the new requirements, deriving first from Investcorp's management and team and then from Candover's representatives. They accommodate the new owners' goals as in a variety of activities performed in areas of purchasing, production, accounting and finance to contribute with improvements that are shown in increased profitability and productivity. The plot brings to life the experience of representatives of the new owners. The 'otherness' of the owners' past takes shape in goals and strategic activities that clearly require receptivity from and the engagement of Hilding Anders people.

Hilding Anders practitioners apparently subordinate themselves to the claims of Investcorp and Candover in their endeavors to make improvements in productivity throughout the organization and the production process while also realizing positive synergies between the subsidiaries that constitute Hilding Anders. In accordance with the actantial schema, collective agents are narratively framed that buy shares, encourage the acquired object to develop and grow before they exit. A binary opposition consisting of the destinator and the destinatee suggests a subject–object relationship. The quest for value is here triggered first by the mandate of the destinator Investcorp and then by Candover taking over the role as destinator in the relationship with the destinatee Hilding Anders. The owners, acting as destinators, provide the destinatee with financial resources, expertise and strategic guidance.

The Investcorp and Candover ownership plot reflects a financial logic that obviously brings in the firm as an object. In order to grow the Hilding Anders firm, the Investcorp and the Candover owners both see it is necessary to expend more effort on productivity improvement and rationalization through the reconfiguration of resources and decreases in costs. From the perspectives of the owners, the competence of the Hilding Anders management plays a crucial role then. In connection with the Investcorp turning point and route follower, Bengt Adolfsson's management is highly praised. Adolfsson, holding the position as CEO all through 1987–2002, is ascribed a unique ability. 'As the business grew in terms of increases in turnover, and whether the turnover amounted to SEK62 million or reached the level of nearly SEK4 billion, Bengt performed well,' Arne Karlsson, CEO of Ratos, underlined. In connection with the Candover turning point and route follower, the Anders Pålsson management is greatly appreciated. From 2003 Pålsson held the position of CEO of Hilding Anders. A focus is intercollectively communicated that actualizes the application of firm-growth theory. As Ghoshal, Hahn and Moran (1997) argue, management competence leads to growth of the firm and is associated with the ability to perceive resource combination and exchange potential. Management competency thereby accounts for entrepreneurial judgment (Penrose, 1959) and organizational capability (Naldi, 2008).

Collective in character, entrepreneurial judgment implies exchanges of ideas and knowledge among organizational participants. In line with the position taken by Penrose (1959), and the more recent resource-based view and capability approaches, a firm can be described as a bundle of resources and capabilities (Erramilli, Agarwal and Dev, 2002). The Penrosian position holds that the knowledge resource is at the center of management competence. The ownership exercised by Investcorp especially signals the importance of sharing knowledge among people, learning about and from each other. A move beyond a firm-growth focus, a knowledge resource view and a subject–object relationship is open to stories embedded in the turning points and route followers that make up the Investcorp and Candover ownership plot. As indicated, these stories help preserve and enhance a calculative rationality.

Narrative Fragments

Narrative fragments provided by practitioners and documents construct a reality that communicates sense and meaning about business growth in reference to turning points, route followers and plots. It should also be remarked that voices of practitioners that are not heard in this study might speak of some disadvantages of the merger between Apax and Hilding Anders, the acquisitions of brand and companies, and of Investcorp and Candover as owners. A story can be recounted from various standpoints. As Buchanan and Dawson (2007: 670) point out, 'multiple stories are an integral part of the complex dynamic of changing in the experiences that they capture, and in the influence that they have on the shape, direction and outcomes of change, as well as on "after-the-change" accounts.' There could be self-serving, politically motivated stories (Leitch and Davenport, 2005) where the story that 'wins' depends on the narrator's credibility, political tactics and skilled storytelling performances (Ng and De Cock, 2002).

Although limited to narrative fragments, the study could bring about some insights about business growth from looking into the son of the founder plot, the Apax-Hilding Anders merger plot, the brand portfolio-building plot and the Investcorp and Candover ownership plot. The son of the founder plot elevates changes in terms of turning points grounded in human interaction with calculative rationality and emotions included. The Apax-Hilding Anders merger plot brings in collective agents and their exchanges. In reference to catalytic elements, a turning point is revealed, indicating the influence of calculative rationality and emotions. The brand portfolio-building plot, extending from route followers, refers to the profit-driven focused growth strategy, which apparently serves the purposes of the Hilding Anders managers to make rational preparations and plans for expansion and acquisitions of brands in order to become one of the world's leading bed and mattress producers. The Investcorp and Candover ownership plot, combining turning points and route followers, further emphasizes the calculative rationality. As indicated, a move from the son of the founder plot toward the Investcorp and Candover ownership plot increasingly strengthens the focus on calculative rationality.

Business growth as a dynamic phenomenon, constantly in motion, unfolds in contexts constructed out of what takes place between humans and collective agents through their interactions and activities. Following Sztompka (1993), just the acknowledgement of movement does not provide dynamism, however. We need to add another dimension, namely time. The business growth narrative establishes interaction and activity within context and time. It attends not only to the present but also actualizes what has passed, making the past real at present (Polkinghorne, 1988). To account for growth, the narrative must stretch beyond the present, considering turning points, route followers and plots that bring the past to the present.

Through temporal extension, the narrative reveals that growth-oriented activities are inherently calculative as well as emotionally influenced and charged. The narrative contextualization of interactions and activities suggests a space that as Bakhtin ([1981] 2002:15) puts it 'becomes charged and responsive to the movements of time, plot, and history.' Time–space relations are inherent in all human interactions (Giddens, 1979) and intrinsically related to social change (Sztompka, 1993). In narratives, there are chronotypes associated with physical and imagined places in intersection with time, differing in scope and emotional intensity, Bakhtin points out. Exploited outside literature and art, a chronotype could serve to highlight further the multidimensional and dynamic business growth phenomenon. A polyvoiced and polyplotted business growth narrative passes through more than one chronotype.

The son of the founder plot defines a chronotype saturated with the time of the historical past. The historical past plays an important role in the stories told in the present by the son of the founder. In these stories, the geographical place Hästveda provides a context for interactions among people and activities lived. The chronotype of Hästveda is also characterized by emotional intensity, as illustrated by turning points. In the merger plot, the brand portfolio-building plot, and the Investcorp and Candover ownership plot, a broader time–space emerges, characterized by socio-historical heterogeneity. Nonfamily members are increasingly involved in growth-oriented activities. Human interaction and activity take place in encounters with people representing companies and brands located in European and Asian countries. The historical and emotional intensity of the Hästveda chronotype apparently gains a diminishing role. The broader scope chronotype also brings in the company as a collective calculating agent. Mainly colored by a rationalistic discourse, attention focuses on the creation of economic value and competitiveness (Vaara and Tienari, 2002).

The study is rooted in a participatory narrative approach that mediates an ontology that consistently permeates the empirical–theoretical interlaced discussions in this book. An interpretation and understanding of business growth encloses the existential dimension of intersubjectivity and relationality. On this abstract level, the different plots require the furthering of the notion of the practitioners' rationally calculative activities through adding the concept of narrative rationality. Narrative rationality, including emotion, allows for a richer substantiation of business growth.

NARRATIVE RATIONALITY

Narrative rationality opens up a narrative truth that regards emotions as rational. The social world is filled with emotions (Albrow, 1997; Fineman, 2000), and emotions cannot be ignored, denied, suppressed or omitted because of evidence and verifiable knowledge.

'In the beginning was the word or, more accurately, the *logos*,' Fisher (1985: 74) reminds us. From being a generic term that included different forms of human expression and communication, logos transformed into a specific form that excluded mythos. Logos and mythos have parallels with intellect and sense, calculative rationality and emotion. Ever since the days of the Greek philosophers, Plato (424/423–348/347 BC) and Aristotle (384–322 BC), the idea that logos is superior to mythos has been reinforced, ensuring the validation of truth, knowledge and reality. Plato and Aristotle attributed rationality primarily to the logic of reasoning and to the ability to argue and control. Emotions were restricted to unpredictable actions of excitement, underlying which was the assumption that a human being is capable of forming the world in agreement with a self-focusing, rationally calculated ambition (Lübcke, 1987).

The Cartesian Distinction

The western European rationalistic view can be traced back in the history of philosophy to Descartes (1596–1650), who claimed that body and mind exist apart, conveying the idea that rationality can be put forward as a contrast to emotion. From the viewpoint of Descartes ([1637] 1968), emotion is nothing more than a certain confused way of thinking. From history and philosophy one learns that acting appropriately means acting in accordance with rationality. The demarcation between rationality and emotion, embedded in culture, confines emotions in a narrow channel separated from the much-praised intellect. This represents a lopsided view of rationalization and intellectualization, according to the philosopher Max Scheler (1874–1928). While deeply rooted in Western culture and embedded in organizational thinking and acting, rationality seems to have taken on a normative character. 'In contrast to Eastern culture, it lost contact with emotive undercurrents of reason,' Scheler ([1915] 1994: 5) explains. The growth strategy of a firm is part of an institutional arrangement and, at least officially, described as governed by the norm of calculative rationality. To express the growth strategy in the discourse of strict economic reasoning, dispelling narratives and emotions, is thus legitimate. Consistent with the principle of noncontradiction is the intention to reduce ambiguity to a minimum, brushing aside irrational elements such as emotions. As Carr (2001: 422) submits: 'Indeed, acting rationally, according to the principle of non-contradiction necessarily excluded that bad guy called emotion and would, at the same time, appear to require no other validation – such as pervasiveness of this touchstone.' Rational models look scientific and most respectable while providing the practitioners with a rationalization of their successes and failures. What they experience emotionally is filtered through the efficiency language (Buono and Bowditch, 1989; Guillet de Monthoux, 1980) and how they construct success or failure in their stories seems not to be taken seriously (Vaara, 2002). Emotion proposes a deviation from what is intelligent (Calori, 1998) and should therefore be avoided, leaving rationality 'along with its cousin "efficiency"' (Carr, 2001: 421) in an incontestable position.

The appropriation of logos to a scientific discourse that only accepts a verified truth downplays the narrative rational side of a human being. Because of this, intellect and sense, (calculative) rationality and emotion are dissociated from each other. To move beyond the hegemonic struggle between logos and mythos, Fisher (1985) proposes a narrative paradigm that aligns logos and mythos. This particular paradigm intends to further the notion of humans' reasonable action by adding the concept of narrative rationality. In the words of Fisher:

> Human communication in all of its forms is imbued with mythos – ideas that cannot be verified or proved in an absolute way, including metaphors, values, gesture, and so on as well as aesthetic significance. Liberation of the human spirit would seem to call for an acceptance of these facts. They are intrinsic to the narrative paradigm, which is a response to the exigency created by their denial. (Fisher, 1985: 88)

Narratively framed rationality reconciles intellect with sense, calculative rationality with emotion and is open to the mythos-like side of humans. Growth and strategy scholars easily commit the 'Descartes' error' (Damasio, 1994), however, when elevating rational acting and cognitive abilities of an individual at the expense of emotions. A dualistic split of ontology is promoted, paralleling the Cartesian distinction between human mind and body with the human mind representing the rational and the body representing the irrational (Descartes [1637] 1968).

Although severe criticism has been leveled against the rational explicit view of strategy (Chakravarthy and White, 2002; Cyert and March, 1963; Levinthal and March, 1993; Lindblom, 1959; Mintzberg, 1978; Quinn, 1980) and a more detailed understanding of strategy process including emotion has been sought (Berg, 1979; Brundin, 2002; Ericson, 1991; Hall, 2003; Hellgren and Melin, 1993; Sjöstrand, 1997), the critique has not gone far enough, claims King (2000). To embrace rational and irrational action simultaneously should be 'natural'. The dividing line between the rational and the irrational is fraught with uncertainty and ambiguity and in some situations even paradoxical action might occur, meaning that rational is defined as irrational and vice versa, as Sjöstrand (1997) posits.

In the dualistic relationship that can mostly be identified between rationality and emotion, it is evident that one side has elevated itself to a superior status (Domagalski, 1999). Often regarded as being of doubtful value, the benign evaluative and constructive functions of emotions are not much appreciated. Cognition, in the form of logic, conceptualization, rational calculation, estimation and sense-making, is considered as more valuable and, in comparison with emotion, often receives undeserved credit for precision, clarity and relevance (Isaacs, 1998). Studies of strategy largely stress the practitioner's abilities, de-emotionalizing an understanding of what is played out in organizations (Carr, 2001), allowing the cognitive lens to be the prime guide of future actions (Rajagopalan and Spreitzer, 1997). Studies centering their focus on growth largely address the firm level, and scholars focusing on entrepreneurship emphasize the individual level, but only direct limited interest to 'relational selves' and to calculative rationality in combination with emotion.

Inviting Relational Selves

To try to deal with emotions by tolerating, controlling, suppressing or fighting them, merely using intellectual tools would obviously be a serious mistake (Isaacs, 1998). The practitioners may also need to rely on their feel for a situation to guide their strategic acting (Agor, 1989; Harper, 1989). Rather than viewing emotion as the dysfunctional antithesis of (calculative) rationality, one must recognize their complementarity (Ashforth and Humphrey, 1995). Yet, the concept of emotion not only serves physical and psychological purposes (Langer, 1967). In 'the rich fabric of social life woven not by physical beings whose actions are caused by mental entities harbored under their skulls, but rather social beings' (Wood and Kroger, 2000: xii), the communicative dimension calls for attention. It builds on the notion that 'human beings have a built in drive to relate to each other' (Ellis, Gates and Kenworthy, 2003: 3) and that it is impossible for one not to communicate (Watzlawick, Bavelas and Jackson, 1967).

A better understanding of what occurs between individuals can be gained by using the information on the significance and meaning of activities that emotions bring (Isaacs, 1998). Emotion is not an individual's private possession but a property of relationships between individuals, the relational selves, as Gergen (1999) points out. There is no such thing as an emotion per se; Brundin (2002: 274) also emphasizes: 'It is in the social interaction that emotions are interpreted or translated, applying a performative vocabulary. From this translation, emotions are transformed in one way or the other, more or less consciously and thereby transformed into emotions or actions, subject to new translations in the inter-personal interplay.' As relational selves, we believe in a dialogically structured world. Such a world 'grows from relationship, and is embedded not within individual minds but within interpretative or communal traditions' (Gergen, 1999: 122). *Homo narrans* as relational selves become part of the world and coexist with it. Implied in this is the existential subjectivity that denotes intersubjectivity (Gadow, 1999).

Relational rationality contextualizes rationality, placing in focus individuals' rationales for action as embedded in their needs, and as shaped by historically situated values, Hall (2003) maintains. In her words: 'Relational rationality is evoked by, and preoccupied with, the individuals' notion of them as part of a social collective, and their way of relating to the members of that collective' (2003: 235).

With a focus on a linguistically manifest and narratively communicated world of business growth practice, I believe that it is important to attach the label 'narrative' to (relational) rationality. The narrative turn taken in this book entails an approach that stresses the language used by narrators to construct sense. Because language is action (Austin, 1962), different uses of language constitute a world differently. The world of growth practice, manifested in lived activities, does not exist for people independently of the language they use. It cannot be treated as an indifferent flow of information, being subjected to decomposition into a set of atomic proportions (Bruner, 1990). The constituting role of lived experience challenges the view that the human mind equals a computational program and that cognition forms the world. The integration of language into life suggests an ontologically grounded understanding of business growth so that there is no historical objectivity and no activity of a single subject. Hence, the practitioners as relational selves engage in storytelling that answers not to a cognitive representation of the world but to the way they have been socialized. As Chia (2004), drawing on the philosopher Heidegger (1889–1976) and on Bourdieu's (1990) concept of habitus,[21] purports, every encounter that takes place with another person is an encounter with the lived experience of that person.

IN RELATION TO EARLIER STUDIES ON CHANGE AND GROWTH PATTERNS

Growth studies mainly attend to the growth of the firm[22] without directing much interest at change as difference implied in human interaction and activity, and to how 'pattern' dynamically emerges through practitioners' stories. The concept of growth is often linked with change in percentage sales, employment profitability, market share, return on capital employed and productivity. Change also refers to the move from one stage to another in the life of a firm, accounting for a number of interrelated firm-, management-, and market-oriented factors (Gibb and Davies, 1990; Merz, Weber and Laetz, 1994). As argued in literature on strategic and organizational change, change is influenced by 'diverse units and actors, both inside and outside the organization' (Van de Ven and Poole, 1995: 526). By virtue of the focus on the inner–outer-context design, organizational becoming (Tsoukas and Chia, 2002) and narrating practitioners receive little attention. The dualistic ontological orientation implied in this binary logic (Calori, 1998), separates organization from environment and the past from the future without noting that an organization can be conceptualized as 'a pattern that is constituted, shaped, *emerging* from change' (Tsoukas and Chia, 2002: 570) and that there is a need for a more performatively defined knowledge (Hjorth, 2007).

A variety of change processes have been outlined in earlier research but with little attention paid to narrative voices. Since the 1980s there has been a conceptual transfer between choice and change theorists, providing linkages between context, content and process and their interconnectedness through time (Hellgren and Melin, 1993; Johnson, 1987; Melin, 1989; Pettigrew, 1992; Pettigrew and Whipp, 1991). Studies also direct attention to strategizing and organizing processes, micro and macro processes through the use of activity- and practice-based approaches (Achtenhagen, Melin and Müllern, 2003; Dougherty, 2004; Jarzabkowski, 2003; Jarzabkowski and Wilson, 2002; Johnson, Melin and Whittington, 2003; Lounsbury and Leblebici, 2004; Løwendahl and Revang, 2004). The political, cultural, cognitive, learning and sense-making dimensions (Barr, Stimpert and Huff, 1992; Gioia and Chittipeddi, 1991; Johnson, 1987; Lant, Milliken and Batra, 1992; Lyles and Schwenk, 1992; Mintzberg and Waters, 1986; Mintzberg and Westley, 1992; Normann, 1985; Pettigrew and Whipp, 1991) as well as the emotion dimension (Brundin, 2002; Ericson, 1991; Hall, 2003; Hellgren and Melin, 1993; Sjöstrand, 1997) are incorporated. Although the aspects of sense-making and emotion are closely related to narrative, little room is provided for the narrating sense-making and feeling practitioner.

Moreover, organizational change is analyzed with a focus centering on the logics underlying change processes. Van de Ven (1992) presents four ideal types of theories based on fundamentally different process logics, also referred to as 'motors' (Van de Ven and Poole, 1995). These are teleological, dialectic, evolutionary and life-cycle process theory. A teleological process builds on the assumption that human beings are purposeful and able to make strategic choices. Dialectic process theory explains change in terms of internal and external oppositions. Change is propelled by tensions between revolutionary and evolutionary forces. Evolutionary process theory explains cumulative changes in structural forms of populations of organizations (Carroll and Hannan, 1989; Hannan and Freeman, 1989). Theorists influenced by Darwinian evolutionism emphasize a continuous, incremental process of change while other evolutionists argue for punctuated equilibrium (Gersick, 1991). Evolutionary processes also draw on systems theory and encompass changes of a unit's traits (Nelson and Winter, 1982). Life-cycle process theory posits that progression occurs according to an immanent logic as driven by a 'genetic code'. This means that the organization in a unidirectional manner follows a number of phases, from birth and start-up through maturity to decline and death, with each phase representing a specific behavioral pattern and style of management (Adizes, 1988).

Any one process theory, referred to above, offers only a limited view of explanation of dynamic organizational life, which is why Van de Ven and Poole (1995) arrange the teleological, dialectic, evolutionary and life-cycle motors into a typology that builds on the dimensions of unit and mode. The typology classifies organizational change and development by their outcomes, proposing a scheme of logical explanations of change and development. But to gain a further appreciation of dynamic organizational life, it is important, according to Van de Ven and Poole, to develop nonlinear models that permit feedback loops among two or more single motors of change and development. However, as Langley (1999: 694) argues: 'The general and banal insight that organizational processes involve opposing forces, nonlinear relationships, and feedback loops needs fleshing out.' As I have emphasized elsewhere (Ericson, 2006), nonlinearity stems from some kind of dynamically increasing return through the enforcement of a system's processes of cumulative causation. Unidirectional causality (Bassanini and Dosi, 2001) yields deviations that amplify into complex outcomes through nonlinear self-reinforcing cycles (Weick, 1979).

Following Melin and Hellgren (1994), models that are more elaborate are needed to capture the apparent nonrational and multidimensional character of change. Through longitudinal studies of the complexity of strategic change processes in the pharmaceutical and biotechnological industries and in the consumer electronics industry, Melin and Hellgren conclude that the degree of change intensity and the degrees of voluntarism in CEOs' actions taken must be considered. By combining the evolutionary–revolutionary dichotomy with the proactive–reactive dimension, they present a typology that accounts for different kinds of revolutionary change and continuous adaptation.

To enhance further the descriptive value, based on a more comprehensive language for a description of strategic change processes, Melin and Hellgren (1994) analyzed the characteristics of different periods of longitudinal change. This resulted in a typology that binds together various epochs in the life of a company, such as the incremental type of epoch, the politicking, the visionary, the paralytic and the action type. The incremental permits actions to be taken in small steps and deals with complexity through a bounded rationality approach. The politicking refers to political activities that include power struggles. The visionary appeals to emotion, and it connects with an imaginative future, open to action outside the current strategic direction. The paralytic characterizes a period during which a company loses its freedom of strategic action. As opposed to the action type of epoch, allowing for big steps and sudden and radical strategic reorientation, the paralytic type describes a period devoid of strategic actions. A processual description of long cycles of change, marking out various types of epochs, has 'the potential for understanding how different mechanism are related to and interact with each other,' Melin and

Hellgren (1994: 268) argue. In the recognition of multiple progressing, development and change processes follow more than one single path that could be parallel, divergent or convergent. Cumulative, conjunctive or iterative progression could also occur. Cumulative progression presupposes that more than one stage belongs to a unit at a time. Elements found in earlier stages add to and provide the basis to build on in subsequent stages. Conjunctive means that there are causally related events that influence events in other paths, and progression characterized as iterative suggests repetition of activities over time (Van de Ven, 1992).

To gain an insight into longitudinal growth and change one could also employ a narrative approach as suggested in this book. It too can help in grasping the multidimensional character of growth while opening it up to emotion. As Melin and Hellgren (1994) emphasize, the rational logic is an insufficient device to understand the complexity of actions. It needs to conjoin with the emotion dimension. Even if the request for advancing our understanding of the strategic change process more recently has encouraged strategy scholars to pay attention to cross-fertilization between different streams of strategy research, there has not been much effort expended on the multidimensional character of strategic change. There is a need to provide a theoretical understanding that 'does not betray the richness, dynamism, and complexity' of strategy process, Langley (1999: 694) contends.

Hutzschenreuter and Kleindienst (2006) advocate an approach that interrelates contextual factors and dynamic organizational factors. To break new ground, they see it as important to link process to content, exploring 'best practice' for combining issue characteristics such as crisis decision and individuals' involvement in decision-making with process characteristics. From the viewpoint of Hutzschenreuter and Kleindienst, it is necessary to integrate content and process research, investigating the effects of the individuals involved in a process as well as the phase prior to and after decision-making. However, little effort is put into providing a narrative-based conception of change and pattern that accounts for human interaction and activity in a dialogically and intersubjectively grounded world. Largely unaddressed are questions regarding how strategic change in reference to growth constitutes in activities with an ontological concern for the relationship between individual and world, the past and the future, organization and environment, and actor and activity.

Dynamism linked with time–space is also largely unaddressed with regard to Bakhtin's ([1981] 2002) chronotype. In the strategic change and business growth literature, this kind of dynamism receives little attention. In strategic change research, time is often exposed in reference to path dependence, which suggests that an organization's future strategic choices are shaped linearly by the path the organization metaphorically travels over time (Booth, 2003). The dynamic capability perspective applied to strategic change emphasizes integration, building and reconfiguration of internal and external routines and resources over time (Eisenhardt and Martin, 2000; Teece, Pisano and Shuen, 1997). Drawing inspiration from evolutionary economics (Nelson and Winter, 1982), it brings in time and the irreversible characteristic of time in relation to path dependence (Ghemawat, 1991).

The polyplotted business growth narrative combines turning points and route followers that appear in different chronotypes. Although the plots, in the main, each follow a linear time logic, the plots are not reducible to the representation of linear time. Akin to path dependence, a route follower extends in time, but unlike path dependence, it assimilates time and space in a more complicated sense, not taking the organization for granted. Path dependence does not account for a space that appears narratively, intrinsically connected with time. Closely connected with turning points is the chronotype of threshold, designating a moment of crisis and a decision that changes life (Bakhtin, [1981] 2002). The business growth plots illustrate emotionally charged turning points that become part of the chronotype of threshold. In this chronotype, time is essentially experienced as instantaneous. The polyplotted business growth narrative thus brings to the fore an alternative view of time. Time is articulated through narrating (Ricoeur, 1983). It is marked by turning points and route followers in which, following Sztompka (1993), we encounter time in interactions and activities rather than interactions and activities in time. This proposes a shift in focus away from a path-dependent time, ascribed to which are deterministic and nonnarrative features.

TOWARD A NARRATIVE DYNAMIC CONCEPTUALIZATION OF BUSINESS GROWTH

A dynamic conceptualization of business growth based on a study that uses a participatory narrative approach could make a valuable complement to the existing body of growth research. It helps broaden the scope of growth inquiries, permits a closer look at growth on the intersubjective level and encourages people as learners to become aware of various aspects of growth while not forgetting about the emotional aspect. The study draws attention, not only to the bigger strategic change issues concerning the rerouting of production, merger and acquisition, brand portfolio-building and ownership, but also to details of practice entailing change, a basis on which a quite colorful and elaborate understanding of business growth can be built. It permits a closer look at growth on the intersubjective level when drawing on the bits and pieces practitioners narratively provide about the activities they engage in. Further, the study conveys the ontological notion of belongingness to a world of practice, offering a nondualistic, interrelated interpretation and understanding.

Growth activities lived by the practitioners are shown in their relationships and the situations they face and construct. The practitioners as relational selves make explicit the intersubjective and relational features of business growth. Growth is living forms of practice, originating in and developing out of an 'in-between of embodied practice' (Küpers, 2005: 118). Growth also takes place intercollectively. As revealed, companies play a significant role as interacting collective agents. The firm or company is a collective agent that serves as a point of reference in some of the practitioners' stories. From the viewpoints of the practitioners, there is often a collective agent that grows while expanding its operations and improving performance.

The business growth narrative is worked out through a heterogeneous set of voices. In the course of the interpretation and understanding, I gloss a variety of concepts grounded in both narrative and nonnarrative theory that help clarify what occurs in the practice people recount. The practitioners' stories lead me to various concepts that help capture changes as turning points and route followers with regard to time–space dynamics. As a dialogical companion to the practitioners, I go where they take me. In a continuous unending stream of activities, turning points and route followers suggest direction. Inherent in this is an accentuation of a pervasive dynamic quality of social reality, proposing a focus on fluctuating figuration rather than on rigid patterns (Sztompka, 2003). In the recognition of constant processes of change, business growth in reference to change – or rather business growing – implies difference in the direction of activities. The basic idea of change is thus 'difference' and, depending on what is seen as changing in time, various aspects of change can be highlighted, as Sztompka argues. Interconnected, these differences form fluctuating figurations, which in this study I refer to as plots.

The business growth narrative thus uses plots to interconnect dynamically the bits and pieces that are narratively communicated. On a more abstract level, such a narrative elevates the underlying narrative rationality, which conjoins calculative rationality with emotion. Narrative (relational) rationality holds a claim of truth about business growth, although different from calculative rationality but certainly not inferior to it. Emotion is not merely a mental process or a state of mind but realizes in social interaction and time in association with calculative rationality. Emotions are not self-contained and derived from the world as it 'really is' but anchored in social interaction (Brundin, 2002; Ericson, 2000; Hall, 2003; Harré, 1986; Saarni, 1999; Sjöstrand, 1997). Consistent with the participatory narrative approach is the notion of a flow of emotion (Brocklesby and Cummings, 2003), which means that emotions are constructed by relational selves (Gergen, 1999).

Language, including emotion, carries business growth, allowing practice to emerge but not in the dualistic sense of a practice separated from the practitioner. Such separation neglects the ontological standpoint concerning

narrative rationality and the belongingness to the world of practice. The practitioner lives practice (Ericson, 2007). Practice thus loses its objective representational abilities (Cummings, 2002). Since much of growth practice takes
place through language there is no need to distinguish between talk and practice as an object that exists independently of the individual. Language is a
means through which the practitioner lives and constructs reality (Gadamer,
[1960] 1989).

A story has 'a life far beyond the single occasion of its telling' (O'Connor,
2000: 177). Although tied to the time and space where their physical bodies
are, storytellers overcome the restrictions of time and space in the sense that
we can imagine different times and spaces (Lämsä and Sintonen, 2006). In the
dynamic repetition of past activities, the past gains contemporeanity with the
present (Gadamer, [1960] 1989). The actors' use of language actualizes a
notion of time that makes the past and the future extensions of the present. The
present articulates the temporal qualities of the past and the future. Through
the practitioner's narrative voice we are carried back into past time and places
through present repetition. The antenarrative pathway of narrative construction cannot warrant a chronology in time. The moves and flows take us beyond
linearity of time toward different chronotypes.

A narrative dynamic conceptualization has normative implications for the
development of knowledge about a strategic change issue such as business
growth. These are inherent in so-called surrogate experiences (Sole and
Wilson, 2002), which means that even though the reader is not directly
involved in the activities displayed, the reader could feel involved and, based
on that feeling of involvement, develop an understanding that helps guide
action.

> When one reads a novel, one often feels as if one is living the experience described
> in the novel. So too when a story is recounted, the narrative form offers the listener
> an opportunity to experience in a surrogate fashion the situation that was experi-
> enced by the storyteller. The listener can acquire an understanding of the situation's
> key concepts and their relationships in the same progressive or cumulative manner
> that the storyteller acquired that understanding (Sole and Wilson, 2002: 5).

This study could enrich both practitioners' and theorists' understanding of
growth. Not fashioned as a testable truth, the study yields an interpretative
truth that the practitioners and the researcher as *homo narrans* jointly impart
about business growth in order to promote new trains of thought (Barry and
Elmes, 1997) and new understanding. The study allows for making sense of,
learning about and in a surrogate way experiencing a variety of growth activities and their dynamic relationships with regard to turning point, route
follower, plot, narrative rationality and chronotype.

Storytelling is a fundamental feature of human life, which is why it is essential to incorporate this feature in a study of business growth, embracing the ability of a story and a narrative to attend to both the rational-calculative and the emotional dimension. By implication, the firm-level curtain is pulled back and the firm questioned as a predefined context within which activities take place and entrepreneurship is encouraged. To strengthen the dynamic character of growth, one needs to turn one's attention to a participative and dialogically structured world, training the spotlight on the narrating practitioner, as suggested in this book.

Notes

1. It should also be mentioned that the 'account' concept is closely related to story and narrative. It was developed by sociologists in the 1970s. 'Account' was employed in studies on how individuals verbally experienced unanticipated or deviant behavior. Scott and Lyman (1968: 46) define account as 'a linguistic device employed whenever an action is subjected to valuative inquiry.' Influenced by the argument put forward by Goffman (1959), that people present themselves in a self-protective manner, sociologists argued that account provides an excuse for a certain behavior. Account-making processes too were examined. These were thought to be of help when dealing with major life events and in hindering psychosomatic illness (Orbuch, 1997).

2. *Academy of Management Journal, Administrative Science Quarterly, American Sociological Review, Entrepreneurship Theory and Practice, Journal of Business Venturing, Journal of Management, Journal of Management Studies, Journal of Small Business Management, Management Science, Organization Science* and *Strategic Management Journal.*

3. I discuss dualism and its relation to duality in Ericson (2004).

4. Life-cycle models are further discussed in Ericson (2007) in reference to growing and aging, and the evolutionary imperative.

5. Formed by trust, commitment and compatibility, social capital constitutes a productive resource. Trust facilitates exchange among alliance partners. Commitment refers to the creation of a structure that constrains opportunism and makes the partner look to long-term gains, forgoing short-term losses. Compatibility depends on how well internal and external resources supplement each other and on positive synergies released between the resources (Moore, Autry and Macy, 2007).

6. To avoid repeating earlier work in the present discussion, see my study in Ericson (2007), where internationalization is related to mergers and acquisitions and to some theories of the firm's involvement in a foreign market.

7. See Chapter 1.

8. 'Premodern discourse is a mythic and nomadic journey, defending artisan craftsmanship, spirituality, family and a strong sense of community over economic rationality' (Boje, 1995: 1002).

9. See Chapter 1.
10. Scapa Bedding became a subsidiary to the Hilding Anders Group in 1999. Scapa Inter joined the Swedish competitor Temas RS Möbler.
11. Demers, Giroux and Chreim (2003) refer to the canonical schema in terms of a transformational model that incorporates the announcement of a merger and acquisition, the catalyst in the form of an opportunity, threat or project, the strategic dynamics with reference to initiating contacts, negotiating, signing contracts and implementing changes, the integration and the final state, that is, the desired strategic position.
12. See Chapter 4.
13. A collection consists of products linked to power brands or local jewels but is also endorsed by other brands (Hilding Anders, 2008a).
14. Dan Meinerts Petersen was managing director for Scandi Sleep during 2001–6. Scandi Sleep, a Danish producer founded in 1990, was brought to Hilding Anders through the merger with Apax in 1999 (*Hilding Anders News*, 2004a, No. 3).
15. In 2004 the headquarters moved from Helsingborg to Malmö (see Chapter 7).
16. The new owner is presented in Chapter 7.
17. The long-term aim is a 50–50 balance but as Pia Rasmussen says: 'If we end up with a brand share of 55%, we wouldn't, of course, regard that as negative in any way' (*Hilding Anders News*, 2004a, No. 2: 14).
18. See Chapter 6.
19. Owen Wilson left his position in 2009.
20. See Chapter 5.
21. Habitus refers to '*a modus operandi*, a predisposed style of engagement that does not presume a means–ends logic or a prior need for mental representations' (Chia, 2004: 31).
22. See Chapter 2.

References

Aaker, D.A. (1991), *Managing Brand Equity: Capitalizing on the Value of a Brand Name*, New York: Free Press.

Achtenhagen, L., L. Melin and T. Müllern (2003), 'Learning and continuous change in innovating organizations', in A. Pettigrew, R. Whittington, L. Melin, C. Sánchez-Runde, F.A.J. van den Bosch, W. Ruigrok and T. Numagami (eds), *Innovative Forms of Organizing*, London: Sage, pp. 72–94.

Adizes, I. (1988), *Corporate Lifecycles. How and Why Corporations Grow and Die and What to Do about It*, Englewood Cliffs, NJ: Prentice Hall.

Agor, W.H. (ed.) (1989), *Intuition in Organizations. Leading and Managing Productivity*, Thousand Oaks, CA: Sage.

Ahl, H. (2007), 'Sex business in the toy store: a narrative analysis of a teaching case', *Journal of Business Venturing*, **22** (5), 673–93.

Albrow, M. (1997), *Do Organizations Have Feelings?*, London: Routledge.

Alchian, A.A. and H. Demsetz (1972), 'Production, information costs, and economic organization', *American Economic Review*, **62** (5), 777–95.

AllBusiness (1998), 'Atle – together with Nordic Capital and others – forms the third largest bed manufacturer in Europe', 21 October. Retrieved 20 November 2008, from http://www.allbusiness.com/company-activities-management-structures.

AllBusiness (2007), 'Hilding Anders continues its expansion by acquiring the Croatian bedding company Perfecta', 9 May. Retrieved 13 November 2008, from http://www.allbusiness.com/services/business-services/4342048-1.html.

Allen, M. and R. Hodgkinson (1987), *Buying Business*, London: Graham and Trotman.

Allen, R.E. (ed.) (1990), *The Concise Oxford Dictionary of Current English*, Oxford: Clarendon Press.

AltAssets (2006), 'Candover acquires mattress and beds manufacturer Hilding Anders from Investcorp', 27 October. Retrieved 13 November 2008, from http://www.altassets.com/news/arc/2006/nz9620.php.

Alvesson, M. (2003), 'Beyond neopositivists, romantics, and localists: a reflexive approach to interviews in organizational research', *Academy of Management Review*, **28** (1), 13–33.

AME Info (2003), 'Investcorp to acquire Hilding Anders', 7 December. Retrieved 13 November 2008, from http://www.ameinfo.com/31950.html.

Andersson, R. and D. Reeb (2003) 'Founding family ownership and firm performance: evidence from the S&P 500', *Journal of Finance*, **58**, 1301–28.

Anselmsson, J., U. Johansson and N. Persson (2007), 'Understanding price premium for grocery products: a conceptual model of customer-based brand equity', *Journal of Product and Brand Management*, **16** (6), 401–14.

Arab News (2006), 'Investcorp sells Hilding Anders', 31 October. Retrieved 13 November 2008, from http://www.arabnews.com.

Argyris, C. and D.A. Schön (1978), *Organizational Learning*, Reading: Addison-Wesley.

Ashforth, B.E. and R.H. Humphrey (1995), 'Emotion in the workplace: a re-appraisal', *Human Relations*, **48** (2), 97–125.

Atle (1998), 'Atle forms the third largest bed manufacturer in Europe', 21 October. Retrieved 23 October 2009, from http://www.cisionwire.com/atle/atle-forms-the-third-largest-bed-manufacturer-in-europe, pp. 1–3.

Atle (1999), press release, 9 February. Retrieved 24 November 2009, from http://feed.ne.cision.com/wpyfs.

Atle (2001), 'Hilding Anders AB creates a European bed giant!', 29 March. Retrieved 5 December 2009, from http://www.cisionwirre.se/atle/hilding-anders-ab-bildar-europeisk-sangjatte.

Austin, J.L. (1962), *How to Do Things with Words*, Oxford: Clarendon Press.

Avlonitis, G.J. and H.E. Salavou (2007), 'Entrepreneurial orientation of SMEs, product innovativeness, and performance', *Journal of Business Research*, **60** (5), 566–75.

Bakhtin, M.M. ([1981] 2002), 'Forms of time and the chronotype in the novels: notes toward a historical poetics', in B. Richardson (ed.), (2002), *Narrative Dynamics, Essays on Time, Plot, Closure, and Frames*, Ohio: Ohio State University Press, pp. 15–24.

Ballantyne, D. (2004), 'Dialogue and its role in the development of relation-ship specific knowledge', *Journal of Business and Industrial Marketing*, **19** (2), 114–23.

Bamford, C.E., T.J. Dean and T.J. Douglas (2004), 'The temporal nature of growth determinants in new bank foundings: implications for new venture research design', *Journal of Business Venturing*, **19** (6), 899–919.

Barney, J. (1991), 'Firm resources and sustained competitive advantage', *Journal of Management*, **17** (1), 99–120.

Barr, P., S.J.L. Stimpert and A.S. Huff (1992), 'Cognitive change, strategic action and organizational renewal', *Strategic Management Journal*, **13**, 15–25.

Barry, D. and M. Elmes (1997), 'Strategy retold: toward a narrative view of strategic discourse', *Academy of Management Review*, **22** (2), 429–52.

Bartlett, C.A. and S. Ghoshal (1991), *Managing across Borders. The Transnational Solution*, Boston: Harvard Business School Press.

Bassanini, A. and G. Dosi (2001), 'When and how chance and human will can twist the arms of Clio: an essay of path-dependence in a world of irreversibilities', in R. Garud and P. Karnøe (eds), *Path Dependence and Creation*, Mahwah: Lawrence Erlbaum, pp. 41–68.

Bateman, T.S. and J.M. Crant (1993), 'The proactive component of organizational behavior: a measure and correlates', *Journal of Organization Behaviour*, **14**, 103–18.

Baumol, W. (1959), *Business Behavior, Value and Growth*, New York: Harcourt, Brace & World.

BedTimes Bulletin (2007), 'Hilding Anders takes majority in Asia firm', January. Retrieved 13 November 2008, from http://www.sleepproducts.org/Template.cfm, pp.1–3.

Begley, T.M. and D.P. Boyd (1987), 'Psychological characteristics associated with performance in entrepreneurial firms and smaller businesses', *Journal of Business Venturing*, **2**, 79–93.

Berg, P.-O. (1979), *Emotional Structures in Organizations*, Lund: Studentlitteratur.

Berger, L.P. and T. Luckmann (1966), *The Social Construction of Reality*, Harmondsworth: Penguin.

Bergh, D.D. (1997), 'Predicting divestiture of unrelated acquisitions: an integrative model of *ex ante* conditions', *Strategic Management Journal*, **18** (9), 715–34.

Berglund, K. (2007), *Jakten på entreprenörer. Om öppningar och låsningar i Entreprenörskapsdiskursen*, Västerås: School of Business, Mälardalen University.

Bernstein, R.J. (1983), *Beyond Objectivism and Relativism: Science, Hermeneutics, and Praxis*, Philadelphia: University of Pennsylvania Press.

Bertrand, M. and A. Schoar (2006), 'The role of family in family firms', *Journal of Economic Perspective*, **20**, 73–96.

Beveridge, W.E. (1980), 'Retirement and life significance: a study of the adjustment to retirement of a sample of men at management level', *Human Relations*, **33** (1), 69–78.

Bico (2008), 'Bico – a company with a history'. Retrieved 20 November 2008, from http://www.bico.ch/en/documents/index/pressrelease.pdf.

Blombäck. A. (2005), *Supplier Brand Image – A Catalyst for Choice. Expanding the B2B Discourse by Studying the Role Corporate Brand Image Plays in the Selection of Subcontractors*, Jönköping: Jönköping International Business School.

Boeker, W. (1997), 'Strategic change: the influence of managerial characteristics and organizational growth', *Academy of Management Journal*, **40** (1), 152–70.

Boje, D.M. (1991), 'The storytelling organization: a study of story performance', *Administrative Science Quarterly*, **36** (1), 106–28.

Boje, D.M. (1995), 'Stories of the storytelling organization: a postmodern analysis of Disney as "Tamara-Land"', *Academy of Management Journal*, **38** (4), 997–1035.

Boje, D.M. (2000), 'Narrative methods for organizational and communication research'. Retrieved 19 May 2009, from http://cbae.nmsu.edu.

Boje, D.M., J.T. Luhman and D.E. Baack (1999), 'Stories and encounters between storytelling organizations', *Journal of Management Inquiry*, **8** (4), 340–60.

Boland, R.J. Jr (1984), 'Sense-making of accounting data as a technique of organizational diagnosis', *Management Science*, **30**, 868–82.

Bollen, B. (2007), 'Anders Hilding goes to the mattresses'. Retrieved 13 November 2008, from http://www.brianbollen.com.

Booth, C. (2003), 'Does history matter in strategy? The possibilities and problem of counterfactual analysis', *Management Decision*, **4** (1), 96–104.

Bowles, M.L. (1989), 'Myth, meaning and work organization', *Organization Studies*, **10** (3), 405–21.

Boyce, M.E. (1995), 'Collective centring and collective sense-making in the stories and storytelling of one organization', *Organization Studies*, **16** (1), 107–37.

Boyce, M.E. (1996), 'Organizational story and storytelling: a critical review', *Journal of Organizational Change Management*, **9** (5), 5–26.

Bradely, J.W. and D.H. Korn (1984), 'The changing role of acquisition', *Journal of Business Strategy*, **12** (4), 30–42.

Bratnicki, M. (2005), 'Organizational entrepreneurship: theoretical background, some empirical tests, and directions for future research', *Human Factors and Ergonomics in Manufacturing*, **15** (1), 15–33.

Brocklesby, J. and S. Cummings (2003), 'Strategy as systems thinking', in S. Cummings and D. Wilson (eds), *Images of Strategy*, Oxford: Blackwell, pp. 266–300.

Brown, A.D., M. Humphreys and P.M. Gurney (2005), 'Narrative, identity and change: a case study of Laskarina Holidays', *Journal of Organizational Management*, **18** (4), 312–26.

Brown, A.D., P. Stacey and J. Nadhakumar (2008), 'Making sense of sense-making narratives', *Human Relations*, **61** (8), 1035–62.

Brundin, E. (2002), *Emotions in Motion. The Strategic Leader in a Radical Change Process*, Jönköping: Jönköping International Business School.

Brundin, E., H. Patzelt and D.A. Shepherd (2007), 'Managers' emotional displays and employees' willingness to act entrepreneurially', *Journal of Business Venturing*, **23** (2), 221–43.

Bruner, J. (1990), *Acts of Meaning*, Cambridge, MA: Harvard University Press.

Brush, C.G., T.S. Manolova and L.F. Edelman (2008), 'Separated by a common language? Entrepreneurship research across the Atlantic', *Entrepreneurship Theory and Practice*, **32** (2), 249–66.

Buchanan, D. and P. Dawson (2007), 'Discourse and audience: organizational change as multi-story process', *Journal of Management Studies*, **44** (5), 669–86.

Buono, A.F. and J.L. Bowditch (1989), *The Human Side of Mergers and Acquisitions*, San Francisco: Jossey-Bass.

Burgelman, R.A. (1983), 'A process model of internal corporate venturing in the diversified major firm', *Administrative Science Quarterly*, **28**, 223–44.

Business Wire (2007a), 'Hilding Anders enhances its board of directors in connection to change in ownership', 8 January. Retrieved 17 February 2007, from http://www.findarticles.com/p/articles/mi_m0EIN/is_2007_Jan_8/ai_n17095742, pp. 1–3.

Business Wire (2007b), 'Hilding Anders makes an historical acquisition by acquiring Myer's, one of UK's leading bedding companies', 6 August. Retrieved 13 November 2008, from http://www.findarticles.com./p/articles/mi_m0EIN/is_/ai_n19396094, pp. 3–4.

Bygrave, W. and M. Minniti (2000), 'The social dynamics of entrepreneurship', *Entrepreneurship Theory and Practice*, **24** (3), 25–36.

Calori, R. (1998), '*Essai*: philosophizing on strategic management models', *Organization Studies*, **19** (2), 281–306.

Campbell, A. and K.S. Luchs (1998), *Strategic Synergy*, London: International Thomson Business Press.

Candover (2008), 'The company'. Retrieved 13 November 2008, from http://www.candover.com/english/about-candover/the-company, pp.1-2.

Cardel Gertsen, M.C., A.-M. Søderberg and J.E. Torp (eds) (1998), *Cultural Dimensions of International Mergers and Acquisitions*, Berlin: Walter de Gruyter.

Carlotti, S.J. Jr., M.E. Coe and J. Perrey (2004), 'Making brand portfolios work', *McKinsey Quarterly*, November, 1–8.

Carr, A. (2001), 'Understanding emotion and emotionality in a process of change', *Journal of Organization Change Management*, **14** (5), 421–34.

Carroll, G.R. and M.T. Hannan (1989), 'Density dependence in the evaluation of populations of newspaper organizations', *American Sociological Review*, **54**, 524–41.

Carson, A.M. (2001), 'That's another story: narrative methods and ethical practice', *Journal of Medical Ethics*, **27**, 198–202.

Cartwright, S. and C.L. Cooper (1990), 'The impact of mergers and acquisitions on people at work: existing research and issues', *British Journal of Management*, **1**, 65–76.

Cartwright, S. and C.L. Cooper (1996), *Managing Mergers Acquisitions &*

Strategic Alliances: Integrating People and Cultures, Oxford: Butterworth-Heinemann.

Case No IV/M.1357 – Nordic Capital/Hilding Anders, 2 April 1999, Luxemburg: Office for Official Publications of the European Communities L-2985.

Case No COMP/M.3315 – Investcorp Group/Hilding Anders AB, 17 December 2003, Luxemburg: Office for Official Publications of the European Communities L-2985.

Case No COMP/M.4468 – Candover Partners/Hilding Anders, 22 November 2006, *Official Journal of the European Union*.

Case No IV/M.1026 – Nordic Capital/Apax Industri, 06 November 1997, *Offical Journal of the European Union*.

Casson. M. (1982), *The Entrepreneur*, Oxford: Martin Robertson.

Chailan, C. (2008), 'Brands portfolios and competitive advantage: an empirical study', *Journal of Product & Brand Management*, **17** (4), 254–64.

Chakravarthy, B. and R.E. White (2002), 'Strategy process: forming, implementing and changing strategies', in A.M. Pettigrew, H. Thomas and R. Whittington (eds), *Handbook of Strategy and Management*, London: Sage, pp.182–205.

Chandler, G.N. and S.H. Hanks (1994), 'Market attractiveness, resource-based capabilities, venture strategies and venture performance', *Journal of Business Venturing*, **9** (4), 331–49.

Chatterjee, S. (1986), 'Types of synergy and economic value: the impact of acquisitions on merging and rival firms', *Strategic Management Journal*, **7** (2), 119–39.

Chell, E. (2000), 'Toward researching the "opportunistic entrepreneur": a social constructionist approach and research agenda', *European Journal of Work and Organizational Psychology*, **9** (1), 63–80.

Chia, R. (2004), 'Strategy-as-practice: reflections on the research agenda', *European Management Review*, **1**, 29–34.

Chia, R. and R. Holt (2006), 'Strategy as practical coping: a Heideggerian perspective', *Organization Studies*, **27** (5), 635–55.

Cho, H.-J. and V. Pucik (2005), 'Relationship between innovativeness, quality, growth, profitability, and market value', *Strategic Management Journal*, **26** (6), 555–75.

Choi, Y.R., M. Lévesque and D.A. Shepherd (2007), 'When should entrepreneurs expedite or delay opportunity exploitation?', *Journal of Business Venturing*, **23** (3), 333–55.

Christopher, M. (1996), 'From brand values to customer value', *Journal of Marketing Practice: Applied Marketing Science*, **2** (1), 55–66.

Churchill, N.C. and V.L. Lewis (1983), 'The five stages of small business growth', *Harvard Business Review*, May–June, 2–11.

Claver, E., R. Andreu and D. Quer (2006), 'Growth strategies in the Spanish hotel sector: determining factors', *International Journal of Contemporary Hospitality*, **18** (3), 188–205.

Covin, J.G. and D.P. Slevin (1991), 'A conceptual model of entrepreneurship as firm behavior', *Entrepreneurship Theory and Practice*, **16** (1), 7–25.

Crites, S. (1986), 'Storytime: recollecting the past and projecting the future', in T.R. Sarbin (ed.), *Narrative Psychology: The Storied Nature of Human Conduct*, New York: Praeger, pp. 152–73.

Crotty, M. (2003), *The Foundations of Social Research. Meaning and Perspective in the Research Process*, London: Sage.

Crown Bedding (2008), 'Crown bedding'. Retrieved 19 November 2008, from http://www.crownbedding.be/ENG/AboutUs.htm, pp. 1–2.

Cummings, S. (2002), *Recreating Strategy*, London: Sage.

Cummings, S. (2003), 'Strategy as ethos', in S. Cummings and D. Wilson (eds), *Images of Strategy*, Oxford: Blackwell, pp. 41–73.

Curran, J. and R. Blackburn (2001), *Researching the Small Enterprise*, London: Sage.

Cyert, R.M. and J.G. March (1963), *A Behavioral Theory of the Firm*, Englewood Cliffs, NJ: Prentice-Hall.

Czarniawska, B. (1997), *Narrating the Organization*, Chicago: University of Chicago Press.

Czarniawska, B. (2002), *A Tale of Three Cities or the Glocalizaton of City Management*, Oxford: Oxford University Press.

Czarniawska, B. (2004), *Narratives in Social Science Research*, London: Sage.

Czarniawska-Joerges, B. and R. Wolff (1991), 'Leaders, managers, entrepreneurs on and off the organizational stage', *Organization Studies*, **12** (4), 529–46.

Dagens Industri (2002), 'Daily economic journal', 6 August.

Dahlgren, G. and P. Witt (1988), *Ledning av fusionsförlopp*, Stockholm: EFI, Stockholm School of Economics.

Dale, A. (1991), 'Self-employment and entrepreneurship: notes on two problematic concepts', in R. Burrows (ed.), *Deciphering the Enterprise Culture. Entrepreneurship, Petty Capitalism and the Restructuring of Britain*, London: Routledge, pp. 35–52.

Damasio, A. (1994), *Descartes' Error: Emotion, Reason and the Human Brain*, New York: Avon Books.

Dandridge, T.C., I. Mitroff and W.F. Joyce (1980), 'Organizational symbolism: A topic to expand organizational analysis', *Academy of Management Review*, January, 77–82.

Darling, J.R. and T.J. Kash (1998), 'Developing small business operations in foreign markets: foundation-building strategies for steady growth and profitability', *European Business Review*, **98** (3), 151–9.

Datta, D.K. (1991), 'Organizational fit and acquisition performance: effects of post-acquisition integration', *Strategic Management Journal*, **12** (4), 281–97.

Davidsson, P. (1991), 'Continued entrepreneurship: ability, need, and opportunity as determinants of small firm growth', *Journal of Business Venturing*, **6**, 405–29.

Davidsson, P., M.B. Low and M. Wright (2001), 'Editor's introduction: Low and MacMillan ten years on: achievements and future directions for entrepreneurship research', *Entrepreneurship Theory and Practice*, **25** (4), 5–15.

Davis, J.A. and R. Tagiuri (1989), 'The influence of life stage on father-son work relationships in family companies', *Family Business Review*, **2** (1), 47–74.

Davis, P.S. and P.D. Harveston (2000), 'Internationalization and organzational growth: the impact of internet usage and technology involvement among entrepreneur-led family business', *Family Business Review*, **13** (2), 107–20.

Dawar, N. (2004), 'What are brands good for?', *MIT Sloan Management Review*, **46** (1), 31–7.

Dean, T.J., R.L. Brown and C.E. Bamford (1998), 'Differences in large and small firm responses to environmental context: strategic implications from a comparative analysis of business formations', *Strategic Management Journal*, **19** (8), 709–28.

Delgado-Ballester, E. and J.L. Munuera-Alemán (2005), 'Does brand trust matter to brand equity?', *Journal of Product and Brand Management*, **14** (3), 187–96.

Delmar, F. (2000), 'Innovation, growth and entrepreneurship', in B. Green (ed.), *Risk Behaviour and Risk Management in Business Life*, Dordrecht: Kluwer Academic Publishers, pp. 197–213.

Delmar, F., P. Davidsson and W.B. Gartner (2003), 'Arriving at the high-growth firm', *Journal of Business Venturing*, **18**, 189–216.

Demers, C., N. Giroux and S. Chreim (2003), 'Merger and acquisition announcements as corporate wedding narratives', *Journal of Organizational Change Management*, **16** (2), 223–42.

Dennett, D.C. (1992), 'The self as a center of narrative gravity', in F.S. Kessler, P.M. Cole and D.L. Johnson (eds), *Self and Consciousness: Multiple Perspectives*, Hillsdale, NJ: Lawrence Erlbaum, pp. 103–15.

Denning, S. (2002), 'Using stories to spark organizational change', *Journal of Storytelling and Business Excellence*, February, 1–10.

Dennis, D. and J. McConnell (1985), 'Corporate mergers and security returns', *Journal of Financial Economics*, **16**, 143–87.

Descartes, R. ([1637] 1968), *Discourse on Method and the Meditations*, London: Penguin Books.

Dobbs, M. and R.T. Hamilton (2007), 'Small business growth: recent evidence and new directions', *International Journal of Entrepreneurial Behaviour and Research*, **13** (5), 296–322.

Dodgson, M. (1991), 'Technology learning, technology strategy and competitive pressures', *British Journal of Management*, **2** (3), 133–49.

Domagalski, T.A. (1999), 'Emotion in organizations: main currents', *Human Relations*, **52** (6), 833–52.

Dougherty, D. (2004), 'Organizing practices in services: capturing practice-based knowledge for innovation', *Strategic Organization*, **2** (1), 35–64.

Downing, S. (2005), 'The social construction of entrepreneurship: narrative and dramatic processes in the coproduction of organizations and identities', *Entrepreneurship Theory and Practice*, **29** (2), 185–204.

Doyle, P. (1997), 'The three R's of growth strategies: radical, rational or robust', *Antidote Issue*, **4**, 29–30.

Dumas, C. (1989), 'Understanding of father–daughter and father–son dyads in family-owned businesses', *Family Business Review*, **2** (1), 31–46.

Dunlopillo (2008), 'About us'. Retrieved 14 November 2008, from http://www.dunlopillo.co.uk/about/.

Dutta, D.K. and S. Thornhill (2007, 'The evolution of growth intentions: toward a cognition-based model', *Journal of Business Venturing*, **23** (3), 307–32.

Eastborn Marine (2009), 'History'. Retrieved 18 February 2009, from http://www.eastbornmarine.com/history.htm.

Easterby-Smith, M. (1997), 'Disciplines of organizational learning: contributions and critiques', *Human Relations*, **50** (9), 1085–113.

Eisenhardt, K.M. and J.A. Martin (2000), 'Dynamic capabilities: what are they?', *Strategic Management Journal*, **21** (10/11), 1105–21.

Ekens (2008), 'Hilding brands'. Retrieved 30 November 2008, from http://www.hildinganders.se/media/hilding_brands.swf.

Ellis, R., B. Gates and N. Kenworthy (2003), *Interpersonal Communication in Nursing. Theory and Practice*, Oxford: Churchill Livingstone.

Ericson, M. (1991), *Iggesundsaffären. Rationaliteter i en strategisk förvärvsprocess*, Stockholm: EFI, Stockholm School of Economics.

Ericson, M. (2000), *Strategi, kalkyl, känsla*, Stockholm: EFI, Stockholm School of Economics.

Ericson, M. (2004), *Strategic Change – Dualism, Duality, and Beyond*, Malmö and Copenhagen: Liber and Copenhagen Business School Press.

Ericson, M. (2006), 'Exploring the future exploiting the past', *Journal of Management History*, **12** (2), 121–36.

Ericson, M. (2007), *Business Growth: Activities, Themes and Voices*, Cheltenham, UK and Northampton, MA, USA: Edward Elgar.

Erramilli, M.K., S. Agarwal and C.S. Dev (2002), 'Choice between non-equity entry modes: an organizational capability perspective', *Journal of International Business Studies*, **33** (2), 223–42.

Feldman, M.S., K. Sköldberg, R.N. Brown and D. Horner (2004), 'Making sense of stories: a rhetorical approach to narrative analysis', *Journal of Public Administration Research and Theory*, **14** (2), 147–70.

Fichtner, B. (1999), 'Activity revisited as an explanatory principle and as an object of study – old limits and new perspectives', in S. Chaiklin, M. Hedegaard and U.J. Jensen (eds), *Activity Theory and Social Practice*, Aarhus: Aarhus University Press, pp. 51–65.

Findlay, M.C. and G.A. Whitmore (1974), 'Beyond shareholder wealth maximization', *Financial Management*, Winter, 25–35.

Fineman, S. (ed.) (2008), *The Emotional Organization – Passions and Power*, Malden, MA: Blackwell.

Fischer, E. and A.R. Reuber (2003), 'Support for rapid-growth firms: a comparison of the views of founders, government policymakers, and private sector resource providers', *Journal of Small Business Management*, **41** (4), 346–65.

Fisher, W.R. (1985), 'The narrative paradigm: in the beginning', *Journal of Communication*, **35** (4), 73–89.

Fisher, W.R. (1989), *Human Communication as Narration: Toward a Philosophy of Reason, Value, and Action*, Columbia, SC: University of South Carolina Press.

Fletcher, D. (2007), 'Toy story: the narrative world of entrepreneurship and the creation of interpretative communities', *Journal of Business Venturing*, **22** (5), 649–72.

Frank, H. and M. Lueger (1998), 'Reconstructing development processes', *International Studies of Management & Organization*, **27** (3), 34–63.

Gadamer, H.-G. ([1960] 1989), *Wahrheit und Methode*, reprinted in J. Weinsheimer and D.G. Marshall (eds) (1989), *Truth and Method*, New York: Continuum.

Gadow, S. (1999), 'Relational narrative. The postmodern turn in nursing ethics', *Scholarly Inquiry for Nursing Practice. An International Journal*, **13** (1), 57–70.

Gartner, W.B. (2001), 'Is there an elephant in entrepreneurship? Blind assumptions in theory development', *Entrepreneurship Theory and Practice*, Summer, 27–39.

Gergen, K.J. (1999), *An Invitation to Social Construction*, Thousand Oaks, CA: Sage.

Geroski, P.A. (1999), 'The growth of firms in theory and in practice', discussion paper 2092, London: Center for Economic Policy Research.

Gersick, C.J. (1991), 'Revolutionary change theories: a multilevel exploration of the punctuated equilibrium paradigm', *Academy of Management Review*, **16** (1), 10–36.

Gersick, K.E., J.A. Davis, M. McCollom Hampton and I. Landsberg (1997), *Generation to Generation. Life Cycles of the Family Business*, Boston, MA: Harvard Business School Press.

Ghemawat, P. (1991), *Commitment: The Dynamic of Strategy*, New York: Free Press.

Ghoshal, S., M. Hahn and P. Moran (1997), 'An integrative theory of firm growth implications for corporate organization and management', working paper 87, Fontainebleau, Paris: INSEAD.

Gibb, A. and L. Davies (1990), 'In pursuit of frameworks for the development of growth models of the small business', *International Small Business Journal*, **9** (1), 15–31.

Giddens, A. (1979), *Central Problems in Social Theory. Action, Structure and Contradiction in Social Analysis*, London: Macmillan.

Gioia, D.A. and K. Chittipeddi (1991), 'Sensemaking and sensegiving in strategic initiation', *Strategic Management Journal*, **12**, 433–48.

Glaser, B.G. and A.L. Strauss (1967), *The Discovery of Grounded Theory: Strategies for Qualitative Research*, Chicago: Aldine.

Glete, J. (1988), 'Long-term firm growth and ownership organizations – a study of business histories', occasional paper 8, Stockholm: SNS.

Goddard, J., M. Tavakoli and J.O.S. Wilson (2009), 'Sources of variation in firm profitability and growth', *Journal of Business Research*, **62**, 495–508.

Goffman, E. (1959), *The Presentation of Self in Everyday Life*, Garden City, NJ: Doubleday-Anchor.

Golann, B. (2006), 'Achieving growth and responsiveness: process management and market orientation in small firms', *Journal of Small Business Management*, **44** (3), 369–85.

Grant, R.M. (1991), 'The resource-based theory of competitive advantage: implications for strategy formulation', *California Management Review*, Spring, 114–35.

Gregory, B.T., M.W. Rutherford, S. Oswald and L. Gardiner (2005), 'An empirical investigation of the growth cycle theory of small firm financing', *Journal of Small Business Management*, **43** (4), 382–92.

Greiner, L.E. (1972), 'Evolution and revolution as organizations grow', *Harvard Business Review*, July–August, 37–46.

Greiner, L.E. (1998), 'Evolution and revolution as organizations grow', *Harvard Business Review*, May–June, 55–67.

Guillet de Monthoux, P. (1980), *Doktor Kant och den oekonomiska rationaliseringen*, Gothenburg: Korpen.

Guth, W.E. and A. Ginsburg (1990), 'Guest editors' introduction: corporate entrepreneurship', *Strategic Management Journal*, **11** (4), 5–15.

Hall, A. (2003), *Strategising in the Context of Genuine Relations. An Interpretative Study of Strategic Renewal through Family Interaction*, Jönköping: Jönköping International Business School.

Hall, P. and D. Kyriazis (1997), 'Wealth creation and bid resistance in UK takeover bids', *Strategic Management Journal*, **18** (6), 483–98.

Hannan, M.T. and J. Freeman (1989), *Organizational Ecology*, New Haven, CT: Harvard University Press.

Hardy, B. (1968), 'Towards a poetics of fiction. An approach through narrative', *Novel*, **2**, 5–14.

Harper, S.C. (1989), 'Intuition: what separates executives from managers', in W.H. Agor (ed.), *Intuition in Organizations. Leading and Managing Productivity*, Thousand Oaks, CA: Sage.

Harré, R. (ed.) (1986), *The Social Construction of Emotions*, New York: Basil Blackwell.

Harrington, L.J. (2007), 'Leveraging emotions in value management of brands and products', in C. Hartel and N. Ashkanasy (eds), *Functionality, Intentionality and Morality. Research on Emotion in Organizations*, Volume 3, Oxford: JAI Press, pp. 121–40.

Hart, P.E. (1998), 'Theories of firms' growth and the generation of jobs', discussion papers in economics and management 11, Reading: Reading University.

Haspeslagh, P. and D. Jemison (1987), 'Acquisitions – myths and reality', *Sloan Management Review*, Winter, 53–8.

Haspeslagh, P. and D. Jemison (1991), *Creating Value through Corporate Renewal*, New York: Free Press.

Hellgren, B. and L. Melin (1993), 'The role of strategists' ways-of-thinking in strategic change processes', in J. Hendry, G. Johnson and J. Newton (eds), *The Strategic Management Society*, Chichester: John Wiley, pp. 47–68.

Helms, M. and T.W. Renfrow (1994), 'Expansionary processes of the small business: a life-cycle profile', *Management Decision*, **32** (9), 43–5.

Herman, D. (ed.) (2003), *Narrative Theory and the Cognitive Sciences*, USA: CSLI Publication, Leland Stanford Junior University.

Herman, V. (1995), *Dramatic Discourse Dialogue as Interaction in Plays*, London: Routledge.

Hilding Anders (2003a), press release, 8 September. Retrieved 10 February 2009, from http://www.hildinganders.se/pressPressreleases.asp.

Hilding Anders (2003b), press release, 24 November. Retrieved 2 February 2009, from http://www.hildinganders.se/pressPressreleases.asp.

Hilding Anders News (2004a), Nos 1, 2 and 3, 2004.

Hilding Anders (2004b), press release, 16 April. Retrieved 10 February 2009, from http://www.hildinganders.se/pressPressreleases.asp.

Hilding Anders (2004c), group presentation, Malmö: Hilding Anders International AB.

Hilding Anders (2006a), board. Retrieved 18 September 2006, from http://www.hildinganders.se/companyBoard.asp.

Hilding Anders (2006b), press release, 15 November. Retrieved 10 February 2009, from http://www.hildinganders.se/pressPressreleases.asp.

Hilding Anders (2007a), press release, 8 January. Retrieved 10 February 2009, from http://www.hildinganders.se/pressPressreleases.asp.

Hilding Anders (2007b), press release, 18 January. Retrieved 29 January 2007, from http://www.hildinganders.se/pressPressreleases.asp.

Hilding Anders (2007c), press release, 9 May. Retrieved 10 February 2009, from http://www.hildinganders.se/pressPressreleases.asp.

Hilding Anders (2007d), press release, 1 June. Retrieved 10 February 2009, from http://www.hildinganders.se/pressPressreleases.asp.

Hilding Anders (2007e), press release, 4 July. Retrieved 14 November 2008, from http://www.hildinganders.se/pressPressreleases.asp.

Hilding Anders (2007f), press release, 7 November. Retrieved 10 February 2009, from http://www.hildinganders.se/pressPressreleases.asp.

Hilding Anders (2008a), brand architecture. Retrieved 13 November 2008, from http://www. hildinganders.se/companyBrandArchitecture.asp.

Hilding Anders (2008b), brands. Retrieved 20 November 2008, from http://www.hildinganders.se/media/hilding_brands.swf.

Hilding Anders (2008c), business concept. Retrieved 13 November 2008, from http://www.hildinganders.se/companyBusinessConcept.asp.

Hilding Anders (2008d), message from the CEO. Retrieved 13 November 2008, from http://www.hildinganders.se/companyCEO.asp.

Hilding Anders (2008e), press release, 8 January. Retrieved 10 February 2008, from http://www.hildinganders.se/pressPressreleases.asp.

Hilding Anders (2008f), press release, 11 March. Retrieved 22 June 2008, from http://www.hildinganders.se/pressPressreleases.asp.

Hilding Anders (2008g), press release, 27 June. Retrieved 13 November 2008, from http://www.hilding anders.se/pressreleases.asp.

Hilding Anders (2008h), press release, 8 October. Retrieved 13 November 2008, from http://www.hilding anders.se/pressreleases.asp.

Hilding Anders (2008i), press release, 24 November. Retrieved 10 February 2009, from http://www.hilding anders.se/pressreleases.asp.

Hilding Anders (2009a), history. Retrieved 10 June 2009, from http://www.hildinganders.se/companyHistory.asp.

Hilding Anders (2009b), organization. Retrieved 6 November 2009, from http://www.hildinganders.se/companyOrganization.asp.

Hilding Anders (2009c), overview. Retrieved 6 November 2009, from http://www.hildinganders.se/financialInfoOverview.asp.

Hilding Anders (2009d), press release, 19 November. Retrieved 9 January 2010, from http://www.hildinganders.se/pressreleases.asp.

Hilding Anders (2010a), brand vision. Retrieved 9 January 2010, from http://www.hildinganders.se/companyBrandVision.asp.

Hilding Anders (2010b), product development policy. Retrieved 9 January 2010, from http://www.hildinganders.se/companyPolicies.asp.

Hjorth, D. (2007), 'Lessons from Iago: narrating the event of entrepreneurship', *Journal of Business Venturing*, **22** (5), 712–32.

Hjorth, D. and B. Johannisson (2000), 'Entreprenörskap som skapelseprocess och ideologi', in B. Czarnaiwska (ed.), *Organisationsteori på svenska*, Malmö: Liber Ekonomi, pp. 86–104.

Hobbs, D. (1991), 'Business as a master metaphor: working class entrepreneurship and business-like policing', in R. Burrows (ed.), *Deciphering the Enterprise Culture. Entrepreneurship, Petty Capitalism and the Restructuring of Britain*, London: Routledge, pp. 107–25.

Hummel, R.P. (1991), 'Stories managers tell: why they are as valid as science', *Public Administration Review*, **51** (1), 31–41.

Hunt, J.W. (1990), 'Changing pattern of acquisition behavior in takeovers and the consequences for acquisition processes', *Strategic Management Journal*, **13**, 69–77.

Hutzschenreuter, T. and I. Kleindienst (2006), 'Strategy-process research: what have we learned and what is still to be explored', *Journal of Management*, October, 673–720.

IDS (2006), press release, 14 November. Retrieved 10 February 2009, from www.idsgroup.com.

Ingersoll, V.H. and G.B. Adams (1986), 'Beyond organizational boundaries. Exploring the managerial myth', *Administration and Society*, **18** (3), 360–81.

Invest in Sweden Agency (2006), 'Candover to fund Hilding Anders expansion', 8 November. Retrieved 13 November 2008, from http://www.isa.se/templatres/News_55950.aspx.

Investcorp (2003a), 24 November 2003, 'Private equity'. Retrieved 13 November 2008, from http://www.investcorp.com/Template1a.aspx?pageid=OB2.0.

Investcorp (2003b), message from the CEO. Retrieved 13 November 2008, from http://www.investcorp.com.

Investcorp (2008), message from the CEO. Retrieved 13 November 2008, from http://www.investcorp.com.

investigate, 26 October 2006, 'Candover investments (CDI)'. Retrieved 13 November 2008, from http://www.investigate.co.uk/Article.aspx.

Isaacs, K.S. (1998), *Uses of Emotion: Nature's Vital Gift*, New York: Praeger.

Jarzabkowski, P. (2003), 'Strategic practices: an activity theory perspective on continuity and change', *Journal of Management Studies*, **40** (1), 22–55.

Jarzabkowski, P. and D.C. Wilson (2002), 'Top teams and strategy in a UK university', *Journal of Management Studies*, **40** (1), 23–55.

Jemison, D. and S. Sitkin (1986), 'Acquisitions: the process can be a problem', *Harvard Business Review*, **64** (2), 107–16.

Jennings, D.F. and J.L. Lumpkin (1989), 'Functionally modeling corporate entrepreneurship: an empirical integrative analysis', *Journal of Management*, **15** (3), 485–503.

Jensen, M.C. and W.H. Meckling (1976), 'Theory of the firm, managerial behavior, agency costs and ownership structure', *Journal of Financial Economics*, **3**, 305–60.

Jiang, P. (2004), 'The role of brand name in customization decisions: a search vs experience perspective', *Journal of Product and Brand Management*, **13** (2), 73–83.

Johanson, J. and L.-G. Mattsson (1988), 'Internationalization in industrial systems – a network approach', in N. Hood and J.-E. Vahlne (eds), *Strategies in Global Competition*, New York: Croom Helm, pp. 287–314.

Johanson, J. and J.-E. Vahlne (1977), 'The internationalization process of the firm: a model of knowledge development and increasing foreign market commitments', *Journal of International Business Studies*, **8** (1), 23–32.

Johanson, J. and F. Wiedersheim-Paul (1975), 'The internationalization of the firm – four Swedish cases', *Journal of Management Studies*, **12** (3), 305–22.

Johnson, G. (1987), *Strategic Change and the Management Process*, Oxford: Blackwell.

Johnson, G., L. Melin and R. Whittington (2003), 'Micro strategy and strate-gizing: towards an activity-based view', *Journal of Management Studies*, **40** (1), 3–22.

Keller, K.L. (1993), 'Conceptualizing, measuring, and managing customer-based brand equity', *Journal of Marketing*, **57** (1), 1–22.

Keller, K.L. (2002), *Branding and Brand Equity*, Cambridge, MA: Marketing Science Institute.

Kim, W.C. and R. Mauborgne, (1997), 'Value innovation: the strategic logic of high growth', *Harvard Business Review*, January–February, 103–12.

King, C.S. (2000), 'Talking beyond the rational', *American Review of Public Administration*, **30** (3), 271–91.

King, S.W., G.T. Solomon and L.W. Fernald Jr (2001), 'Issues in growing a family business: a strategic human resource model', *Journal of Small Business Management*, **39** (1), 3–13.

Kirzner, L.M. (1973), *Competition and Entrepreneurship*, Chicago: University of Chicago Press.

Kitching, J. (1967), 'Why do mergers miscarry?', *Harvard Business Review*, November–December, 84–101.

Knights, D. (1997), 'Organization theory in the age of deconstruction: dual-ism, gender and postmodernism revisited', *Organization Studies*, **18** (1), 1–19.

Kumar, S. and K. Hansted Blowqvist (2004), 'Mergers and acquisitions:

making brand equity a key factior in m&a decision-making', *Strategy and Leadership*, **32** (2), 20–7.

Küpers, W. (2005), 'Phenomenology of embodied implicit and narrative knowing', *Journal of Knowledge Management*, **9** (6), 114–33.

Lämsä, A.-M. and T. Sintonen (2006), 'A narrative approach for organizational learning in a diverse organisation', *Journal of Workplace Learning*, **18** (2), 106–20.

Langer, S.K. (1967), *Mind: An Essay on Human Feeling*, Baltimore, MD: Johns Hopkins University Press.

Langley, A. (1999), 'Strategies for theorizing from process data', *Academy of Management Review*, **24** (4), 691–710.

Lant, T.K., F.J. Milliken and B. Batra (1992), 'The role of managerial learning and interpretation in strategic persistence and reorientation – an empirical exploration', *Strategic Management Journal*, **13**, 585–608.

Larsson, R. and A. Risberg (1998), 'Cultural awareness and national versus corporate barriers to acculturation', in M.C. Cardel Gertsen, A-M. Søderberg and J.E. Torp (eds), *Cultural Dimensions of International Mergers and Acquisitions*, Berlin: Walter de Gruyter, pp. 39–56.

Le Breton-Miller, I. and D. Miller (2008), 'To grow or to harvest? Governance, strategy and performance in family and lone founder firms', *Journal of Strategy and Management*, **1** (1), 41–56.

Leitch, S. and S. Davenport (2005). 'The politics of discourse: marketization of the New Zealand science and innovation system', *Human Relations*, **58**, 891–912.

Levinson, D.J. (1978), *The Seasons of Man's Life*, New York: Ballantine Books.

Levinthal, D.A. and J.G. March (1993), 'The myopia of learning', *Strategic Management Journal*, **14** (52), 95–112.

Lindblom, C. (1959), 'The science of muddling through', *Public Administration Review*, **19** (2), 79–88.

Lindell, M. and L. Melin (1991), 'Internationalization through acquisition: the realization of corporate vision', paper presented at the EAM conference, Managing in Global Economy IV.

Lockett, A. and S. Thompson (2004), 'Edith Penrose's contribution to the resource-based view: an alternative perspective', *Journal of Management Studies*, **41** (1), 193–203.

Louis, M.R. (1980), 'Surprise and sense making: what newcomers experience in entering unfamiliar organizational settings', *Administrative Science Quarterly*, **25** (2), 226–51.

Lounsbury, M. and H. Leblebici (2004), 'The origins of strategic practice: product diversification in the American mutual fund industry', *Strategic Organization*, **2**, 65–90.

Løwendahl, B.R. and Ø. Revang (2004), 'Achieving results in an after modern context: thoughts on the role of strategizing and organizing', *European Management Review*, **1**, 49–54.

Lübcke, P. (ed.) (1987), *Vår tids filosofi*, Stockholm: Forum.

Lumpkin, G.T. and G.G. Dess (1996), 'Clarifying the entrepreneurial orientation construct and linking it to performance', *Academy of Management Review*, **21** (1), 135–72.

Lyles, M.A. and C.R. Schwenk (1992), 'Top management, strategy and organizational knowledge structure', *Academy of Management Review*, **29**, 155–74.

McCann, J.E. (1991), 'Patterns of growth, competitive technology, and financial strategies in young ventures', *Journal of Business Venturing*, **6** (3), 189–208.

McGee, J.E., M.J. Dowling and W.L. Megginson (1995), 'Cooperative strategy and new venture performance: the role of business strategy and management experience', *Strategic Management Journal*, **16** (7), 565–81.

MacIntyre, A. (1981), *After Virtue*, London: Duckworth.

McKelvie, A., J. Wiklund and P. Davidsson (2006), 'A resource-based view on organic and acquired growth', in J. Wiklund, D. Dimov, J.A. Katz and D.A. Shepherd (eds), *Entrepreneurship: Frameworks and Empirical Investigations from Forthcoming Leaders of European Research, Advances in Entrepreneurship, Firm Emergence and Growth*, Volume 9, Amsterdam: Elsevier, pp. 175–94.

McMahon, R.G.P. (2001), 'Business growth and performance and the financial reporting practices of Australian manufacturing SMEs', *Journal of Small Business Management*, **39** (2), 152–64.

McWhinney, W. (1984), 'Alternative realities: their impact on change and leadership', *Journal of Humanistic Psychology*, **24** (4), 7–38.

Madhok, A. (1997), 'Cost, value and foreign market entry mode: the transaction and the firm', *Strategic Management Journal*, **18** (1), 39–61.

Mahajan, V. and Y. Wind (2002), 'Got emotional product positioning? There's more to positioning than just features and benefits', *Marketing Management*, **11** (3), 36–41.

Mahoney, J.D. and J.T. Mahoney (1993), 'An empirical investigation of the effect of corporate amendments on stockholder wealth', *Strategic Management Journal*, **14**, 17–31.

Malmö Trade and Industry (2008), *Hilding Anders Controls the Global Market from Malmö*, Malmö: Malmö stad.

Markham Shaw, C.L. (1997), 'Personal narrative revealing self and reflecting other', *Human Communication Research*, **24** (2), 302–19.

Mazzarol, T. (2003), 'A model of small business HR growth management', *International Journal of Entrepreneurial Behavior and Research*, **9** (1), 27–49.

Melin, L. (1989), 'The field-of-force metaphor', *Advances in International Marketing*, **3**, 161–79.

Melin, L. and B. Hellgren (1994), 'Patterns of strategic processes: two change typologies', in H. Thomas, D. O'Neal, R. White and D. Hurst (eds), *Building the Strategically Responsive Organization*, Chichester: Wiley, pp. 251–71.

Merz, R.G., P. Weber and V.B. Laetz (1994), 'Linking small business management with entrepreneurial growth', *Journal of Small Business Management*, **32** (4), 48–60.

Miller, D. and P.H. Friesen (1984), 'A longitudinal study of the corporate life-cycle', *Management Science*, **30**, 1161–83.

Mintzberg, H. (1978), 'Patterns in strategy formation', *Management Science*, **24**, 934–48.

Mintzberg, H. and J.A. Waters (1986), 'Of strategies, deliberate and emergent', *Strategic Management Journal*, **6** (3), 257–72.

Mintzberg, H. and F. Westley (1992), 'Cycles of organizational change', *Strategic Management Journal*, **13**, 39–59.

Moore, C.B., C.W. Autry and B.A. Macy (2007), 'Interpreneurship: how the process of combining relational resources and entrepreneurial resources drives competitive advantage', in G.T. Lumpkin and J.A. Katz (eds), *Entrepreneurial Strategic Processes. Advances in Entrepreneurship, Firm Emergence and Growth*, Volume 10, St Louis, MO: Saint Louis University, Cook School of Business, pp. 65–102.

Morgan, G. (1997), *Images of Organization*, Thousand Oaks, CA: Sage.

Moustakas, C. (1994), *Phenomenological Research and Methods*, Thousand Oaks, CA: Sage.

Mumby, D.K. (ed.) (1993), *Narrative and Social Control: Critical Perspectives*, London: Sage.

Nahavandi, A. and A.R. Malekzadeh (1988), 'Acculturation in mergers and acquisitions', *Academy of Management Review*, **13** (1), 79–90.

Naldi, L. (2008), *Growth through Internationalization. A Knowledge Persperctive on SMEs*, Jönköping: Jönköping International Business School.

Napier, N.K. (1989), 'Mergers and acquisitions, human resource issues and outcomes: a review and suggested typology', *Journal of Management Studies*, **26** (3), 271–89.

Nelson, R.R. and S.G. Winter (1982), *An Evolutionary Theory of Economic Change*, Cambridge, MA: Harvard University Press.

Ng, W. and C. De Cock (2002), 'Battle in the boardroom: a discursive perspective', *Journal of Management Studies*, **39**, 23–49.

Nisker, J. (2004), 'Narrative ethics in health care', in J.L. Storch, P. Rodney and R. Starzamski (eds), *Toward a Moral Horizon: Nursing Ethics in Leadership and Practice*, Toronto: Prentice Hall Malmö, pp. 285–309.

174   *A narrative approach to business growth*

Nordic Capital (2007), 'In brief'. Retrieved 17 February 2007, from http://www.nordiccapital.com/aboutus.asp.

Nordic Capital Ratos (2003), press release, 24 November. Retrieved 13 November 2008, from http://www.investcorp.com/template1a.aspx.

Nordqvist, M. (2005), *Understanding the Role of Ownership in Strategizing. A Study of Family Firms*, Jönköping: Jönköping International Business School.

Normann, R. (1985), 'Developing capabilities for organizational learning', in M. Pennings (ed.), *Organizational Strategy and Change*, San Francisco: Jossey-Bass, pp. 217–48.

Norra Skåne (1969), 12 June, 'Produktarbete i Hästveda gav skandinaviskt rekord' (local newspaper, Hässleholm, Sweden).

Norra Skåne (1978), 25 October, 'Olle Andersson 50 år' (local newspaper, Hässleholm, Sweden).

Norra Skåne (1997), 18 November, 'Hilding Anders bästa leverantör i Norden' (local newspaper, Hässleholm, Sweden).

Norra Skåne (1998), 17 January, 'Stor sängaffär klar' (local newspaper, Hässleholm, Sweden).

Nystrom, H. (1995), 'Creativity and entrepreneurship', in C.M. Ford and D.A. Gioia (eds), *Creative Action in Organizations. Ivory Tower Visions and Real World Voices*, Thousand Oaks, CA: Sage, pp. 65–70.

O'Connor, E.S. (2000), 'Plotting the organization: the embedded narrative as a construct for studying change', *Journal of Applied Behavioral Science*, **36** (2), 174–92.

O'Connor, E.S. (2007), 'Reader beware: doping business with a store(y) of knowledge', *Journal of Business Venturing*, **22** (5), 637–48.

Oliveira, B. and A. Fortunato (2006), 'Firm growth and liquidity constraints: a dynamic analysis', *Small Business Economics*, **27**, 139–56.

Orbuch, T.L. (1997), 'People's accounts count: the sociology of accounts', *Annual Review of Sociology*, **23**, 455–78.

Oviatt, B.M. and P.P. McDougall (1994), 'Toward a theory of international new ventures', *Journal of International Business Studies*, **25** (1), 45–64.

Øyhus, A.O. (2003), 'The entrepreneurial self-image: lonely rider or social team player? Comparing entrepreneurs in Tanzania and Indonesia', *Journal of Entrepreneurship*, **12** (2), 201–23.

Pattison, S., D. Dickenson, M. Parker and T. Heller (1999), 'Do case studies mislead about the nature of reality?', *Journal of Medical Ethics*, **25**, 42–6.

Peay, T.R. and W.G. Dyer Jr (1989), 'Power orientations of entrepreneurs and succession planning', *Journal of Small Business Management*, **27** (1), 47–52.

Peng, M.W. (2001), 'The resource-based view and international business', *Journal of Management*, **27** (6), 803–29.

Peng, M.W. and P.S. Heath (1996), 'The growth of the firm in planned economies in transition: institutions, organizations, and strategic choice', *Academy of Management Review*, **21** (2), 492–528.

Penrose, E. (1959), *The Theory of the Growth of the Firm*, Oxford: Oxford University Press.

Perfecta (2008), 'Perfecta'. Retrieved 20 November 2008, from http://www.hildinganders.se/media/hilding_brands.swf.

Perfecta Dreams (2008), 'About us'. Retrieved 19 November 2008, from http://www.perfecta.hr/index.php.

Petromilli, M., D. Morrison and M. Million (2002), 'Brand architecture: building brand portfolio value', *Strategy and Leadership*, **30** (5), 22–8.

Pettigrew, A.M. (1992), 'The character and significance of strategy process research', *Strategic Management Journal*, **13**, 5–16.

Pettigrew, A.M. and R. Whipp (1991), *Managing Change for Competitive Success*, Oxford: Blackwell.

Pfeffer, J. (1972), 'Merger as a response to organization interdependence', *Administrative Science Quarterly*, **17**, 382–94.

Pfeffer, J. (2005), 'Producing sustainable competitive advantage through the effective management of people', *Academy of Management Executive*, **19** (4), 95–106.

Polkinghorne, D.E. (1988), *Narrative Knowing and the Human Sciences*, New York: State University of New York Press.

Pondy, L.R., P.J. Frost, G. Morgan and T.C. Dandridge (eds) (1983), *Organizational Symbolism*, Stamford, CT: JAI Press, pp. 3–35.

Ponsonby-Mccabe, S. and E. Boyle (2006), 'Understanding brands as experiential spaces: axiological implications for marketing strategists', *Journal of Strategic Marketing*, **14**, 175–89.

Porac, J.F., H. Thomas and C. Baden-Fuller (1989), 'Competitive groups as cognitive communities: the case of Scottish knitwear manufacturers', *Journal of Management Studies*, **26**, 397–416.

Prus, R. (1996), *Symbolic Interaction and Ethnographic Research: Intersubjectivity and the Study of Human Lived Experience*, Albany, NY: State University of New York Press.

Quinn, J. (1980), *Strategies for Change, Logical Incrementalism*, Burr Ridge, IL: Richard B. Irwin.

Rae, D. (2005), 'Entrepreneurial learning: a narrative-based conceptual model', *Journal of Small Business and Enterprise Development*, **12** (3), 323–35.

Rajagopalan, N. and G.M. Spreitzer (1997), 'Toward a theory of strategic change: a multi-lens perspective and integrative framework', *Academy of Management*, **22** (1), 48–79.

Ratos (2002), 17 October. Retrieved 12 October 2009, from http://www.cisionwire.se/ny-vd-i-hilding-anders.

Ratos (2008), business concept and targets. Retrieved 6 November 2009, from http://www.ratos.se/en/Startpage.

Ravenscraft, D. and F. Scherer (1987), *Mergers, Sell-Offs and Economic Efficiency*, Washington, DC: Brooking Institution.

Reissner, S.C. (2005), 'Learning and innovation: a narrative analysis', *Journal of Organizational Change*, **18** (5), 482–94.

Rhodes, C. (1996), 'Researching organizational change and learning: a narrative approach', *Qualitative Report*, **2** (4), 17.

Richardson, B. (ed.) (2002), *Narrative Dynamics, Essays on Time, Plot, Closure, and Frames*, Columbus, OH: Ohio State University Press.

Ricoeur, P. (1983), *Time and Narrative*, Volume 1, Chicago: University of Chicago Press.

Riessman, C.K. (1993), *Narrative Analysis*, Newbury Park, CA: Sage.

Rossiter, M. (1999), 'A narrative approach to development: implications for adult education', *Adult Education Quarterly*, **50** (1), 56–71.

Rotfeld, H.J. (2008), 'Beyond product's brand management. Brand image of company names matters in ways that can't be ignored', *Journal of Product and Brand Management*, **17** (2), 121–2.

Roulac, S.E. (2007), 'Brand + beauty + utility = property value', *Property Management*, **25** (6), 428–46.

Rouse, M.J. and U.S. Daellenbach (1999), 'Rethinking research methods for the resource-based perspective: isolating sources of sustainable competitive advantage', *Strategic Management Journal*, **20**, 487–94.

Rovio-Johansson, A. (2007), 'Post-acquisition integration: ways of sensemaking in a management team meeting', *Qualitative Research in Organizations and Management: An International Journal*, **2** (1), 4–22.

Rugman, A.M. and A. Verbeke (2004), 'A final word on Edith Penrose', *Journal of Management Studies*, **41** (1), 205–17.

Saarni, C. (1999), *The Development of Emotional Competence*, New York: Guilford Press.

Salvato, C., U. Lassini and J. Wiklund (2006), 'Dynamics of external growth in SMEs: a process model of acquisition capabilities emergence', in J. Wiklund, D. Dimov, J.A. Katz and D.A. Shepherd (eds), *Advances in Entrepreneurship, Firm Emergence and Growth, Volume 9. Entrepreneurship: Framework and Empirical Investigations from Forthcoming Leaders of European Research*, Oxford: JAI Press, pp. 229–66.

Scapa Inter (2009), 'Om Scapa'. Retrieved 4 December 2009, from http://www.scapainter.com.

Scheler, M. ([1915] 1994), *Ressentiment*, Milwaukee, WI: Marquette University Press.

Schmidt, D.R. and L.K. Fowler (1990), 'Post-acquisition financial performance and executive compensation', *Strategic Management Journal*, **11** (7), 559–69.

Schumpeter, J.A. (1934), *The Theory of Economic Development*, Cambridge, MA: Harvard University Press.

Schumpeter, J.A. (1951), *Essays of J.A. Schumpeter*, Cambridge: Addison-Wesley Press.

Sciascia, S. and L. Naldi (2004), 'Corporate entrepreneurship: a literature review', in S. Sciascia (ed.), *Exploring Corporate Entrepreneurship. Entrepreneurial Orientation in Small and Medium-sized Enterprises*, JIBS Research Report Series, No 2004-4, Jönköping: Jönköping International Business School, pp. 47–74.

Scott, M.B. and S. Lyman (1968), 'Accounts', *American Sociological Review*, **33**, 46–62.

Senge, P.M. (1990), *The Fifth Discipline. The Art and Practice of the Learning Organization*, London: Century Business.

Sexton, D.L. and F.I. Seale (1997), *Leading Practices of Fast Growth Entrepreneurs. Pathways of High Performance*, Missouri: National Center for Entrepreneurship Research.

Sexton, D.L. and R.W. Smilor (1986), *The Art of Science of Entrepreneurship*, Cambridge: Ballinger.

Shane, S. and S. Venkataraman (2000), 'The promise of entrepreneurship as a field of research', *Academy of Management Review*, **25** (1), 217–26.

Shepherd, D.A. and J. Wiklund (2005), *Entrepreneurial Small Business: A Resource-based Perspective*, Cheltenham, UK and Northampton, MA, USA: Edward Elgar.

Shepherd, D.A. and J. Wiklund (2009), 'Are we comparing apples with apples or apples with oranges? Appropriateness of knowledge accumulation across growth studies', *Entrepreneurship Theory and Practice*, **33** (1), 105–23.

Shklovsky, V. ([1909] 1990), *Theory of Prose*, Elmwood Park, IL: Dalkey Archive Press.

Shotter, J. (2003), '"Real presences": meaning as living movement in a participatory world', *Theory Psychology*, **13** (4), 435–68.

Sievers, B. (1986), 'Beyond the surrogate of motivation', *Organization Studies*, **7** (4), 335–51.

Singh, K. and W. Mitchell, (2005), 'Growth dynamics: the bidirectional relationship between interfirm collaboration and business sales in entrant and incumbent alliances', *Strategic Management Journal*, **26** (6), 497–521.

Sjöstrand, S.-E. (1997), *The Two Faces of Management. The Janus Factor*, London: International Thomson Business Press.

Slumberland (2008), 'About us'. Retrieved 14 November 2008, from http://www.slumberland.co.uk/about/.

Smallbone, D., R. Leigh and D. North (1995), 'The characteristics and strategies of high growth SMEs', *International Journal of Entrepreneurial Behavior and Research*, **1** (3), 44–62.

Smircich, L. (1983), 'Concepts of culture and organizational analysis', *Administrative Science Quarterly*, **28**, 229–358.

Smircich, L. and G. Morgan (1982), 'Leadership: the management of meaning', *Journal of Applied Behavioral Science*, **18**, 257–73.

Sole, D. and D.G. Wilson (2002), 'Storytelling in organizations: the power and traps of using stories to share knowledge in organizations', paper presented at the Harvard Graduate School of Education.

Spence, P.D. (1982), *Narrative Truth and Historical Truth. Meaning and Interpretation in Psychoanalysis*, New York: W.W. Norton & Company.

Staahl Gabrielsen, T. and L. Sørgard (2007), 'Private labels, price rivalry, and public policy', *European Economic Review*, **51** (2), 403–24.

Starbuck, W.H. and F.J. Milliken (1988), 'Executives' perceptual filters: what they notice and how they make sense', in D.C. Hambrick (ed.), *The Executive Effect: Concepts and Methods for Studying Top Managers*, Greenwich, CT: JAI Press, pp. 35–65.

Steiner, P. (1975), *Mergers, Motives, Effects, Policies*, East Lansing, MI: University of Michigan Press.

Steinmetz, G. (1992), 'Reflections on the role of social narratives in working-class formation: narrative theory in the social sciences', *Social Science History*, **16** (3), 489–516.

Stevenson, H.H. and J.C. Jarillo (1990), 'A paradigm of entrepneurship: entrepreneurial management', *Strategic Management Journal*, **11** (5), 17–27.

Steyaert, C. (2007), 'Of course that is not the whole (toy) story: entrepreneurship and the cat's cradle', *Journal of Business Venturing*, **22** (5), 733–51.

Storey, D. (1994), *Understanding the Small Business Sector*, London: Routledge.

Sztompka, P. (1993), *The Sociology of Social Change*, Oxford: Blackwell.

Taylor, J.R. and E.J. Van Every (2000), *The Emergent Organization. Communication as Its Site and Surface*, Mahwah, NJ: Lawrence Erlbaum.

Taylor, S.S., D. Fisher and R.L. Dufresne (2002), 'The aesthetics of management storytelling', *Management Learning*, **33** (3), 313–30.

Teece, D., G. Pisano and A. Shuen (1997), 'Dynamic capabilities and strategic management', *Strategic Management Journal*, **18** (7), 509–33.

Thompson, J.D. (1967), *Organizations in Action*, New York: McGraw Hill.

Thurik, R. and S. Wennekers (2004), 'Entrepreneuship, small business and economic growth', *Journal of Small Business and Enterprise Development*, **11** (1), 140–49.

Timmons, J.A. (1994), *New Venture Creation*, Burr Ridge, IL: Richard B. Irwin.

Tollington, T. (1998), 'Brands: the asset definition and recognition test', *Journal of Product & Brand Management*, **7** (3), 180–92.

Treacy, M. and F. Wiersema (1993), 'Customer intimacy and other value disciplines', *Harvard Business Review*, January–February, 84–93.

Tropico (2008), 'Tropico'. Retrieved 20 November 2008, from http://www.hildinganders.se.

Tsoukas, H. and R. Chia (2002), 'On organizational becoming: rethinking organizational change', *Organization Science*, **13** (5), 567–82.

Turkel, S. (2006), 'George Mortimer Pullman: builder of hotel rooms on wheels'. Retrieved 14 November 2008, from http://www.ishc.com/uploadedFiles/PublicSite/Resources/Library/Articles/GeorgeMortimer Pullman BuilderofHotelRoomsonWheels31506.pdf.

Urde, M. (2001), 'Core value-based corporate brand building', *European Journal Marketing*, **37** (7/8), 1017–40.

Vaara, E. (2002), 'On the discursive construction of success/failure in narratives of post-merger integration', *Organization Studies*, **23** (2), 211–48.

Vaara, E. and J. Tienari (2002), 'Justification, legitimization and naturalization of mergers and acquisitions: a critical discourse analysis of media texts', *Organization*, **9** (2): 275–304.

Van de Ven, A.H. (1992), 'Suggestions for studying strategy process. A research note', *Strategic Management Journal*, **13**, 169–88.

Van de Ven, A.H. and M.S. Poole (1995), 'Explaining development and change in organizations', *Academy of Management Review*, **20** (3), 510–40.

Van Maanen, J. (1979), 'On the understanding of interpersonal relations', in W. Bennis, J. Van Maanen, E.H. Schein and F.I. Steele (eds), *Essays in Interpersonal Communication*, Homewood, IL: Dorsey Press, pp. 13–42.

Varadarajan, R., M.P. DeFanti and P.S. Busch (2006), 'Brand portfolio, corporate image, and reputation: managing brand deletions', *Journal of the Academy of Marketing Science*, **34** (2), 195–205.

Very, P., M. Lubatkin and R. Calori (1998), 'A cross-national assessment of acculturative stress in recent European mergers', in M.C. Cardel Gertsen, A.-M. Søderberg and J.E. Torp (eds), *Cultural Dimensions of International Mergers and Acquisitions*, Berlin: Walter de Gruyter, pp. 111–27.

Vickers, D. (2008), 'Beyond the hegemonic narrative – a study of managers', *Journal of Organizational Change Management*, **21** (5), 560–73.

Walsh, J.P. and G.R. Ungson (1991), 'Organizational memory', *Academy of Management Review*, **16** (1), 57–91.

Walter, G.A. and J.B. Barney (1990), 'Management objectives in mergers and acquisitions', *Strategic Management Journal*, **11** (1), 79–86.

Watson, T.J. (2002), *Organising and Managing Work. Organisational, Managerial and Strategic Behavior in Theory and Practice*, Harlow: Prentice Hall, Pearson Education.

Watzlawick, P., J.B. Bavelas and D.D. Jackson (1967), *Pragmatics of Human Communication. A Study of Interactional Patterns, Pathologies and Paradoxes*, New York: W.W. Norton.

Weber, M. (1947), *The Theory of Social and Economic Organisation*, New York: Oxford University Press.

Weick, K. (1979), *The Social Psychology of Organizing*, Reading, MA: Addison-Wesley.

Weick, K.E. (1995), *Sensemaking in Organizations*, Thousand Oaks, CA: Sage.

Welter, F. and F. Lasch (2008), 'Entrepreneurship research in Europe: taking stock and looking forward', *Entrepreneurship Theory and Practice*, **32** (2), 241–48.

Wifor (2008), 'Wifor'. Retrieved 20 November 2008, from http://www.hildinganders.se.

Wigren, C. (2003), *The Spirit of Gnosjö – The Grand Narrative and Beyond*, Jönköping: Jönköping International Business School.

Wiklund, J., P. Davidsson and F. Delmar (2003), 'What do they think and feel about growth? An expectancy-value approach to small business managers' attitudes toward growth', *Entrepreneurship Theory and Practice*, **27** (3), 247–70.

Wiklund, J., H. Patzelt and D.A. Shepherd (2009) 'Building an integrative model of small business growth', *Small Business Economics*, **32** (4), 351–74.

Wilkins, A.L. (1984), 'The creation of company cultures. The role of stories and human resource systems', *Human Resource Management*, **23** (1), 41–60.

Wilkinson, D. (2007), 'Slumberland closure will cost 260 jobs'. Retrieved 13 November 2008, from http://www.rochdaleobserver.co.uk/news/.

Williamson, O. (1975), *Markets and Hierarchies: Analayis and Antitrust Implications*, New York: Free Press.

Wood, L.A. and R.O. Kroger (2000), *Doing Discourse Analysis. Methods for Studying Action in Talk and Text*, Thousand Oaks, CA: Sage.

Wright, A. (2006), 'The role of scenarios as prospective sensemaking devices', *Management Decision*, **43** (1), 86–101.

Index

employees
  care by management, and business
    growth narrative beginning
    60–61
  information sharing by management,
    and merger activities 64, 135
  treatment as family members 64
  we-feeling and merger activities
    77–8, 135
entrepreneurship
  at individual level 29–33
  and corporate setting 27–8
  entrepreneurial actions by employees
    132
  entrepreneurial self 59–62, 133
  and growth 21, 22–3, 25–9
  judgment and risk-taking, and
    business growth narrative
    beginning 59–60, 133
  and management judgment 27–8
  and resource allocation 29
  social constructionist perspective
    27–8, 29–33
Erramilli, M. 24, 140
evolutionary process theory 147–8
existential dimension, participatory
  narrative approach 15, 16, 28, 33,
  35, 46, 142, 145

Feldman, M. 5, 11, 13, 41
Fichtner, B. 2
Findlay, M. 109, 139
Fineman, S. 142
Fischer, E. 32
Fisher, W. 5–6, 143, 144
Fletcher, D. 3, 14, 32
Fortnato, A. 21
Fowler, L. 77
Frank, H. 10
Freeman, J. 147
Friesen, P. 20
Frye, N. 6

Gadamer, H.-G. ix, 6, 7, 13, 14, 33, 35,
  36, 38, 42, 45, 130, 152
Gadow, S. 35, 145
Gallagher, C. vi, vii
Geertz, C. vii, viii
Gergen, K. 31, 46, 145, 151
Geroski, P. 20

Gersick, K. 20, 147
Ghemawat, P. 150
Ghoshal, S. 19
Gibb, A. 18, 19, 20, 146
Giddens, A. 10, 142
Ginsburg, A. 28
Gioia, D. 147
Glaser, B. 36
Glete, J. 29
Goddard, J. 2, 30
Goffman, E. 154
Golann, B. 19, 136
Grant, R. 22
Greenblatt, S. vi, ix
Greiner, L. 20
growth
  and belief in growth 132
  continuous, and brand portfolio
    building 81–96, 136, 137
  and entrepreneurship 21, 22–3, 25–9
  expectations of continued, and,
    merger activities 74–8
  and firm's linear moves 20
  and internal–external distinction
    (dualism) 18, 21–2, 29, 30–32,
    147–8, 150
  and internationalization 23–5
  patterns and change, relating to
    earlier studies on 146–50
  and performance measurement 18–29
  and research and development 129
  and resource and capability 21–3, 24
  strategy, pursuing aggressive 96–102,
    136–7, 138
Guillet de Monthoux, P. 143
Guth, W. 28

Hall, A. 50, 144, 145–6, 147, 151
Hamilton, R. 21
Hanks, S. 19
Hannan, M. 147
Hansted Blomqvist, K. 82, 90, 103
Hardy, B. 5
Harper, S. 145
Harré, R. 151
Harrington, L. 80, 105, 137, 138
Haspeslagh, P. 134
headquarters move, importance of 109
Heath, P. 19
Hellgren, B. 144, 147, 148, 149

188